JOHN BELLEW, A SEVENTEENTH-CENTURY MAN OF MANY PARTS

To My Wife Lily

John Bellew, a Seventeenth-Century Man of Many Parts

Harold O'Sullivan

IRISH ACADEMIC PRESS
DUBLIN • PORTLAND, OR

First published in 2000 by
IRISH ACADEMIC PRESS
44, Northumberland Road, Dublin 4, Ireland
and in the United States America by
IRISH ACADEMIC PRESS
c/o ISBS, 5804 NE Hassalo Street, Portland,
OR 97213–3644

Website: www.iap.ie

© Harold O'Sullivan 2000

British Library Cataloguing in Publication Data
O'Sullivan, Harold
  John Bellew , a Seventeenth-Century Man of Many Parts.
  1. Bellew, John 2. Gentry – Ireland – Biography 3. Ireland – History –
17th century
  I. Title
  941.5'06

  ISBN 0–7165–2622–0

Library of Congress Cataloging-in-Publication Data
O'Sullivan, Harold.
  John Bellew , a Seventeenth-Century Man of Many Parts.
      p.   cm.
  Includes bibliographical references and index.
  ISBN 0–7165–2622–0
  1. Bellew, John, 1606–1679. 2. Administration of estates—Ireland—History—17th century. 3. Ireland—History—Rebellion of 1641 Biography. 4. Ireland—History—17th century Biography. 5. Galway (Ireland : County) Biography. 6. Louth (Ireland : County) Biography. 7. Legislators—Ireland Biography. 8. Landowners—Ireland Biography. 9. Lawyers—Ireland Biography. I. Title.
  DA940.5.B45088 1999
  941.706'092—dc21   99–36754
  [B]   CIP

All rights reserved. Without limiting the rights under copyright reserved
alone, no part of this publication may be reproduced, stored in or introduced
into a retrieval system, or transmitted, in any form or by any means
(electronic, mechanical, photocopying, recording or otherwise),
without the prior written permission of both the copyright
owner and the above publisher of this book.

Typeset in 11 pt on 13 pt Sabon
by Carrigboy Typesetting Services, County Cork
Printed by Creative Print and Design, (Wales), Ebbw Vale

Contents

Preface	vii
Abbreviations	xii
List of Illustrations	xiii

Chapter One
    Old English Gentleman   1

Chapter Two
    Irish Parliamentarian   10

Chapter Three
    From King's Sheriff to Irish Rebel   25

Chapter Four
    Lieutenant-General of Artillery in the
    Confederate Army of Leinster   38

Chapter Five
    'Being a people, if driven from the coast
    of Israel must of necessity perish'   54

Chapter Six
    'It being repugnant to all reason that the
    estates of such as served his majesty, should now
    be the reward of those who fought against him'   71

Chapter Seven
    Agent to Theobald Taaffe, Earl of Carlingford   97

Chapter Eight
    'The Earl of Carlingford is the most
    powerful man in the country'   108

Chapter Nine
    'It were hard that your petitioner, who showed
    his affections to his majesty's interest, should now,
    himself and his family perish'   123

Contents

Epilogue   140

Appendices   161

  I To the Honourable the Knights, Citizens and Burgesses of the House of Commons in this Present Parliament Assembled in his Majesty's Kingdom of England. The Humble Petition of [several] of the Knights, Citizens and Burgesses of the Commons of the Parliament of Ireland whose names are underwritten   161

  II To the King's most Excellent Majesty the Humble Petition of the Knights Citizens and Burgesses, of the Commons House of Parliament of Ireland whose names are underwritten   163

  III The Account Touching the Train of Artillery c.1645–46   168

  IV A Collection of Documents Relating to John Bellew's Transplantation to Connacht   170

  V John Bellew's Critical Commentaries on the Proposals for the Land Settlement 1660–61   180

  VI Patrick Bellew's Affidavit to the Commission of Grace 1684   184

  VII The Marriage Settlement of Patrick Bellew and Elisabeth Barnewall   189

  VIII Copy of Bond dated 7 January 1664 between John Bellew and Sir Richard Barnewall   191

Notes   193

Glossary   211

Bibliography   215

Index   223

Preface

John Bellew was typical of his class, an Old Englishman of the landed gentry of Ireland, a lawyer and parliamentarian with deep roots in the old Pale establishment, which lost political power to the New English in the late sixteenth and early seventeenth centuries. His ancestor, Roger Bellew of Yorkshire, came with Hugh de Lacy into Ireland in 1172, and subsequently settled at Duleek in County Meath, where the family had two-and-a-half carucates of land in 1332. They later spread to Castletown-Dundalk where their fifteenth-century tower house still stands. The family had many branches throughout Louth and Meath. John belonged to the Lisrenny branch where his grandfather Patrick, the second son of Sir John Bellew of Castletown-Dundalk, had an estate of inheritance granted him by his father about 1575. Like his grandfather, John was educated in England where he studied law at Gray's Inn in London in 1627. Upon his return to Ireland he came into the inheritance of his late father's estate of 700 acres at Lisrenny, north of Ardee, and established himself in a legal practice which soon prospered. He married Mary, daughter of Robert Dillon of Clonbrock County Galway, and the couple settled at Willistown Drumcar. By the outbreak of insurrection in 1641 he was a member of parliament, justice of the peace, sheriff of the county of Louth and had a landed estate of 1,460 acres. Wrongfully suspected of collaboration with the insurrectionists, he was expelled from parliament and outlawed.

After he joined the Catholic Confederacy at Kilkenny, he served with some distinction as Preston's lieutenant-general of artillery until the Ormond Peace of 1648 when he transferred into the royalist forces then confronting the English Parliamentarian garrisons at Dublin. As captain of the train of artillery, he was in the force under Ormond which was routed by Michael Jones at the battle of Rathmines where he was captured. After paying the required ransom, he was released into the 'Irish Quarters' in September 1649. Commissioned by Ormond as lieutenant-general of artillery in 1650, he continued in service until 1652 when, having assisted in the negotiations of the Articles of Kilkenny, he surrendered at Mullingar and returned home to Louth. His subsequent struggle to avoid confiscation of his lands and transplantation to Connacht, relying upon the terms of the Articles of

Kilkenny, though unsuccessful, reveals fresh insights into the management of that transplantation by the English Commonwealth administration in Ireland. Later in the Restoration period, his activities on his own and on the Earl of Carlingford's behalf, for whom he acted as agent during the restoration land settlement, reveals a great deal of new information on the proceedings of that settlement. His involvement in those proceedings represents a case study of the legal, administrative and political aspects of the settlement, which was a watershed in Irish history. Thanks to his abilities both as a lawyer and as a negotiator, he was instrumental in the recovery by Carlingford of much of his ancestral estates in Louth and Sligo as well as the acquisition of additional lands in these counties and in Wexford. He too recovered part of his ancestral estates in Louth as well as additional lands in that county while at the same time retaining the estate allocated to him by the English Commonwealth in Galway.

After his death in 1679, he was succeeded by his sons Patrick of Barmeath and Christopher of Galway who, taking the Jacobite side during the Williamite wars, demonstrated that they were, like their father, great survivors. The implementation of the Jacobite Repeal Act was a severe setback, particularly for Patrick, much of whose estates were lost under the terms of the Act and whose house and lands at Barmeath were looted while he sat with James II before the wall of Derry. Nonetheless, they remained loyal to their king, and having been adjudged as serving inside the walls of Limerick, on 3 October 1691 they had the benefit of the Treaty which brought the wars to an end. Reversing their Williamite outlawries, they managed to recover their estates and to found families who survived the rigours of the eighteenth-century Penal Laws against Catholic landowners. One branch of the family is still in occupation of the ancestral home at Barmeath Castle, County Louth.

Men such as John Bellew have been little studied by historians. Most have concentrated either on local studies of the early seventeenth century or of the restoration land settlement. While such studies can isolate large-scale processes, they fail to focus on the individual experience of survival in a turbulent age. In this case the study of an individual is made possible only because of a uniquely detailed collection of family papers not hitherto published, which provides documentary evidence for many aspects of the socio-political developments of the period. These range from the fall of Wentworth in the 1630s, the insurrection of 1641 and the more than a decade of warfare which ensued, through to the Articles of Kilkenny, which brought the war to an end in 1653. The English Commonwealth, the restoration land settlement and the Jacobite-Williamite periods described in the biography are equally dependent upon manuscript material hitherto unpublished. A selection from these papers, which are important for the life of John Bellew, are published in Appendix V.

The Bellews were careful about their family papers; those of the Galway branch now rest in the National Library of Ireland while a substantial deposit of the Barmeath papers are in the National Archives. The greater part of the Barmeath family papers, however, is retained in private keeping at Barmeath Castle. I was fortunate to have been given access to them by Mr Bryan Bellew, the present proprietor and direct descendant of John Bellew's eldest son Patrick, from whom, and from whose wife Rosemary, I have received both help and hospitality on the many occasions I accessed the collection. I also wish to thank Mr Bertie Grattan-Bellew, Bryan's distant cousin, and direct descendant of John Bellew's son Christopher, for giving me permission to make use of his family papers, now known as the Mountbellew Papers, in the National Library, for the purposes of this biography. To both I owe a great debt of gratitude, and without their help this book could not have been written.

I am particularly grateful to Dr Raymond Gillespie for all the help, encouragement and practical assistance he gave me over the years and especially for reading the text over and alerting me to necessary corrections and amendments. I doubt if I could have completed the work without his support. I also wish to thank Professor Aidan Clarke, whose advice and assistance was a boon on many occasions.

I also wish to acknowledge with sincere thanks the help given me by the staffs of the National Library and the National Archives who despite cutbacks in staff and pressures of work were always courteous and helpful, particularly Gerry Lyne and Dr Noel Kissane of the Library and Aideen Ireland of the Archives. My sincere thanks are also due to Siobhan Rafferty of the Royal Irish Academy, Ann Ward and Kathy Murphy of the Louth County Library, and Noel Ross the always helpful editor and secretary of the Louth Archaeological and Historical Society. Finally, to my wife Lily, to whom this book is dedicated, thanks for all your help and never-ending patience.

In expressing my thanks to the foregoing I must emphasise also that any inaccuracies or defects are my responsibility alone.

NOTES ON DATING

Dates throughout the text are in accordance with the Old or Julian Calendar. The beginning of each year is taken, however, as the 1st January, rather than the 25th March. Dates occurring within this period give the Old Calendar year followed after slash / by New Calendar year. Thus 7 January 1663 Old Calendar is 7 January 1964 New Calendar, or 1663/4.

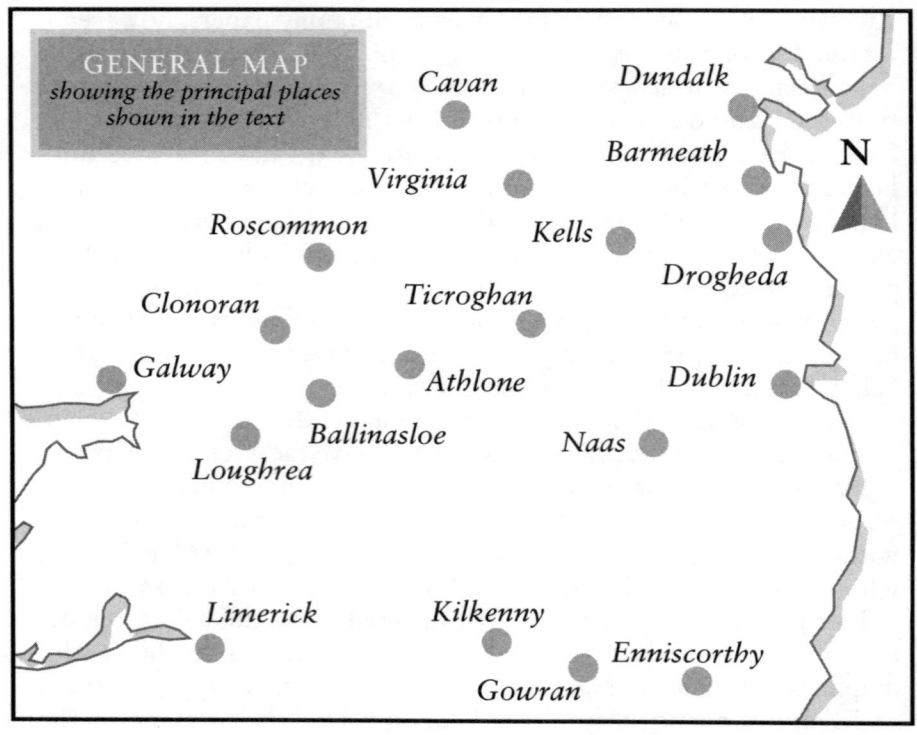

1. General map showing the principal places mentioned in the text.

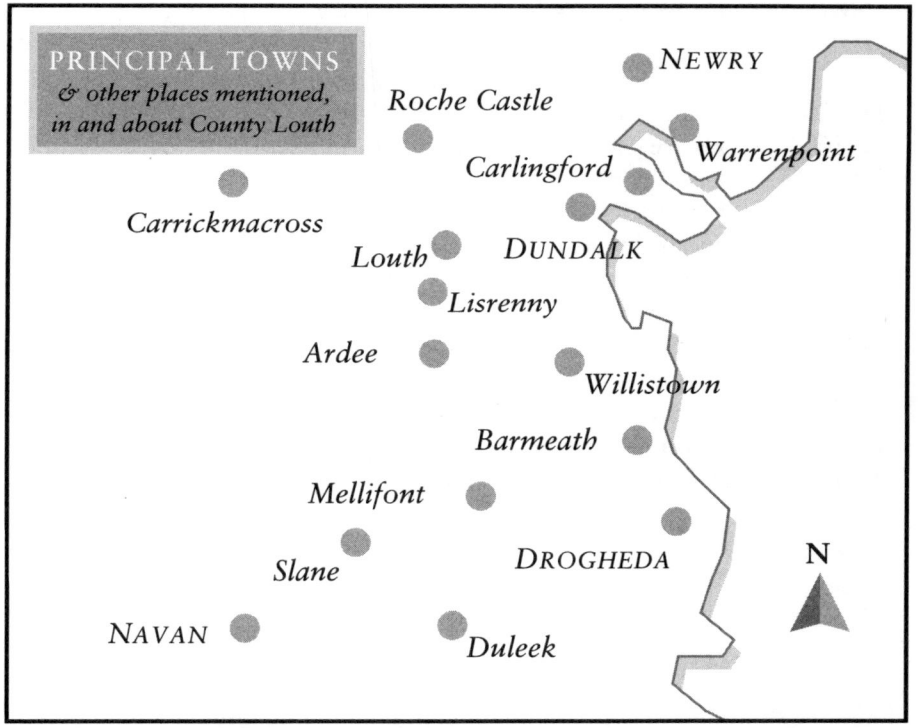

2. Map showing the principal towns and other places mentioned, in and about the county of Louth.

Abbreviations

AH	*Analecta Hibernica*
BP	Bellew Papers in private keeping.
BL	British Library
BSD	Book of Survey and Distribution
CSP	*Calendar of State Papers Ireland*
JHC	*Journal of the House of Commons of Ireland*
JHCE	*Journal of the House of Commons of England*
DNB	*Dictionary of National Biography*
HMC	Historical Manuscripts Commission
IORCHA	*Inquisitionum Officia Rotulorum Canncellariae Hibernice Asservatorum Lagena* (Dublin 1826–1829)
JLAHS	Journal of the Louth Archaeological and Historical Society
NAI	National Archives of Ireland
NLI	National Library of Ireland
PROE	Public Record Office, London
PRONI	Public Record Office, Belfast
TCD	Trinity College Manuscripts Department

List of Illustrations

1. General map showing the principal places mentioned in the text. — x
2. Map showing the principal towns and other places mentioned, in and about the county of Louth. — xi
3. Copy of original warrant to the 'Knights, esquires, gentry and freeholders of the county of Louth to assemble at the Chapple of Toullihskear'. — 30
4. Owen Roe O'Neill's commendation of John Bellew's service at Portlester. — 41
5. The 'runey littel house' to which Lady Carlingford was consigned in May 1665 after her husband returned to the Court in London. — 121
6. Aerial view of Barmeath Castle. — 159

CHAPTER ONE

Old English Gentleman

Of all the various strands that constitute the weave of the modern Irish nation, few have been more enduring or have contributed more than the descendants of those of the Anglo-Norman settlement of the twelfth and thirteenth centuries. Unlike in England, where the Norman conquest proceeded apace after the watershed Battle of Hastings in 1066, the Normans never completed their conquest of Ireland, so that by the fourteenth century Ireland was neither wholly native Irish nor wholly Anglo-Norman. For those who had settled along the east coast, the Lordship of Ireland, with its capital at Dublin, provided a bridgehead with their homelands in England and Wales. However, many of the original magnates of that settlement founded dynasties and semi-autonomous lordships outside the immediate area of settlement in Leinster. Some became more Irish than the Irish themselves, as exemplified by the Clanricards of Connacht, the Desmonds of west Munster and the Ormonds of east Munster and south Leinster. Only in the province of Ulster were the Old Irish to hold the ascendancy, although vestiges of the De Courcy earldom of Ulster survived to the early modern period in the coastal areas of Down and Antrim.

It would be wrong, however, to assume that the acculturation process between 'Gael' and 'Gall' was all one-sided. By the beginning of the sixteenth century, for example, the two great houses of the O'Neills of Ulster and the Fitzgeralds of Leinster had close family ties which were to influence state policies in Ulster during the brief ascendancy of the Fitzgeralds in the early sixteenth century. From this time forward the influence of the Englishry upon the native Irish lords of that province became more noticeable, particularly in those of the Marchland areas of Down, south Armagh, Monaghan and Cavan.[1] As the century progressed and especially after the introduction of the 'surrender and re-grant' policies of St Leger, the acculturation process proceeded apace. By the end of the century the ancient Irish lordships of the 'March and Maghery' of south east Ulster, the McCartans and

1

Magennises of Down, the O'Neills and O'Hanlons of south Armagh and the McMahons of Monaghan had all been irretrievably bonded with the Englishy. Not one of these journeyed with O'Neill of Tyrone to the fateful battle of Kinsale, and apart from O'Hanlon, who was to suffer confiscation by a legal trick of the new British administration of the early Stuart period, none of these was to know the escheats and plantations of the rest of middle and west Ulster.[2] Instead they were to accept the division and bounding of their respective lordships into freehold tenures under the English Common Law, resulting in the creation of a patchwork of landed estates, stretching across the landscape from the counties of Cavan and Monaghan through south Armagh to the former lordships of the Magennises of Iveagh and the McCartans of Kinelarty in County Down. While the greater part of these freehold estates were held by the native Irish, there were others, held in the main by ex-soldiers of Elizabeth's armies, which had been formed from lands, formerly monastic properties, which had come into the possession of the crown in the early Stuart period. Examples of these were the Bagenals of Newry, the Blaneys of Cremorne in County Monaghan and the Moores of Orier in County Armagh.

While the system of land tenures introduced into the former Irish lordships at this period was grounded on the English Common Law, the model had already been in existence in Ireland for many centuries. This was especially true in the case of the contiguous counties of Meath and Louth where the colonial settlement of the Anglo-Normans had been established for more than four-and-a-half centuries and where the system could be said to have had its own indigenous development. The readiness with which the northern Irish adapted themselves to the new system must be accounted for, in part at least, by their knowledge of its workings in these nearby areas, especially the advantages which it conferred on the individual freeholder, as against the old Irish system based on the common ownership of land. Further evidence of this borrowing of the experience of the Englishry of Louth and Meath was the employment by the Irish freeholders of Old English lawyers, descendants of the Anglo-Norman colonists, in the conduct of their legal affairs, men such as the Gernons of Killencoole and Stabannon, the Chamberlains of Nistlerath [Rathneestin] and the Hadsors of Cappock.[3] Thus by a form of legal osmosis the principles and practices of the Common Law, including the Common Law Courts in Dublin, so long the resort of the Old English of the Pale, readily transferred to the Old Irish in the early Stuart period. The modifications, which later arose from the experiences of the Restoration land settlement later in the century, provided, in time, the modern Irish State with its basic laws of land tenure.[4] A similar influence can be detected in our political institutions and in our constitutional laws.

Unlike other parts of Ireland, which had been similarly colonised in the twelfth and thirteenth centuries, the northern Marchland counties of Leinster never came under the patronage or domination of an aristocratic magnate such as an Ormond or a Kildare. Instead they dealt directly with the central organs of government, maintained their shrievalty by the direct appointment of the chief governor of the Lordship and conducted their business and legal systems in accordance with laws and practices which had evolved as part of their English heritage.[5] In the period preceding the commencement of the Tudor era in the late fifteenth century, these counties, while theoretically within the 'land of peace' of the English Lordship, were themselves divided between the settled lands of the Pale where English law was supreme, and the adjoining areas of the 'March and Maghery' which were the frontiers between the Irishry of Ulster and the Englishry of Leinster.[6] In these areas both communities had settlements which derived their titles from the period of the great Norman settlements of De Lacy in Meath, the later De Verdons in Meath and Louth and the De Courcy/De Burgo Earldoms of Ulster. Examples of these were the O'Hanlons who held great tracts of lands in the Faughart-Omeath areas of north Louth and the McMahons of Farney in County Monaghan who also held tracts of lands in the western borderlands of Louth. Intermixed with them were such Old English families as the Flemings of Slane, who had intruded into Farney by the sixteenth century, where they built a castle at Bellahoe, on the Lagan river boundary with Monaghan.[7] The Darcys of Platten acquired the manor of Stonetown in the same district in 1407, formerly held by the de Verdons while the Talbots of Malahide acquired the manors of Louth, Castlering and Ash from the Darcys in 1465. By 1591 the Darcys were reported as 'having built a house of strength in these borders'. On the northern March with Armagh Richard Bellew of Castletown-Dundalk and Roche had by 1458, after many years of violent action against the O'Neills of the Fews, succeeded in expelling them from their southern lands of south Armagh, now incorporated into the north-western parts of the county of Louth as the 'five towns of the Fews'. This dispute erupted again in the early seventeenth century after Sir Turlough O'Neill had his 'country of the Fews' granted to him by letters patent of the crown. Among the disputes that arose from this event was Turlough's claim to lands incorporated into Bellew's manor of Roche and described as 'Liscarrevick, Carriggnesyogy and Shillagh'. Turlough's claim was based upon inheritance from his ancestors while Bellew's claim was that the lands in question were in County Louth. On this occasion the issue was tried, not by battle, but by an action in the Common Law Court of Chancery in 1614 and while details of the outcome have not survived, it is clear that Bellew won the day.[8] The Bellews had earlier acquired title to lands in the western March in 1399 when a John Kenefer granted to John Bellew knight and John Boscome junior 'his lands in Kenvickrath, Lisrenny, Little Arthurstown, Nicholastown, Much Lisrenny, Louth, Ardee and all his other lands in the county of Louth'.[9]

By the beginning of the Tudor era, the English of Louth were the dominant community of the March. Such was their strength that in 1524 the Lord Deputy, Ormond, found it necessary to curb their more aggressive tendencies by the imposition of recognisances on twenty-five of their leading men varying in sums from 100 marks to £40.[10] The objective was to ensure that they kept the peace and made restitution 'for all manners of thefts, robberies, trespasses, extortion and riots' and that they retained no more fighting men than those allowed by the deputy. Numbered amongst these were Walter Bellew of Roche for 100 marks, William Bellew of Verdonstown near Dundalk for £40 and Philip Bellew of Haynestown Dundalk also for £40. The former can be identified as Sir Walter Bellew, the son of Richard, conqueror of the Fews. The Bellews had been settled in the Dundalk area of north Louth since 1366 when John fitz John Bellew appointed John Dowdall his seneschal in the manors of Dundalk and le Roche. The latter had formed part of the de Verdon estates, which in 1332 had been partitioned between the four daughters and co-heiresses of Theobald de Verdon who died without male heir in 1316, and which was included in the property which had been assigned to the eldest daughter Joan, who had married a Thomas de Furnivalle.[11] By this time the Bellews had been long settled in Ireland, tracing their descent from a Roger Bellew of Yorkshire. According to family tradition, Roger married a near relation of Hugh de Lacy's and having accompanied him to Ireland in 1172, he participated in the reduction of east Meath and settled subsequently at Duleek south of Drogheda.[12] In 1332 a John Bellew held two-and-a-half carucates of land in Duleek – probably the original grant made by de Lacy.[13] The Bellews claimed their earlier ancestry from a Roger Bellew who was one of the knights who accompanied William the Conqueror to England who, after participation in the Battle of Hastings, settled principally in Yorkshire spreading later on into Derbyshire, Lincolnshire, Northampton, Kent, Buckinghamshire and Worcester.[14] Possessed of such an ancestry and with extensive estates in the counties of Meath and Louth, the Bellews were a prominent gentry family of the Pale throughout the turbulent years of the Tudor era of the sixteenth century. They were also numbered amongst the shrievalty and commissions of the peace for the county of Louth in this period.[15] John's grandfather Walter had survived his father Christopher, who died about 1532 while he was still a minor, and it was not until 1541 that he came into his inheritance. Sir John married three times, firstly Margaret Plunkett, daughter of Oliver Plunkett, the first baron Louth, secondly Ismay Gay née Nugent, daughter of John and Eleanor Nugent of Phillipstown-Nugent near Dundalk and thirdly Janet Plunkett née Sarsfield, daughter of Roger Sarsfield of Sarsfieldstown County Meath. He was her sixth husband and she predeceased him in 1582, while he survived until 1600.

Sir John had a large family by his first two wives, of whom nine can be identified. These were Christopher, his heir, born 1545, John, his second son, styled of Lisrenny near Ardee, Robert, vicar of Dundalk 1576, Richard of Stameen who died in 1596 and daughters Maud, who married Patrick White of Richardstown Dunleer, Alison, who married Martin Blake of Athboy, County Meath, Mary, who married a Plunkett, Elisabeth, who married William Moore of Barmeath and Margery, who married an Elcock of Drogheda. Of these, John of Lisrenny established his own family line which survives to this day as the Bellews of Barmeath, County Louth. As the younger son, not likely to succeed as his father's heir, John's upbringing was conditioned to him acquiring a career as a lawyer, which was a common practice amongst the younger sons of the landed gentry of the period. He had been born about 1548 and in 1566 was admitted to Oxford University in England where, in 1570, as a Master of Arts, he was a supplicant for the degree of Bachelor of Laws, after which he returned to County Louth to settle at Port near Dunany.[16] In 1575 he married Joan Lynham, daughter of Richard Lynham of Adamstown Drumcar. On foot of this marriage his father John established a trust to uses, settling on trustees Thomas Gernon of Gernonstown, Patrick Stanley and Martin Blake of Athboy County Meath, all the former Kennefer lands of Lisrenny, Little Arthurstown, Nicholastown, Graftonstown and Hitchestown to the use of his son John. John Bellew did not live very long and when he died aged 41 in November 1589, he left his widow with five children, Patrick, the eldest and heir, Nicholas, later of Dunleer, Ismay, Margery, who married Robert Fitz-Symons in 1601 and Joan, who married Patrick Verdon of Clonmore. Patrick was about twelve years of age when his father died. He married Mary, a daughter of the Warrens of Warrenstown (now Dillonstown) in 1603. In May of that year a trust to uses was established, the trustees of which were Martin Blake of Athboy, Thomas Brandon of Dublin, Christopher Verdon of Clonmore, Richard White of Richardstown, Edmond Harold of Kilmachioke and William Warren of Warrenstown.[17]

The intent of the trust was that the estate would be held to Patrick's own use for his lifetime and thereafter, the lands of Lisrenny, Little Arthurstown and Kenvicsrath would pass for her lifetime, to his wife Mary. Alternatively she could receive £20 yearly from all his lands in consideration of her jointure as well as a third part of all his lands at her choice. Following her death the estate was to be held to the use of the male heirs in tail, with successive remainders to the use of the heirs male of his father John and to the uses of the last will of his grandfather, Sir John Bellew. As Patrick died in 1610 at the relatively young age of thirty-four years, he may have been in ill health at this period and may have found it necessary to make provision for his wife and family in the event of his death. His will is dated 18 January 1610 and is signed by his mark and witnessed by Roger Chamberlain, suggesting that he was not at that time able to write.[18] He appointed his wife Mary and his son John as 'executors' of all his goods and chattels and asked to be buried in the 'Church of Tallonstown'. He also appointed as executors William Moore (Barmeath) and Christopher Verdon of Clonmore. There were four children of the marriage, John, the eldest, born in 1605, Matthew, Richard and Anne.

The Lisrenny estate was relatively small, consisting of about 700 acres. Apart from the lands in Graftonstown, Hitchestown and Scobbagh Tullydonnell, which were in the barony of Ferrard, it was located in the barony of Ardee. This suggests that the lands in Ferrard may have come with the marriages of John and Patrick. Patrick's widow, Mary, remarried Patrick Russell of Brownstown County Dublin, probably one of the Old English Russells of Lecale County Down who had settled in north County Dublin. Despite the setbacks suffered by the early deaths of John and Patrick, the family seems to have prospered sufficiently for the eldest son John to be educated in England where he was admitted to study law at Gray's Inn in London at the age of twenty-one years in November 1627.[19] Nothing is known of his earlier upbringing or of his time in England, which may have included a period of apprenticeship in the office of an attorney-at-law. This possibility is suggested by a bond dated November 1630 in the sum of £500 which William Warren of Warrenstown, one of the feoffees of Patrick Bellew's trust to uses of 1603 and John Bellew of Lisrenny, entered into with Richard Hadsor of the Inner Temple in London. The bond provided that upon giving six months notice to Hadsor that

> he either was desirous to be discharged of his employment in the said Richard Hadsor's affairs, or gave a new security with a sufficient bond by like security and condition and gave or delivered his account in writing under his hand, and paid all such sum and sums of money as shall appear to be due unto the said Hadsor for and upon the foot of the said account and perform all the other things mentioned in the said conditions of the said bond, that he the said Richard Hadsor will deliver up the said bond unto the said John Bellew to be cancelled.[20]

As a feoffee of the trust to uses regulating the affairs of Patrick Bellew's estates during John Bellew's minority, this would appear to have been an agreement made by Warren for services rendered or be rendered by Hadsor, who as a lawyer practising in London, might well have included the education and training of John Bellew as a lawyer. The Hadsors were near neighbours of the Bellews of Lisrenny being landowners in Cappoge, north of Dunleer. By this time John Bellew had returned to Ireland, where in July 1630 Messrs Patrick Russell of Brownstown County Dublin, John's stepfather and William Moore of Drogheda, agreed to 'pass assure and convey' to John Bellew of Lisrenny 'all the premises, lands, tithes and hereditaments which the said William and Adam hath in Hitchestown in the county of Louth now in the holding of Patrick McCollier in such sort and manner as the said Patrick Russell's learned counsel shall devise'.[21] By this time John Bellew was twenty-three or twenty-four years of age and may already have begun practising as an attorney-at-law. A successful law practice was then, as it still is, a lucrative business. Apart from handling litigation on behalf of clients in the courts, the landed gentry had much recourse to lawyers in the conduct and management of their estates, handling their testamentary affairs, marriage and other trusts to uses. As has been pointed out the clientele included also the newly created landed gentry of the Ulster borderlands where John's family connections would have been of advantage. With a steady cash flow from fees, lawyers commonly engaged in money-lending through mortgages on lands, bonds and statute staple agreements. John Bellew seems to have conducted a substantial money-lending business, many of the records of which have survived. Some examples of these were a statute staple bond in the sum of £400, advanced by John Bellew to George Russell of Rathmullen County Down and George Taaffe of Rathbody County Louth, through the Drogheda Staple in December 1638. A similar bond in March 1639 was in the sum of £800 advanced to Oliver Plunkett Baron Louth and John Taaffe of Braganstown.[22] On 26 September, 1641 John Bellew advanced the sum of £31.10s. to ten Clogherhead fishermen in a penal bond of 'three score and two pounds', the fishermen being named as Messrs Patrick McEntire 'the younger', Patrick Conlan, Patrick Hoey, Patrick Kenedy, George Fulchagh, Nicholas McEntire, John Crooly, Patrick Crooly, Thomas Frydy and Patrick Dawe, all Irish-English surnames commonly found in the coastal areas of the counties of Down and Louth.[23]

In 1632 John Bellew purchased the lands and fishings of Willistown from George Gernon of Dunmahon where he subsequently established his residence upon his marriage to Mary Dillon, daughter of Robert Dillon of Clonbrock, County Galway. This was a Roman Catholic branch of the Protestant Dillons of Kilkenny-West in County Westmeath, the then head of which Lord Robert Dillon, later Earl of Roscommon and member of the Irish Privy Council, was a prominent supporter of the Lord Lieutenant Wentworth in the 1630–40 period.[24] In her father's will dated 14 December, 1628 he left her 'the interests out of the lands of Ballynadallen' as a marriage portion. By 1641 John Bellew had further acquired forty acres in Drumcar called 'Plunketts land and Simonstown' from William Plunkett of Beaulieu as well as the moiety of Adamstown Drumcar eighty acres, from Simon Orphie.[25] In all, his landed estates by 1641 were estimated at one thousand four hundred and sixty acres plantation measure, not including a thousand-year lease of Reynoldstown and Garmoyle and fishing rights on the river Dee at Drumcar and Braganstown, which were estimated at a yearly value of £50. His success in his business affairs was matched also in his professional career, as he was appointed a Justice of the Peace in 1639 which, as a Roman Catholic, was the highest rank he could have attained in the legal profession.[26] He was also elected one of the two members of Parliament for Louth in the following year, his companion being his cousin, Sir Christopher Bellew of Castletown.

As a lawyer, member of parliament, landed gentleman and member of a family settled in Ireland from the very beginning of the Norman conquest, John Bellew, had times been normal, might well have expected further advancement within the ruling elite. However, times were no longer normal. The elite to which his family had belonged throughout the centuries of English settlement in Ireland no longer existed, having been gradually replaced throughout the Tudor and early Stuart periods by a new elite known as the New English. In contrast to their Old English predecessors this new elite was Protestant in faith and careerist in mentality. Many of them had come into Ireland devoid of landed estate, which was an essential requirement for gentry status, to serve as soldiers or as officials in the retinues of successive viceroys of the crown. Having proved their loyalty to the crown, their objectives, on achieving power, were to acquire landed estate and gentry status in what was fast becoming a new Ireland in which this new Protestant elite would hold the political ascendancy.

Crowded out of the corridors of power by the new elite, the Old English soon found themselves progressively disabled, by virtue of their Roman Catholicism, from participation in large areas of public affairs, including the upper levels of the law. Even their landed tenures which, as in the case of the Bellews dated from the earliest years of the English settlements in Ireland, were in doubt and dependent solely on the grace and favour of the crown. After the cataclysmic decade of warfare following the insurrection of 1641, a losing struggle was begun for the recovery of their ancestral lands, forfeited in the period of the English Commonwealth. It was a struggle that was to extend to the end of the century, but by which date there were few Old English landed survivors. John Bellew's family was one of them.

CHAPTER TWO

Irish Parliamentarian

John Bellew's election to Parliament in 1640 came at the commencement of one of the most fateful periods in Irish history. In the two years that followed, the king's Lord Lieutenant, Thomas Wentworth, Earl of Strafford, and the government which he had established in Ireland since his appointment in 1634, were destroyed and he himself was executed in England's Tower of London. The governmental apparatus he left behind then fell into the hands of his opponents, the rabid anti-Catholic Puritan wing of the English House of Commons, whose revolutionary policies were to precipitate the outbreak of civil war in England in September 1642 – less than twelve months after the tragic outbreak of insurrection in Ireland in October 1641. At the time of his election to Parliament, John Bellew was without question a loyal subject of the Crown, proud of his English ancestry and in his politics anxious only for such constitutional reforms as were necessary to make the executive arm of government more amenable to parliament and the common law. He was also concerned to secure some amelioration in the restrictions imposed on the Catholic Old English in the matter of religion. After six years of the authoritarian government of Wentworth many of these objectives were widely shared, not alone by the Catholic Old Englishry, but also by the Protestant New English. By the 1630s the latter had established themselves in political ascendancy and in extensive landed estates in Ireland, notably in the province of Ulster. During his lifetime John Bellew and the former Old English Catholic establishment to which he belonged experienced the sociopolitical effects of this transformation. Successive governments, through the progressive enforcement of oaths and other tests of religious conformity, gradually eliminated them from participation in public affairs, treating their divergence in the matter of religion as an impairment of the loyalty due by them as the king's subjects.[1] It was a dilemma not unknown in other European countries at this period whether ruled by Catholic or Protestant sovereigns, where local communities, choosing to follow their consciences in matters of religion, rather than the edicts of the monarch, had to pay the price for such aberrant loyalty. In Ireland that price was the loss of privilege and political power as successive king's lieutenants and deputies gradually transferred that privilege and power to the new, and by their lights and standards, more reliable class. The efforts of the Old English to row back the tide had reached some measure of success in 1628 with the grant of the 'Princely Graces' by Charles I, but the subsequent refusal by Wentworth to enact them into law left a void which the Old English would seek to fill in the new Parliament.[2] For them this was their hidden agenda.

The opening session of the new Parliament in March 1640 was all that Wentworth would have wished. The strength of the Roman Catholic representation had been reduced by a third, sixty-eight of whom were Old English and six Old Irish, while the Protestant majority had increased from thirty to eighty-nine.[3] At the outset, the Catholic faction was fully supportive of the government, agreeing to the payment of four subsidies and declaring a willingness to make a further grant if 'the occasions of the war continue'. This was a reference to the king's disputes with the Scots, which had erupted into open warfare in the previous year and concluded in an uneasy peace in June 1639. Not without some criticism, from a section of Protestant dissidents, the subsidies were passed into law on 30 March and were accompanied by an expression of gratitude to the king for having appointed Wentworth as Lord Lieutenant. It was to be the first and last vote of confidence that Wentworth was to receive. When the second session reassembled in June, opposition to Wentworth's policies began to emerge, occasioned by the levying of the first subsidy without the prior approval of the Parliament. There was also opposition to a Bill for securing the recent plantations in Connacht, Clare and Ormond which, having been referred to a committee of the House was never returned by the committee. The opposition now confronting the government under Wentworth's deputy, Sir Christopher Wandesford, was a remarkable coalition of the Catholic Old English and the Protestant New English. These had identified a commonality of interests in opposing Wentworth, sufficient to overcome, at least for the moment, the more fundamental differences in the matter of religion. As matters developed, the Protestant faction came more and more under the influence of the Puritan faction in the English House of Commons, notably through the County Antrim Presbyterian planter, Sir John Clotworthy, who had been a member of the Irish parliament of 1634 and who had been elected to the English House of Commons in November 1640. The hidden agenda of this Protestant faction was to secure, in collaboration with the Old English faction, the destruction of Wentworth, thereby undermining the king's religious policies, and ultimately to wrest power to themselves, in Ireland as well as in England. Their notorious anti-Catholic sentiments, which grew more voluble as their confidence increased, played no small part in unsettling the Catholics in Ireland, notably those in Ulster where further plantation was feared. This fear was to be one of the motivations of the leadership of the insurrection of October 1641.

Probably because he was a newcomer, John Bellew did not figure in the affairs of the House of Commons until the critical third session, which commenced at the beginning of October and ended on 12 November 1640, when the House was prorogued at the instance of the deputy Wandesford. The prorogation followed the adoption of the 'Just Remonstrance' on 7 November, which listed a catalogue of complaints against the arbitrary regime of Wentworth and his deputy, alleging a general decay in trade, failure to give legal effect to the clauses in the Graces regarding security of land tenures, the abuses of the tobacco monopoly and the 'cruel usage' of the Londonderry planters who, it was alleged, had been reduced to such poverty that many had been forced to flee the country. Serious allegations were also made of abuses of power in the administration of the law, including the 'immoderate and unlawful fees' charged by secretaries, clerks and others employed by the administration. Others included, the prohibition of 'men of quality or estate' to pursue complaints by way of petition to the king without the prior consent of the king's lieutenant and the 'powerfulness of some Ministers of State interfering in the natural freedom of Parliament'.[4] In summary, the Remonstrance was a bitter diatribe against Wentworth's rule in Ireland and was a counterpart of a similar movement in the English Parliament, which culminated in his impeachment on 11 November and ultimately in his trial and execution on 12 May 1641. The significance of the Remonstrance was that more than half of the twenty-eight articles of impeachment laid against him in England was related to his service in Ireland. John Bellew, together with his colleague, Oliver Cashell, the member of parliament for the borough of Dundalk, were to play a small, but not insignificant part in Strafford's downfall in that they were the agents who, without the prior permission of the deputy, brought the Remonstrance to England where John Bellew presented it by way of petitions to the English House of Commons and later to the king himself.[5]

The selection of Bellew and Cashell to bring the Remonstrance over to England against the wishes of Wandesford was part of an elaborate plot developed by the opposition factions in the Irish Parliament, probably in collaboration with Clotworthy, Pym and others in the English Parliament, where the plans were being laid for Wentworth's impeachment. Anticipating that Wandesford would reject the Remonstrance and prorogue Parliament, the House decided on 11 November to appoint a Select Committee to travel to England to petition the king regarding the 'grievances of this Kingdom'. This committee was constituted of thirteen members selected from each province, seven of whom were Roman Catholics and six were Protestants. In expectation that this committee would be refused permission to travel, they resorted to a subterfuge by sending John Bellew and Oliver Cashell to England in advance, carrying with them a petition addressed to the English House of Commons, to which a second petition, addressed to the king, was 'annexed'. A copy of these petitions, endorsed by John Bellew as 'the petitions I carried with me to England', are included in Appendices I and II.[6] The second petition repeated all the grievances set out in the Just Remonstrance and ended with a request that the king receive 'a Select Committee from the House of Commons in the Parliament now assembled in this kingdom and in case the Parliament be dissolved certain agents to be chosen by the country from the several parts of this kingdom to attend in person'. This objective was the prime purpose of their mission. Each petition was signed by eighty-four members of the Irish House of Commons, twenty-eight of whom were of the Protestant faction. While the first petition solicited the support of the English Parliament for the objectives set out in the second, the two were interlocked in that the request stated in the first was that the English House of Commons would submit the 'annexed petition of remonstrance' to the king because Wandesford's prohibition on travel prevented the Select Committee 'to make their personal addresses thither'. True to their expectations, Wandesford not alone rejected the Remonstrance and refused permission to travel, but he also had certain pages of the Commons Order Book torn out including the record of the proceedings of 11 November regarding the reduced rate of subsidies decided upon by the House against the wishes of Strafford.

Travel restrictions between Ireland and England had been introduced by Strafford in 1635, requiring the prior consent of the Lord Lieutenant before the journey could be made. The purpose was to limit the right of petition to the king, thus effectively closing off appeals against decisions of the Irish administration, without the prior approval of the Lieutenant. The decision to send Bellew and

Cashell was, therefore, an act of defiance, which could have had serious repercussions for them if they had been discovered. Cashell, like Bellew, had legal training, both having been students at Gray's Inn, and would therefore have had contacts of their own in London. As lawyers and active members of the House of Commons they would have been credible advocates of the matters contained in both petitions. While their prime objective was to secure the reception by the king of the Select Committee, it is evident from the king's reply that other important issues were also dealt with by them. They may also have been selected because it would have been easier for them to travel to England unnoticed from County Louth, possibly with the help of the fishermen of Clogherhead, than it would have been through the port of Dublin. Whether by coincidence or not, the English House of Commons had been debating these travel restrictions in the period prior to their departure and as a result, the English Privy Council decided that they should be lifted. This decision cleared the way for the Select Committee to travel to London where they arrived in several groups between 12 and 19 December.[7] In the meantime Bellew and Cashell, who had arrived in London about 11 November, were busy about their affairs, 'giving in' their petition to the House of Commons on 20 November where they were received ten days later and told that their petitions had been taken into account. They were also received by the king, who on foot of their petition, issued the following letter on 4 January to Messrs William Parsons and John Borlace, who had been appointed Lords Justices of Ireland in succession to Wandesford, who had died suddenly on 3 January:

> Charles R:
> Right trusty and well beloved Counsellors, We greet you well. Having, by the Committee of the House of Commons, assembled in Parliament within our Realm of Ireland, received satisfaction both in their loyalty and affection unto Us, and also in those matters which induced Us to require our Deputy, by our letters of the ninth of November last, to vacate an order, made concerning the levies of our subsidies granted in the same Parliament; We are now graciously pleased, and do hereby authorise and require you, to cause this enclosed, if upon examination you find it to be a true copy, to be again inserted and registered in the same place, to continue and be of equal force, as if the original had still remained there. Whereupon, We do hereby further authorise our Justices and Counsel there, that they give directions to the Speaker of the said House of Commons in that our Realm, that the orders which concern the rating and levying of the said subsidies, with these our letters, be enrolled amongst other acts of the said House; and that,

together with all Commissions to issue for the assessments and levies of the said subsidies, authentick copies of the said order and of these our letters be delivered to the Commissioners in every county and city respectively, for their better direction in the execution of such Commissions, and the satisfaction of the people there: and forasmuch as the said Committee have now humbly besought Us, that from henceforth all letters, directed to our Lieutenant, Deputy, Justices, Chief Governor or Governors, or to any other our Officers and Ministers of that our Realm, either concerning the public affairs, or the private interests of any of our subjects there, may be entered in our Signet office here, to the end they may upon occasion find and take copies for their better information in such public things, as may concern them. We are graciously pleased to condescend thereunto, and give order, that all such letters shall be accordingly recorded and entered here; and that all dispatches, as shall hereafter come from thence, shall be safely kept apart, that like recourse may be had to them for the satisfaction of our subjects, which shall be concerned therein, as occasion shall require: and forasmuch as the Committee aforesaid, John Bellew Esq., and Oliver Cashell, with others employed by them, have made their repair into this our Kingdom of England, to represent their grievances, We, having at all times a gracious disposition to hear all just grievances of our subjects, and to afford them fitting redress, have, for this purpose, given them access to our Royal presence; and therefore, we are graciously pleased to allow of their and every of their comings over without licence, so we do hereby require You, and all other our Officers and Ministers of that our Kingdom, to take notice of this our gracious pleasure, and not to proceed in any wise against them, or any of them, for the same, any former order or direction to the contrary notwithstanding. We do also further declare, that, upon any particular complaint of any of our subjects against any order or decree, they shall and may have, and take such copies of records, certificates, orders of Counsel, public letters, or other entries, as shall be necessary for the declaration of their grievances to us as aforesaid: and these our letters shall be unto you, and every of you, and to all other our Officers and Ministers, whom it may concern, for doing and executing all and singular the premises, a sufficient warrant and discharge. Given under our signet at our palace of Westminster, the fourth day of January, in the sixteenth year of our reign.

Examinater per Warwick.

By his Majesty' commandment H.Veyne.

To Our right trusty and right well beloved our Privy Counsel of our Kingdom of Ireland, and to our right trusty and well beloved Counsellors, Sir William Parsons and Sir John Borlace, knights, designed to be our Justices of that our Kingdom.[8]

Bellew and Cashell had indeed done their work well. By the time of their return to Ireland not alone had the hated Wentworth been impeached but many of the accusations made against him in the 'Petition of Remonstrance' had been incorporated into the articles of impeachment. Furthermore, with the death of Wandesford, his Irish administration had been replaced by Lords Justices, who while the Parliament was in session, would find it necessary to take account of the temper of the House of Commons in their conduct of the affairs of state. In addition to the matters raised in their petitions, other issues, which must have arisen in the interim, were also dealt with. These included the restoration of the pages torn by Wandesford from the Commons Journal, the effect of which was an acceptance by the king of the lower level of subsidy decided by the House, while the administrative reforms introduced by the king, giving greater access to information, regarding king's letters and other Irish state records, would enable the House to exercise a greater vigilance over the executive acts of government. Their mission also cleared the way for the Select Committee to commence their negotiations on the various other issues raised in the 'Petition of Remonstrance'.

Emboldened by the success of the Bellew-Cashell mission, the Parliament in Dublin further instructed the Select Committee to seek additional reforms, such as the enhancement of the role of Parliament in respect of the judicature, and by a substantial modification of Poyning's Law, to secure a greater freedom in the enactment of legislation. Bellew and Cashell were back in Ireland by 9 February 1641 when they were appointed to a Select Committee to treat with the Lords Justices regarding the 'rating of the subsidies, and torn out of the book of orders of this House by Christopher Wandesford Esq., the late Lord Deputy'. Thereafter John Bellew played a full part in the remaining sessions of the Parliament through his participation in the committee system of the House. These included service on such committees as that which was appointed to convey instructions to the Select Committee in London; the committee which dealt with the prosecution of Carpenter and others involved in the tobacco monopoly; the committee appointed for the impeachment of Bolton, Radcliffe and others. He also served on the several committees appointed in connection with the Queries.[9] Involvement in these proceedings gave John Bellew an opportunity to establish personal contacts and friendships across the whole spectrum of political life, and placed him as one of the leaders of the Old English faction in the months preceding the outbreak of the 1641 insurrection. The restoration of the right to petition the king, over the heads of the crown administration in Ireland, had repercussions some one hundred and fifty years later, when in December 1792 Christopher Dillon-Bellew persuaded a timid Catholic Committee to defy the prevailing convention of submitting petitions to the king through the Lord Lieutenant. Dillon-Bellew, who was a direct descendant of John Bellew through his son Christopher, by his defiant stand persuaded the Committee to petition the king directly.[10] He was one of the deputation of five who met the king in London in the following year, the outcome of which was the Catholic Relief Act of 1793. This measure swept away most of the Penal Laws against Roman Catholics then extant and paved the way for the final Act of Catholic Emancipation in 1829. The ancient right of appeal was, however, abolished by the Convention Act enacted later that year.

While in London John Bellew was approached by Robert Maxwell, the Earl of Nithsdale and prominent Roman Catholic recusant, who sought to dissuade him from continuing his mission against Wentworth arguing that if he 'be taken away, our Catholic religion cannot stande'. This was a clear warning of the strong anti-Catholic bias of those in England seeking Wentworth's downfall. John Bellew's reply, that he could not 'departe from my directions with which I am put in trust' by the Parliament could be regarded as naive were it not for the fact that the Old English in their coalition with the anti-Wentworth faction had their own agenda, additional to the destruction of Wentworth's administration.[11] The fourth and twelfth clauses of the 'Petition of Remonstrance', dealing with the 'princely graces' and the right of travel and petition 'to his Sacred Majesty and Privy Council' respectively, were of particular relevance to them. The former had been the subject of negotiation and agreement with the king in the late 1620s and had conferred many benefits on the Old English, notably in the area of land tenures. In particular, Article 24 of the Graces contained a promise to apply in Ireland a Statute of Limitations already in operation in England which provided that the crown's right to resume lands would be limited so as not to extend to lands already in occupation 'above three score years'. This had not been given statutory effect in Ireland, hence its inclusion in the Remonstrance. The subject's right to petition the king was one of long standing in Ireland, 'since the reign of Henry II' as the Remonstrance asserted, and Wentworth's proclamation of 1635 prohibiting travel without licence to 'men of quality or estates to depart this kingdom' had seriously impaired the ability of the Old English to appeal directly to the king over the head of his lieutenant. To secure these and other reforms it was necessary for them to seek what help they could from those whose dislike for Wentworth matched their own. For the greater part of the 1640–1641 Parliament this consensus held good, and was destroyed only at the outbreak of insurrection in October 1641.

The outcome of the negotiations by the Select Committee in England was promulgated by king's letters dated 28 March and 3 April respectively. The former confirmed the continuance of the Parliament and ratified the legality of its proceedings while the latter dealt with the issue of the Graces. These letters were considered by the Parliament by means of a Select Committee of which John Bellew was a member. The proceedings included meetings with the House of Lords and the Lords Justices, culminating in their being read in public by the latter and written into the record of both Houses on 22 May, 'that they may speak, not only to present times, but also to all succeeding ages'.[12] The king's decisions fell short of expectations in regard to the right of judicature of Parliament and the modification of Poyning's Law. He did however confirm his intention to ratify the Graces 'according to the true intention thereof' and as 'may most conduce to the future security of our said subjects estates and the good of that our kingdom'. To this end he required the Lords Justices to prepare the necessary legislation covering such items as the free export of 'corn, grain, malt, oats and oatmeal', the implementation of the Statute of Limitations regarding land tenures and the securing of land titles in Connacht, Clare, Limerick and Tipperary. He also required the submission of a bill conferring the benefits of the fifty-first article of the instructions given for the implementation of the Graces and 'for all other parts of the said Instructions and Graces not herein expressed and for which other particular directions shall not come unto you in the meantime, for transmitting of bills for performance thereof.'[13] This was as ample a response to the Old English expectations as they could have wished for.

The gushing promise, made to Wentworth at the commencement of the Parliament in March 1640, to provide further aid to the king in his quarrel with the Scots 'if the occasions of the war continue' may have provided some comfort to him as he was then in the process of organising the 'New Irish army', a force of eight thousand foot and one thousand horse, officered in the main by Protestant British but with the rank and file predominantly Catholic and Irish. It had begun mustering for training at Carrickfergus, County Antrim, in the summer of 1640 with a view to providing the king with an additional force which could be shipped to England for deployment in the event of a renewal of hostilities with the Scots.[14] While the latter transpired in August, the subsequent ending of the war by the Treaty of Ripon in October rendered the force virtually redundant. However, because of its continued existence after this time, it was to become like a malignant cancer on the whole body politic in Ireland, souring relations with England, introducing instability and distrust at every level and was an important factor in the circumstances leading to the insurrection of October 1641. Despite a lack of funds necessary to maintain it, the king was at first anxious to avoid the disbandment of the force and throughout the early months of 1641 was in communication with the Lords Justices to this effect. The latter, unable to maintain the force and concerned at the growing disorders in Ulster arising from the behaviour of what was by now an unpaid army, argued for their progressive disbandment. In April they were joined by the English Parliament where Pym alleged that the army was being kept in being by the king for eventual service against Parliament in England. Unable to meet these demands, the king then resorted to a plan of disbandment by granting licences to individuals to transport them to the continent for service with Spain, then at peace with England. As well as relieving the pressures created by an unpaid army in Ireland, this might also ensure, as was suspected by his Parliamentarian enemies, its continuance as a force that might become available to the king, if his disputes with Parliament led to open hostilities. This plan was put into effect in May and to this end eight or nine individuals, most of whom were Old English, were licensed to transport the army to Spain. These included Theobald Taaffe, the eldest son of Lord Taaffe of Corren, County Sligo, and Smarmore, County Louth, John Bellew's cousin.

The decision to transport the army abroad was considered by a committee of the Irish House of Commons on 27 July, in association with the House of Lords. As a result, they published 'Reasons for the stay of the sixteen thousand men intended to be sent into Spain,' arguing that the needs of agriculture and manufacture were such that the country could not afford to lose such a body of men and that being thus 'disfurnished' of men might tempt an enemy to invade.[15] The maintenance by the old enemy, the King of Spain, of the survivors of the Old Irish who had fled with the Ulster Earls from Lough Swilly in 1607 was also listed as an objection. While the colonels and captains intended to command the departing army were men of 'known merit, loyalty and integrity', nevertheless 'once the army had passed into Spain they might be relieved of their commands and replaced by some of the said attainted septs who in hope to recover their justly forfeited inheritance might draw the needy unsettled soldier to embrace any motion to return home to their native country to divide the spoils of it amongst them, and if such a mischance do happen, they in their return may be so many spies and guides.' This move was opposed by the Lords Justices, one of whom, Sir William Parsons, suspected an ulterior motive that some might seek to use the force in the event of an insurrection.[16] Following a period of vacillation, the English Parliament finally came down on the side of the Irish Parliament and on 28 August ordered that the ships hired for the transportation be stopped from sailing. By the time this embargo was lifted, insurrection had indeed broken out and a large proportion of the army had passed over to the side of the insurrectionists.

The move to insurrection seems to have occurred in the early summer of 1641 although long before this, as the Irish Parliament clearly suspected, many of the Ulster exiles in Spain and France had cherished the hope of a return to Ireland and, with support from the Continent, the recovery of their long-lost estates. The Old English gentry of the county of Louth, on the other hand, would not have supported insurrection as a solution for their grievances, especially after the receipt of the king's letters of March and April, conveying his consent to the giving of statutory effect to the Graces. The arguments deployed in the petition to the English House of Commons by Bellew and Cashell in the previous November referred to 'the near links and great ties of blood and affinity betwixt the people of this kingdom and the famous people of England, from whose loins they are descended.' Their sincerely held view of themselves was that they were 'flesh of their flesh and bone of their bone'; 'subjects to one gracious sovereign and governed by the same laws'; they had therefore no compelling reason to take other than a constitutional approach. This was further reinforced by the statement in the Preamble to the Petition of Remonstrance to the king,

> that in all ages past, since the happy subjection of this kingdom to the imperial Crown of England, it was, and is a principal study and princely care of his Majesty, and his most noble Progenitors, Kings and Queens of England and Ireland, to the vast expence of treasure and blood, that their loyal and dutiful people of this land of Ireland, (being now for the most part derived from British ancestors), should be governed according to the municipal and fundamental laws of England.

However, the landed gentry was only a part, although an important one, of the total population of the county, which for its size was then, as now, densely populated. That population was a highly segmented one, headed by the landed gentry most of whom were of Catholic Old English stock, interspersed with Protestant British settlers, such as the Moores of Mellifont whose estates were situated along the Boyne valley, Collon, Ballymascanlon and Ardee, the Boltons of Louth and the Bagenals of Carlingford and Omeath. While the estates of the Old English were tenanted in the main by Catholics, many of these were native Irish from the nearby Ulster Marchlands whose forefathers had long been settled in the county. There was also a sprinkling of Protestant British tenants to be found on the Moore and Bagenal estates, many of whom served in the crown forces raised in the aftermath of the insurrection. A similar divide can be traced in the corporate towns of Drogheda, Dundalk, Ardee and Carlingford where the dominant mercantile class was of the Catholic Old English, added to by a growing body of Protestant British newcomers whose main strength lay in the borough of Drogheda.[17] Dean Bernard, in his highly partisan account of the siege of that town in 1641–42, alludes to the divisions between Catholics and Protestants that existed there at that time. While he never resisted the temptation to find fault with the former, whom he accused of resorting to insurrection 'for the utter ruin of the Protestants and the true religion professed by them', he studiously avoided anything that might stand to their favour.[18] Nevertheless, he had been fully aware of the contributions made by the Catholic mercantile class in the defence of the town at that time. In 1653 he was amongst the many Protestants who testified to the Commonwealth authorities of the contribution made by Drogheda's leading merchant, George Peppard, 'for contributing all he could in money and goods for support of that garrison both for setting out of shipping and the relief of the soldiers with clothes and other necessaries'.[19] Nor was Peppard alone in this respect, as ample evidence survives of the contributions made by other Catholic merchants to the defence of the town at that time.

The early decades of the seventeenth century had been relatively prosperous for County Louth, with the manufacture of linen yarn giving employment in the rural areas additional to that provided by the mixture of arable and pasture agriculture then practised. In the port towns in particular, a good deal of employment was provided in the processing of agricultural products into provisions for export, and beer for local consumption. The drinking shops of Dundalk, for example, had a formidable reputation throughout the seventeenth century, while the bulk of the linen yarn then produced in Ireland was exported through the ports of Drogheda or Dundalk.[20] W. J. Smith, in 'Society and Settlement in Seventeenth Century Ireland, the Evidence of the 1659 Census', has concluded that 'a core area in south and mid Louth' was 'not only a society of gentry, farmers and merchants, but also of labourers, ploughmen, husbandmen, cowmen, horseboys, smiths and weavers and even its small towns had their malsters, millers, tanners, butchers and innkeepers'.[21] In an age when word of mouth was the principal means of communication in a society largely illiterate, it is conceivable that the concerns of the landed gentry for the security of their tenures would have been of little interest to the generality of the population. The latter would have been much more concerned with the effects of the recessions in trade, which occurred in the years 1639–40. Their dependence on the landed gentry for political leadership was much less than that afforded by the mendicant friars, particularly the Franciscans, who, as the militant foot soldiers of the Counter Reformation, regarded insurrection as a legitimate means for toppling the Protestant State. This would have been especially true of Dundalk, as described in 1635 by Sir William Brereton.

> This town of Dundalk hath been a town of strength, and is still a walled town, and a company of fifty soldiers are here in garrison under the command of Sir Faithfull Fortesque. This town is governed by two bailiffs, sheriffs and aldermen; the greater part of the inhabitants of the town are popishly affected, and although my lord deputy at the last elections for burgesses for the parliament, commended unto them Sir Faithfull Fortesque and Sir Arthur Terringham yet they rejected both and elected a couple of recusants. One of the present bailiffs is popish. Abundance of Irish both gentlemen and others dwell in this town, wherein they take the boldness to go to mass openly.[22]

The Guardian of the Dundalk Franciscans in the years 1640 to 1644 was Thomas McKiernan. He was an Ulsterman and originally a secular priest who entered the Franciscan Order in 1630, having acted for a time as the Vicar General of the diocese of Clogher where he had been postulated for a bishopric.[23] He was, therefore, a prominent man in the ecclesiastical affairs of the northern Irish at this period and is mentioned in Lord Maguire's confession as having been at the last meeting of the insurrectionists before the abortive attack on Dublin. Another Dundalk resident at this period was Rory O'Moore, the man credited with having organised and developed the plot for insurrection. Maguire described his meetings with him at the early stages of the plot during which O'Moore referred to the smallness of Maguire's 'now estate' 'overwhelmed in debt', compared with the 'greatness of the estate of his ancestors' and to the fears then widespread that the English Parliament was intent on the suppression of the Catholic religion.[24] He mentioned the king's Irish army, which he described as 'all Irishmen and well armed' as a likely source of recruitment and suggested that a date for the rising should be set in 'near winter', when the English could not readily send reinforcements into Ireland. In a reference to the Old English gentry, O'Moore claimed, that while there was some doubt about their willingness to take part, nevertheless it was his view that 'they would not stay quiet and that at least they would not oppose the Irish in anything but be neuters' and 'if in case they did, that the Irish had men enough in the kingdom without them'. O'Moore was a descendant of the native Irish O'Moores of Leix-Offaly who had suffered confiscation of their lands during the reign of Philip and Mary. He had an estate of 954 profitable acres in the parish of Caddamstown, barony of Carbury in County Kildare, which he may have disposed of sometime before 1641.[25] His main landed interests were, however, in Orier in south Armagh where he had a lease or fee farm of the Castlehaven estates of 3,338 acres which included the former lands of Art McBaron O'Neill, half-brother of Hugh, Earl of Tyrone and father of Owen Roe, whose grant in the Plantation of Ulster was only a life interest, the reversion to pass to Lord Audley, made Earl of Castlehaven in 1616. Dundalk was a convenient centre for O'Moore, both to manage his estates in Orier and to maintain contact with many of his co-conspirators, men such as Sir Phelim O'Neill of Kinard in County Tyrone and his brother Turlough, Colonel Brian McMahon of County Monaghan, Philip O'Reilly of Cavan and Sir Con Magennis of Newcastle, County Down. Considering its location as well as the characteristics of its leading inhabitants, it is not surprising that Dundalk was the first town in County Louth to fall to the insurrectionists on 31 October 1641, eight days after the taking of Charlemount and Newry by the forces of Sir Phelim O'Neill and Sir Con Magennis.

John Bellew had been appointed High Sheriff for the county of Louth for the period 1641–1642, an onerous appointment, which carried with it the responsibility for the maintenance of law and order.[26] On 23 July he had been licensed by the House of Commons 'to go into the country about his urgent occasions to be dispatched there, and to return again by Wednesday next'.[27] This is the last mention of him in the House until after the outbreak of the insurrection, although the mention of a petition, which he had lodged in a dispute between himself and Lord Louth later that month, suggests that he was in attendance but did not participate in any of the committees of the House after this date. On 30 October he received a commission from the Lords Justices signed by Borlace and Parsons to execute martial law in County Louth. In addition, he was supplied with arms for three hundred men and about forty more 'for the guard of Dundalk'. Before Bellew could act, the latter town had fallen to the northern Irish with Ardee following a short time afterwards.[28] It would take more than a sheriff's posse to stem the tide of their advance into the county, although twenty-one days elapsed after the fall of Dundalk before Drogheda was besieged. Sir Faithful Fortesque, the governor of Drogheda, was so alarmed at the state of unreadiness in which he found the crown authorities that he resigned his commission. As Dean Bernard put it, 'by his disheartening letters [he] gave us over, who though willing to hazard his life for us yet was loath to lose his reputation also'.[29] In what was to transpire, it was not Fortesque, by deserting his post, nor the crown authorities, by their failure to make adequate provision for the defence of the loyal Englishry of Louth, who were to lose their reputations, but the loyal Englishry themselves. Having been abandoned to meet whatever fate the insurrectionists might visit upon them, they would subsequently lose that reputation for loyalty which had been theirs for over four hundred years and become, in the judgement of the crown authorities, 'Irish Rebels'.

CHAPTER THREE

From King's Sheriff to Irish Rebel

The speed with which Dundalk fell to the insurgents at the end of October 1641 stands in marked contrast with their subsequent advance into County Louth. While individual acts of plundering and spoiling of properties within the county are reported in the depositions as having taken place about the same time or shortly afterwards, it was not until early November that the frontier town of Ardee fell, while the investment of Drogheda did not begin until 21 November, three weeks after the fall of Dundalk.[1] This suggests the possibility that the delay may have been an act of policy on the part of the northern Irish, similar to their approach towards the Ulster Scots, to refrain from attacking in the hope that they might stand neutral or subsequently join with them. Like the Scots, who were initially slow to react in making common cause with their other British neighbours, the Englishry of County Louth seemed to vacillate as if taking a neutral or 'wait and see' attitude. The delay in moving into south Louth was however a boon to the crown authorities, enabling Sir Henry Tichborne to be dispatched with a force of over one thousand men to reinforce the garrison at Drogheda, where the insurgents were to be subsequently bogged down, throughout the winter months, in an ineffectual siege until March 1642, when Tichborne's breakout occurred.

The Parliament had been summoned to meet on 9 November to consider the situation but as the attendance at the Commons was 'but thin' the house adjourned to 16 November when about seventy members were in attendance, including John Bellew.[2] The business of the House was taken up in the preparation and voting on a 'Protestation and Declaration' which, while condemning the outbreak of the insurrection, fell short of condemning those involved as 'rebels', although their actions were described as 'traitorous and rebellious'. It was the kind of compromise which characterised the attitude of the Old English in the early period of the insurrection and which is echoed in Dean Bernard's *Whole Proceedings*. Commenting on the arrival of Tichborne's regiment in Drogheda, he claimed that 'before it was not well taken to call it rebellion but only the act of some discontented gentlemen, but now we took heart to speak as we thought'.[3] That the origins of the insurrection may indeed be traced to 'some discontented gentlemen' of the Ulster Irish can hardly be denied. It was however soon to run out of control as law and order broke down with individuals and groups in localities taking the opportunities offered to work off hidden grievances, engage in lawless acts of violence and plunder or respond to the sectarian urges of the day. Although provided by the Lords Justices with plenary powers of martial law and a supply of arms to equip several hundred men, there is no evidence that John Bellew made use of either and it appears likely that the arms remained in the Drogheda magazine until they were later appropriated by Lord Moore. The martial law powers granted to Bellew were draconian in character.[4] Any persons found to have been active in the rebellion or engaged in 'robbing or spoiling the good subjects' were to be summarily executed. Even where prisoners had been taken, these too were to be executed 'to prevent the danger that may come by keeping them prisoner'. These instructions were qualified so as to restrict the executions to 'men of mean fortunes and the most active'. Nonetheless where 'any of quality' were captured these 'could be reserved in safety', but 'some must be executed for terror to others'. In such cases he was to exercise his discretion, if he thought a 'moderate number will serve, otherwise do as you see cause'.

Bellew had been appointed to a 27-man committee established by the House of Commons on 16 November to treat with the insurrectionists and which included his cousin Sir Christopher Bellew of Castletown-Dundalk, Theobald Taaffe, and Lords Gormanston and Moore of Mellifont.[5] His strict adherence to the brief given him by the House of Commons in the previous November suggests that he was a man who would not depart from a trust reposed in him as a member of parliament. His dilemma was, however, that if he were to execute martial law as required by the Lords Justices he could hardly fulfil the mandate given him by the House to treat with the insurrectionists. In the event he was to take the latter course and, as often happens to mediators, he was to fall foul of one of the parties. For this he paid the price when in February 1642 he was proclaimed a traitor and a rebel and a price of £300 was put on his head. In the following June he was expelled from the House of Commons.[6]

A brief description has survived of Bellew's involvement in negotiations with the Ulster Irish and with Lord Moore of Mellifont, which is contained in a deposition made by him some twenty years later in connection with a petition seeking to establish his 'innocency'. It appears incomplete and perhaps economical with the truth, just as might be expected of a person whose anxiety was to avoid implicating himself in any of the actions of the period alleged against the Old English of acting against the 'English interest' in Ireland.

> Those of Ulster soon after their breaking out came in a very great body to the county of Louth and stormed the late Lord Moore's house, to wit, Mellifont and killed some of his servants and his lordship being then in Dublin went to Tredagh [Drogheda] and I being likewise in Dublin did accompany his lordship and the gates being shut there [Dublin] and all in an uproar, I consulted with his lordship what he thought was best for me to do, whereupon his lordship told me that he was informed that they did no hurt to the country gentlemen or inhabitants, but took meat and drink and desired me to repair home and consult with one Mr Barnewall who lived in the said county, being one in whom his lordship did repose much confidence and that we should labour to find out what the Ulster party would a [sic] been at and thereupon a couple of horsemen were sent with me a good distance of the town and then turned back. This was about eleven of the clock at night and so I went on in byways until I came to my own house where I no sooner alighted than I was met by two strangers and enquiring what they were they told me they were of the Ulster party and were there seeking for me and so coming in with them they told me they were sent to bring the best pledge I had to the camp, in case I could not be met with myself, which was then at a place near Tredagh called Tullyesker, where being accordingly brought the next morning and being put several questions by the Vicar-General McMahon (after bishop of Clogher) and others touching the proceedings then at Dublin by the Parliament and what was done against them there. I told them that had they not come so into the heart of the country, the Parliament had an intention to have treated with them and out of that, falling into discourse, I desired to know what they would be at and observing a willingness in them to have the matter taken up, so the same were well managed for their safety with the king in what had been past, I put them the question what they would offer in that behalf. Whereupon they answered that notwithstanding what was done at Mellifont, for which they would make the Lord Moore what satisfaction he would himself desire, they would intrust his lordship to go to the king on their behalf, whereupon the said Mr Barnewall, unto whom I had communicated what I was commanded as aforesaid, told the said Ulster party that in regard I was with his lordship but the day before, that it

were well done to send me into his lordship to declare their intentions and accordingly the said Ulster party pressed upon me so to do and that they would return into Ulster again, so his lordship went [sic] into England, and would remain there until they had heard from his lordship. Whereupon I went with Mr Barnewall that night, who writt to his lordship touching the premises and within two days after I went into Tredagh and did second the said Mr Barnewall's letter and told his lordship at full what I had understood from them. Whereupon his lordship answered that he was under command as being captain of horse and therefore though he was very willing to undergo the matter, yet he did not think it fit or safe for him to part the kingdom until first he had spoken with the lord of Ormond and to that end he would go in person to Dublin to acquaint his lordship with the business, so they gave him way. The which being propounded by me unto them they (after some consultation) said they would not consent that he should go to Dublin, alleging they feared if his lordship went thither he might be wrought upon there to their prejudice; with which message one Mr James Bath of Athcarne [County Meath], who was near allied to his lordship and myself, went in again to persuade his lordship to go into England and wrought on his lordship as much as we could to go, but his lordship would not, but did advise the said Mr Bath and myself to go to Dublin and to acquaint my lord of Ormond with the matter and his willingness to undergo it as desired and said he doubted not but his lordship would approve thereof. And to that end himself and Sir Henry Tichborne would give us their passes, which was accordingly done. Upon this we departed and having told the said Ulster party thereof, they went into consultation and as it should seem grew suspicious or fearful of us likewise, and so would not permit our going to Dublin. Whereupon we withdrew ourselves and so grew jealous of each other and being in that condition those of the Pale began to consult among themselves what might be best for them to do and in the end sent one Mr Barnewall of Kilbrue [County Meath] to the Lords Justice being a person as was conceived, who had an interest in them, and accordingly he went and that to no other end than to inform them of the sad condition those of the Pale were in and to seek a safety for them from their Lordships and to offer them their service, but the said Mr Barnewall being then racked and after him Sir John Read likewise, the same struck such a terror into all men as made them desperate and so matters fell into a confusion and every one began to consider of his own safety and to draw into remote parts and among the rest I went into Westmeath where some of my wife's friends were.[7]

The period to which this description of events relates ranges from after the investing of Drogheda by the northern Irish on 21 November, to the racking of Sir John Read which took place on 22 March 1642 a few days after the raising of the siege of Drogheda.[8] While the mission of Mr Barnewall may indeed have been to explain the 'sad condition those of the Pale were in' and 'to offer their service' so much distrust had been engendered by the seeming alliance of the Old English of Louth with the northern Irish during the siege of Drogheda and the evident defection of the Meath Old English at the hill of Crufty on 7 December that, for them, the die of their 'traitorous and rebellious' behaviour had been cast. Commenting upon the situation after Crufty, the Lords Justices advised the absentee Lord Lieutenant that 'their discovering of themselves [the Old English] now will render advantage to his majesty and this State and those great counties of Leinster, Ulster and the Pale, now lie the more open to his majesty's free disposal and to a general settlement of peace and religion by introducing of English'.[9] A legal base for such confiscations was enacted in the English Parliament in February under the title the Act for Adventurers in Ireland which was followed on 4 April by the appointment of an English parliamentary commission, consented to by the king, for the management of Irish affairs, including the prosecution of the war and the disposal of confiscated lands.[10] By these means the exercise of the crown prerogative in Ireland was to all intents and purposes rendered null and void.

The evidence of the collaboration of the County Louth gentry with the northern insurrectionists is based upon a number of depositions taken from those who surrendered or were captured in Tichborne's rampage through County Louth in the aftermath of the lifting of the siege of Drogheda. The most notable of these were made by Christopher Barnewall of Rathasker and George Colley, the provost of Ardee, and uncle to Lord Moore of Mellifont on his mother's side. They are dated May 1642 and given as sworn before Robert Meredith, Chancellor of the Exchequer by direction of the Lords Justices and Council.[11] While the possibility cannot be excluded, there is no mention that they were taken on the rack. Barnewall relates that upon the first coming of the insurrectionists into the county under Collogh McBrien (McMahon), Tirlogh Og O'Neill and Colonel Hugh Birne, they 'possessed themselves of all the arms which they could find in the gentlemen's houses', suggesting that no organised resistance could have been given them by the Old English. Considering that the army commander at Dundalk had effectively abandoned the town to the insurrectionists and, that later at Drogheda the governor, Faithful Fortesque, had fled away to England, it is not surprising that the civil population acquiesced in the occupation, being otherwise incapable of resistance. Colley, in his

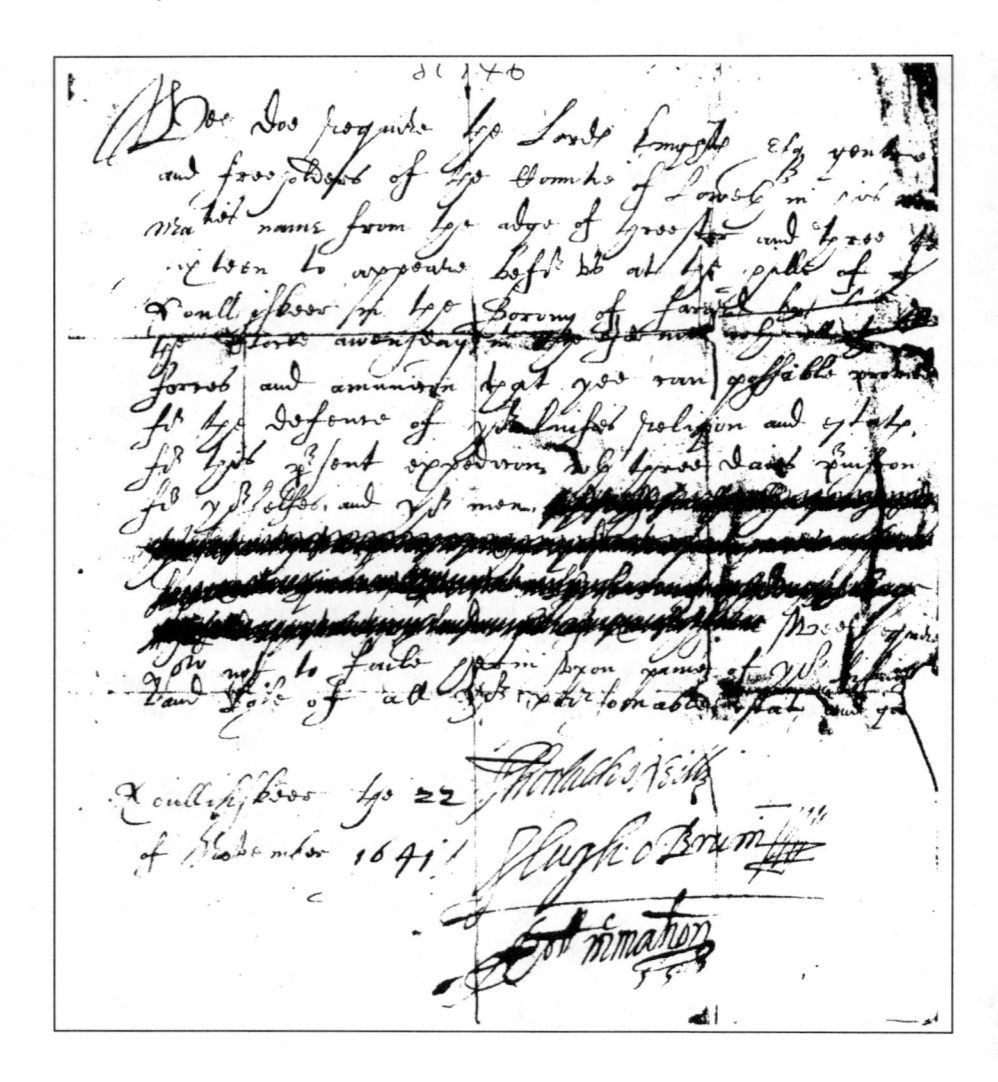

30　*John Bellew, a Seventeenth-Century Man of Many Parts*

3. Copy of original warrant to the 'Knights, esquires, gentry and freeholders of the county of Louth to assemble at the chapple of Toullihskear'.

deposition, stated that the commanders in the county of Louth amongst the rebels required every landowner to contribute one soldier for each forty acres of his holding and as his holding was four score acres he sent a letter to Lord Louth stating that he had sent two soldiers. He claimed that he wrote the letter being 'in fear of his life and in danger of the said northern rebels'. Barnewall referred to warrants issued by the insurrectionists to all persons 'from sixteen to three score' to assemble at Tullyesker within four days, after which a regiment was formed from among the Old English, which subsequently participated in the siege of Drogheda on the north side of the town. The warrant referred to is dated 22 November 1641 at Toullihskear and was signed by Torlough O'Neill, Hugh O'Bruin and Collo McMahon (sic). It was couched in the most peremptory terms:

> We do require the knights, esquires, gentry and freeholders of the county of Louth in his Majesty's name, from the age of three score and three to sixteen to appear before us at the chapel of Toullyisker in the barony of Ferrard by ten of the clock Wednesday next in the forenoon with all such forces and ammunition that you can possibly provide for the defence of your houses, religion and estate for this present expedition with three days provisions for yourself and your men. We require you not to fail herein upon pain of your life and loss of all your personable estate and goods.[12]

By this date, all of the county of Louth, with the exception of Drogheda, was in the hands of the insurrectionists, who had assembled a considerable army, equipped with arms supplied from the captured magazine at Newry and elsewhere, ready for deployment around Drogheda.[13] In these circumstances, abandoned behind enemy lines and left to shift for themselves, it is not surprising that the Old English accommodated themselves to the demands of the insurrectionists, although the first meeting had to be abandoned for want of attendance. The peremptory nature of those demands rule them out as a move towards an alliance between equals and is more reminiscent of the tactics, employed by Mountjoy during the closing years of the Nine Years War, of forcing the Marcher lords in Ulster to put forces in the field against O'Neill and thus to 'put them in blood against him and his confederates'.[14] At the next meeting two days later, a regiment was formed consisting of sixteen companies of foot each captained by one of the local landed gentry or town merchant. Christopher Barnewall of Rathesker was appointed colonel, Bartholomew St Laurence lieutenant-colonel and William Warren sergeant-major. While a number of unsigned depositions give John Bellew as one of the captains appointed at Tullyesker, it is noteworthy that Barnewall's mentions him only as being in attendance. If credence is to be given to one of these unsigned depositions, which was attributed to William Moore of Barmeath, John Bellew 'soon after the sitting of the Parliament at Dublin . . . coming from the said Parliament . . . began to bestir himself and to raise forces to join likewise in the said rebellion, by whose example and labour others of the said county did also join'.[15] This is the only evidence of John Bellew's alleged involvement in the raising of the regiment at Tullyesker while Dean Bernard, who was no friend of Bellew, makes no mention of him in that regard. Notwithstanding the unreliability of the evidence, John Bellew was included as one of the captains of the regiment in the discrimination records made available to the court of claims established under the Act of Settlement of 1662, evidently on the basis of William Moore's unsigned deposition.

Much of John Bellew's deposition can be confirmed from contemporary correspondence, which he managed to retain, as well as from the otherwise hostile source of Dean Bernard's *Whole Proceedings*. John Bellew's offer to go into Drogheda to meet Lord Moore to tell him of the intentions of the northern Irish and their willingness to compensate him for the destruction done by them at Mellifont is confirmed by Bernard although embroidered out of all recognition. Claiming that Bellew was a leader in the rebellion, Barnard described him as coming into the town with 'one Stanley who took himself highly promoted to be a captain with them . . . upon protection as joint commissioners from the rebels upon some pretended treaties'. This conveniently overlooked the fact that Bellew had been appointed by Parliament for such a mission, as was Lord Moore whose appointment Bernard acknowledged.[16] While the account of the proceedings between the parties is a highly coloured one, Barnard does refer to the 'extraordinary affection to my Lord Moore and his family' displayed at the meeting, and to an offer to him 'for his safety, to retreat to Mellifont again or if that was not sure enough, a strong castle was offered him'. The purpose of these offerings was, according to Barnard, to seduce Moore away from Drogheda offering 'to make him General, at least of all Meath and Louth that whatever losses himself or tenants had sustained should all be repaid to a penny'.[17] While it had been agreed at Tullyesker to offer Moore compensation for the destruction of Mellifont, the only other request that Bellew was required to make of him was that he would intercede on their behalf with the king. That this mission was indeed carried out is confirmed in a letter from Moore to Christopher Barnewall dated 6 December and which was a reply to the letter, which the latter undertook to write after the meeting at Tullyesker. As the latter is dated 4 December this seems to fix the date of that meeting.

> Mr Barnewall,
> Yours of the 4th., of this instant I received this day wherein you expressed your and Mr Bellew's care and forwardness in settling an end to these present trouble to which purpose I perceive you have treated with the gentry. Its a matter of great consequence and in conclusion I doubt not but our labours will bend to the content of those that seem to be now discontented, for effecting whereof to attend his majesty which I shall with all cheerfulness do and therein express that which I presume you are not ignorant of, my ever good respects to my country and the gentry thereof. I know you are sensible of the danger which I am in if I should part this kingdom without first acquainting the State therewith, which by letters I cannot do by reason of the late interception of letters, which hath lately happened, so that without some special directions from their party I can neither go nor send to them, either of which upon such directions I shall do and then I with yourself and Mr Bellew will go together and in the end both you and those gentry shall receive no less than what I ever intended, the general good, which will repair the desolations past and prevent the ensuing danger, be the preservation of much blood that will otherwise be spent on this occasion and for those prisoners I have acquainted Sir Henry Tichborne with your desires and he and I are very willing to release, man for man, in the meantime I pray you express my integrity and forwardness in this service which shall readily be performed upon the honour of
>
> Your assured loving friend and servant,
>
>   Moore.
>
> The names of two of the prisoners is one Dowdall [sic]. It is desired that if they have any of my Lord of Ormond's troops you will cause them to be released.
> Drogheda this sixth of December 1641.[18]

This letter confirms in substantial measure John Bellew's account of his dealings with Moore, including the suggested approach to the king. The latter was one of the key objectives of the Pale gentry at this time, not alone to clarify the extent to which the claims of the northern Irish to act in the king's name were justified, but also to assure the king of their continued loyalty to him and to complain against the hard dealings they were experiencing at the hands of the Lords Justices and which was the cause of their seeming alliance with the northern Irish.[19] Moore's insistence that he could not engage in this project without the approval of the State i.e., the Lords Justices, which he must have known would be refused, suggests that he was prevaricating and was not treating seriously the approaches being made by Bellew and Barnewall. More than likely he was seeking instead to garner as much intelligence as possible as to the motives and intentions of the Pale gentry in their apparent alliance with the northern Irish. That Moore was not negotiating in good faith is clearly established by a report from Moore and Tichborne to the Lords Justices stating that they had been informed by Mr Stanley (who accompanied John Bellew in his meeting with Moore in Drogheda) 'an alderman of that town' and 'who had been with the rebels . . . that the whole county of Louth both gentry and others are joined in the rebellion and that the High Sheriff of that county one John Bellew is likewise with them'. This information was subsequently incorporated into the Lords Justices' report of 25 November to Leicester, the absentee Lord Lieutenant.[20] Notwithstanding this identification of John Bellew as being in rebellion, Moore continued to treat with him at Drogheda, providing him and Mr Bath of Athcarne, as late as 10 December with passes to 'travel to Dublin upon special occasions concerning the peace and quietness of the commonwealth and town of Drogheda as their occasions shall or may admit'.[21]

John Bellew, as an able lawyer and experienced politician, must have been only too aware of the precariousness of his position. His companions in the negotiations at Drogheda, John Stanley and James Bath, had already compromised themselves, the former by accepting a captaincy in Barnewall's regiment, the latter by his participation in the proceedings at Crufty and Tara and his subsequent acceptance of a captaincy in Lord Gormanston's regiment.[22] On the face of it, John Bellew's position had many of the characteristics of a double agent, seeming to negotiate on the basis of his mandate from the Parliament while at the same time appearing also, in the eyes of Tichborne and Moore, as an agent of the rebels. Bernard, in *Whole Proceedings*, referred to a present received by Moore on Christmas Day from an unidentified 'captain of their' which was accompanied by a statement of the 'Motives moving the Catholics of Ireland to take arms':

> Our Royal King and Queen are by the puritans curbed and abused and their prerogatives restrained, diminished and almost wholly abolished,

contrary to the rights and power of all monarchical authority and also the duty, allegiance and consciences of all loyal subjects which with grief we take to heart as faithful and loyal subjects ought to do. The Catholic religion suppressed and put down in England and the Catholics persecuted with all rigorous cruelty even to death; the like the puritans of this kingdom threatened to have brought hither.

That there is a law against Catholics in this country whereby the kingdom hath often been impaired and ruined with persecutions, by means whereof the Catholics are made uncapable of any office, or place of commodity or profit, to the great and extraordinary decay of the Catholics in their estates, education and learning.

That the government of the kingdom is wholly in the hands of strangers who in their beginnings are generally poor of birth and means and very quickly become noblemen and men of great estates by oppressing the poor natives.

That there hath been of late threatenings of sending great Scottish forces, with the Bible in one hand and sword in the other to force our consciences or end our lives, besides a private report of a sudden surprisal and cutting the Catholics throats, intending, which way we know not, but it hath been both written and spoken by several Protestants and Puritans.

That the Catholics were not allowed to have any arms or munition (as Protestants and Puritans were) but stood like dead men not able to defend themselves in such desperate dangers.

All which by them considered, they did see no way out but to attempt to seize upon arms, where they could get them, to save their lives, maintain the king and queen, their religion and country.[23]

This statement is a repetition of many of the reasons given for the insurrection by the northern Irish in their 'General Declaration of the Catholics of Ireland', published on 23 October 1641, particularly the references to the curbing of the royal prerogative by the English Parliament, the further legislative restrictions on Roman Catholics in that country and the threat of a Scottish army coming into Ireland with the Bible in one hand and sword in the other.[24] The second and third paragraphs pertaining to the restrictions on the holding of public offices by Roman Catholics and the complaints against the 'strangers' of 'poor birth and means' relates to matters of more concern to the Pale gentry than to the northern Irish and may represent an interpolation by them into the document. Bernard associates Bellew with this statement, whose 'impudence' he condemned when, as 'sheriff of the county of Louth with our Alderman Captain' they came in on parleys, 'as the mouths and legates of the Catholic camp' and 'in their bold assertions and presumptuous hopes in matter of religion', which he described as 'unsufferable'.[25] While making due allowances for Bernard's wild rhetoric, it can hardly be doubted where Bellew's sympathies lay and in his 'parleys' with Moore, it is likely that no amount of dissimulation could hide them. By Barnard's standards he stood condemned as a rebel, as much by the words he spoke, as by the company he kept.

Ormond, who had been plundering and burning the county of Meath with a force of 3,000 foot and 500 horse, arrived at Drogheda on 11 March, thus lifting the siege.[26] Although he was anxious to press northwards into County Louth, he was prevented from doing so by the Lords Justices, who ordered his return to Dublin. Meanwhile the northern Irish with such of the Pale Englishry as remained with them began to regroup. Tichborne, reinforced by Ormond with four additional companies of foot, one of horse and two pieces of artillery, raided the Boyne valley area on 21 March where they burned the town of Slane. Encouraged by this success, they proceeded 'with fire and smoak' towards Ardee on 23 March, which was subjected to an extensive and uncontrolled pillage. On 26 March they assaulted Dundalk and having driven the northern Irish across the bridge north of the town, they subjected the town to an organised pillage which lasted for over four days, 'each captain taking the fortune of his quarter'. The bailiff with many of the burgesses and freemen of the town were hanged. This was to be but one of the many mass killings of civilians carried out by Tichborne and his forces in County Louth throughout 1642. As he himself described the situation many years later, 'the number of the slain I looked not after; but there was little mercy shown in those times.[27]

John Bellew and his family lived in a house at Willistown situated at the end of a long cul-de-sac leading to the river Dee, off the Mullinscross to Adamstown road just east of Drumcar.[28] In some respects this was an out of the way place, although the northern representatives who met him after his return from Dublin seem to have had no difficulty in finding him. Neither had Mrs Cecily Jones and her companions, John Eden and Richard Lawson, who, fleeing from Ardee early in November, came 'accidentally to Mr Bellew of Willistown' and had their lives 'preserved by him and ourselves civilly entertained and safely conveyed by him to Drogheda'. She was to affirm that he and his family were 'as much for the preservation of the English as any could be'.[29] By this time the children of the Bellew marriage may all have been born, Patrick the eldest, Richard, later killed in action while serving with the Jacobite forces in Cavan in 1689, Robert, who became an apothecary, Christopher, who became the agent of his father's properties in Galway, James, who became an attorney in Dunleer and a daughter, Mary, who in January 1665 married Gerald Aylmer, the son of Sir Christopher Aylmer of County Meath.[30] In the wake of Tichborne's advance northwards, it was the turn of the Bellews to take the refugee trail westwards, at first to Virginia in County Cavan and thence to Mrs Bellew's relations in County Westmeath. The Rev George Creighton, vicar of Lurgan, described the flight of the Pale population westwards into Cavan, after the taking of the towns of Dundalk and Trim:

> ... all the inhabitants of the counties of Dublin, Meath and Louth fled with all their goods into the countie of Cavan: day and night they came through Virginia great droves of cattle of all sorts, great carts laden with trunckes and all kinds of good howsholdstuff, great store of wheat and malt. They filled all the empty howses of Virginia full of inhabitants, three or four families making shift with one poor howse. One Robert Baly came to dwell in the low rooms of this Deponent's howse and put in a great deal of his carriage: but one Thomas Plunkett alleged he had leave from the earl of Fingalle to make his choice, and therefore made him remoue to the next house, over against whom was placed Mr Tath of Ecclare [possibly Taaffe of Athclare near Dunleer], Robert Begg of the Navan, Mr Richard Begg, Nicholas Stoakes of Balharry, Russell of Seatowne: all the people of Swords, Christofer Archpoole of Skeaduff, Mr Holliwood of Artane, Mr Blackney of Rickewhore, Barnewall of Lispoppell and Russell of Brunstown. With these there came such plentie of corn that by God's providence wee gott some releefe, the liberality of the Deponent's own parrishioners proveing most scant and beggarly.

Elsewhere in his deposition Creighton identified John Bellew as 'one Mr John Bedlow, which Bedlowe he remembreth to have seen at his, this deponent's house whilst he was prisoner there'. This was probably about April 1642.[31]

Bellew's decision to quit County Louth and to go as a refugee into County Monaghan was forced upon him by Tichborne's murderous campaign. His quitting of his native county and his abandonment of his estates was however interpreted differently by the crown authorities, who found in it a ready pretext to declare him a traitor and an outlaw. Although never formally proclaimed an outlaw, he laboured under the suspicion of it for the rest of his life.

CHAPTER FOUR

Lieutenant-General of Artillery in the Confederate Army of Leinster

Bellew was in Kilkenny in October 1642 where he participated in the first General Assembly of the Confederate Catholics and took the oath of association.[1] However, he did not involve himself in the political affairs of the Confederation, turning instead towards the military, having been commissioned by Lord Gormanston on 14 October 1642 as lieutenant-general of artillery in the 'Confederate Army of Leinster'.[2] According to the military conventions of the day, the lieutenant-general of artillery was the principal field officer responsible for the organisation and management of the train of artillery under the overall but nominal command of the general of ordnance, who was a political figure. Because of the heavy costs involved in the provision of artillery pieces, their munitions and attendant wagons, and the need to provide and command a corps of personnel skilled in the operation of artillery, the office of lieutenant-general of artillery was a senior rank, equivalent, at least, to that of colonel of a foot regiment. Nothing is known of John Bellew's qualifications for the position other than his standing as a prominent member of the gentry class who had demonstrated leadership qualities in a period of crisis. Another and important consideration would have been his capacity to assist directly in the provision of the financial resources necessary to maintain the operational efficiency of his command. In the event, the train of artillery in the Leinster army was to acquit itself well throughout the war years, especially in the reduction of forts and other enemy held strong points.[3] That he had some knowledge and understanding of artillery is suggested by a report made by him on the state of the train of artillery at Athlone and elsewhere (Appendix III). This may have been prepared in the period after receipt of the supplies provided by the papal nuncio Rinuccini for the Leinster Army late in 1645 and the subsequent preparation for Preston's advance into Connacht in the summer of 1646. It displays a good knowledge of the weaponry then available to the Leinster Army and of its condition, with recommendations for improvements, which included criticisms of the failure to provide proper maintenance of equipment and the guard for the train of artillery. Pointing out the need for readiness, he argued that:

> when armies have been ready to advance into the field and gain the opportunity of service, both as to the enemy and time of year, then hath all been at a stand, waiting for the fitting out of these things, whereby the kingdom hath been eaten out and the service lost, for hitherto there was never provision made for those things (let a man solicit as much as if his life lay on it), until the very time of service came and then things were put a work in a hudling manner, hand over head and when the summer service were over, no provision was made for laying up these things from the rain or weather nor yet for the members of the train, but all turned from winter quarters and so every year they were forced to begin anew as if the war were never thought of before.[4]

This was a comment, as much on the desultory and even amateurish quality of the conduct of the army at this period, as it was on the management of the train of artillery and suggests that Bellew took the duties of his command seriously.

In 1642 Colonel Richard Plunkett, the son of the earl of Fingal, was reported as being engaged in the manufacture of cannon either at Virginia, County Cavan, or at the earl's other house at Killeen, County Meath.[5] As Bellew was in Virginia about this time where he could have made the acquaintance of Plunkett, it is tempting to speculate that this could have provided him with his first introduction to artillery. By August 1643 Bellew had taken the field as lieutenant-general of artillery in the forces sent by the Catholic Confederacy under Sir James Dillon, Bellew's relation by marriage, to join with Owen Roe O'Neill's Ulster army in the defence of County Meath. This force included some artillery pieces, one of which was detached to O'Neill and which was put to good use in the capture of several towns and forts in that county, such as Clonabreney and Ballybeg outside Kells where Tichborne's son William was captured.[6] In September Bellew's former parliamentary colleague and negotiator at Drogheda, Lord Moore of Mellifont, marched out from Athboy with a force of about three thousand men to confront O'Neill who, again with the aid of the artillery, had taken Portlester Castle outside Trim. In the ensuing skirmish, which involved a spirited defence of an old mill by a party of O'Neill's musketeers, the artillery was again in action. Moore's forces were heavily defeated and he himself killed by a cannon ball said to have been aimed at him by O'Neill.[7] Sir James Dillon had failed to give the support to O'Neill which had been expected of him, but this was not so in the case of John Bellew, who was specially commended by O'Neill in a testimony dated 19 September 1643, in which he described him as a 'valiant, vigilant and expert gentleman', who 'in a word discharged the duty of his place as well as any man could have done'.[8] High praise indeed, coming from a man who was then the most professional soldier in Ireland. Showing his contempt for Dillon, O'Neill suggested that he should forego a military career, as he was 'more suited to courting ladies'.[9]

The outbreak of the English Civil War on 22 August 1642 changed the whole context of the political situation in Ireland. The king, no longer fettered by his rebel Parliament, sought a rapprochement with his erstwhile 'Irish rebels', so that by bringing hostilities to an end, would enable the shipment of troop reinforcements into England. His agent for this purpose was his newly appointed lieutenant, the Earl of Ormond, whom he instructed to negotiate a truce or cessation with the insurgents. This was accomplished on 15 September, 1643 when a cessation of one year was agreed, the sides to retain control over their respective areas. For the next four years these were to become known as the Irish quarters, when held by the Confederacy, and the English quarters, when held by the Crown forces serving under Ormond. Included in the latter were the areas of east Cork and Cork city held by Murrough O'Brien, Baron Inchiquin, until his defection to the rebel English Parliament in July 1644. In the province of Ulster the Irish quarter, was in middle and west Ulster, and was held by Owen Roe O'Neill on behalf of the Confederacy, while the English quarter, consisting of the greater part of the counties of Antrim, Down, Donegal and Derry was held by the British colonists of these areas, who professed an uncertain loyalty to the king. County Antrim was held by the Scots expeditionary force under Major General Robert Monro, which had been despatched into Ulster in April 1642, under an agreement made between Scots and English parliamentary commissioners with the nominal consent of the king.[10] While the Scots refused to recognise the cessation, the situation in Ulster, including that of supply, was to lead to a chronic state of warfare as the various sides struggled for territory on which to supply a subsistence for their respective forces.

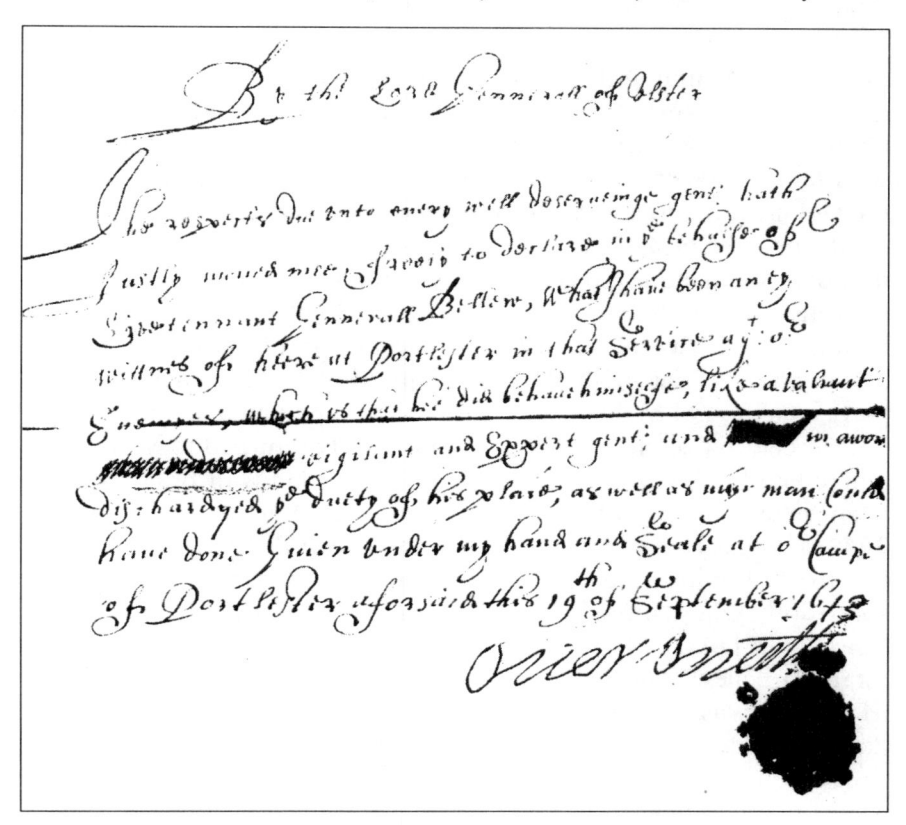

By the Lord Generall of Ulster The respects due unto every well deserving gent hath justly moved me freely to declare on the behalf of Lieutenant Generall Bellew, what I have been an eye witness of here at Portlester in that service against the enemie, which is that he did behave himselfe, like a valiant, vigilant and expert gent, and in a word, discharged the duty of his place as well as anye man could have done. Given under my hand and seal and ye Campe of Portlester aforesaid this 19th., of September 1643. *Owen O'Neill.*

4. Owen Roe O'Neill's commendation of John Bellew's service at Portlester.

The county of Louth, with the possible exception of some areas along the western March with County Monaghan, came within the English quarters. The terms of the cessation provided for the Old English proprietors to recover their estates, outlawry proceedings against them notwithstanding, on condition that they complied with the requirements of the Dublin administration and paid their taxes and other contributions for the maintenance of garrisons. Evidence of their return is to be found in post mortem inquisitions held in the county in March 1644 involving the estates of the Babes of Darver and the Plunketts of Beaulieu.[11] A land dispute between the Gernons of Maine and Drumcath was also investigated by the Irish Parliament in May 1644, which involved Patrick Gernon of Maine, one of the captains appointed at Tullyesker in November 1643.[12] John Bellew and his family returned to Willistown where he obtained a lease of Thomas Dawe's lands in Braganstown, Mansfieldstown, Drumcashel, Milltown and Dundalk in November 1644. Thomas Dawe of Dunany had been one of Bellew's clients during the 1630s and in the lease documents he acknowledged that 'the said John doth relieve myself, my wife and family in these unbearable times'.[13] In January 1645 Dawe conveyed his freehold interests in the estate to Bellew. Another transaction entered into by John Bellew in May 1645 was a mortgage loan of £20 sterling to William Moore of Barmeath secured on certain specified lands in the barony of Ferrard and subject to a right of recovery by Moore if the loan was repaid by the 1 May 1647.[14] In June 1645 a James Darcy of Galway acknowledged that a judgement debt of £36 sterling, due for payment in November 1641 by John Taaffe of Braganstown and his son and heir, Christopher, had been held in trust by him 'for my brother-in-law John Bellew of Willistown'.[15] Darcy testified that, although 'having through the distractions of the times and mislaying of papers forgotten both sureties, time of payment and particular sum', the Taaffes nonetheless acknowledged that a judgement debt of £36 was due to be paid before November 1641. One of the witnesses was a Richard Dillon who may also have been John Bellew's brother-in-law.[16] Whether on the basis of subsequent extensions of the cessation, or through the connivance of the successive Dublin administrations, the Old English of County Louth were allowed to continue the effective occupation of their estates until the mid-1650s. In September 1647, after the occupation of the county by the English parliamentarian forces under Colonel John Moore, the outlawry proceedings were reactivated and while the outcome is not known, no evidence of any general sequestration of Old English lands in the county has been found.[17]

Notwithstanding that John Bellew had returned to the beneficial use of his estates in the English quarters of County Louth, he continued in his duties as lieutenant-general of the artillery in the Leinster army and was located in the garrison at Kilkenny, the headquarters of the Catholic Confederacy. While this would seem to imply that he had to divide his time between Louth and Kilkenny, it seems more likely that his wife Mary had to assume responsibility for the management of their County Louth estates as well as to care for their growing family. This would have been especially true in the later stages of the war when Bellew was on active service. In the period immediately following the cessation, military activity would have been reduced to garrison duties, but as the negotiations for a political settlement dragged on, the changed fortunes of the king, especially after the defeat at Marston Moor in July 1644, necessitated a settlement in Ireland to release badly needed reinforcements for service in England and Wales. However, the capacity of the Confederacy to conclude a peace with the king's lieutenant Ormond was limited, as much by the incapacity of the latter to compromise, as by the influence of the Roman Catholic clergy and their supporters, mainly but not exclusively Old Irish. These held out for the replacement of the Protestant Church Establishment by a Roman Catholic Church Establishment, an inconceivable prospect for a king who was himself Protestant and struggling to maintain himself as king, not alone of Ireland but more importantly from his standpoint, of Protestant England. By contrast, the Old English gentry, already inured to the disabilities imposed upon them by reason of their religious beliefs, were content to accept the de jure status of the Protestant State, provided they were allowed the quiet practice of their religion and security of their landed tenures. The arrival of the papal nuncio, Rinuccini in October 1645 added a further dimension and in time a further obstacle to the conclusion of a peace based upon a compromise that recognised the dangers that could arise from a puritan victory in England. Another factor, which created disunity within the Confederation, was the failure by the Supreme Council to nominate an overall commander of the field forces. This created tensions between Owen Roe O'Neill, the commander of the Ulster army, and Preston, the commander of the Leinster army, which was made more acute by the apparent favouritism shown to the latter by the Council.

In March 1646, agreement was reached for a continuance of the cessation, and in the following June, Owen Roe O'Neill achieved his great victory over Monro at the Battle of Benburb, an event which greatly strengthened the nuncio's position. When the Supreme

Council finally concluded a peace with Ormond in July to which the nuncio was adamantly opposed, the hidden dissensions within the Council and between the army commanders became manifest. Such was the strength of his position that the nuncio had the outgoing Supreme Council arrested and replaced by a provisional Council which he endowed with the same powers as the 'late Supreme Council'.[18] It consisted of the nuncio as president acting with two laymen and one bishop from each province, two laymen selected at large, with the army commanders O'Neill and Preston as ex-officio members. Oliver Plunkett, Lord Louth, was appointed one of the members. In the summer of 1646, Preston's army had been campaigning in Connacht against the forces of the parliamentarian, Sir Charles Coote of Sligo, and his allies, the Laggan army of north-west Ulster. With the aid of Bellew's train of artillery, he succeeded in capturing the strong points of Roscommon and Boyle in July. A contemporary description of the attack on Roscommon Castle indicated that it was not until 'the cannon had made a breach' that the garrison sued terms for surrender.[19] In the following month Preston promulgated the peace agreement in his camp 'with trumpet and a salute of guns'.[20] However while Preston secretly supported the agreement, he feared the nuncio's influence. Pleading his ignorance of the real state of affairs, he revoked his decision and came out in support of the nuncio. Nonetheless when the nuncio's Council decided to move against Ormond and invited Preston as well as O'Neill to take the field, Preston's reaction was a tardy one, pleading difficulties in mustering his forces. However, when he eventually joined with O'Neill at Kilcock, County Kildare, in October, his army was found to be as large as O'Neill's. Evidently he had deliberately delayed his advance on Dublin in order to field an army which would act more as a counter-force to O'Neill rather than as a threat to Ormond. Under heavy suspicion of colluding with Ormond, Rinuccini and his Council called on Preston to promise on oath to act in good faith with O'Neill in the attack on the city. This he refused to do, unless it was agreed beforehand that Ormond be called upon to concede satisfactory conditions for Irish Catholics before any attack was launched. Rinuccini consented to this condition and the two armies marched together to Lucan. An ultimatum was delivered to Ormond demanding the same freedom for Roman Catholics as they enjoyed in France, the purging of the Dublin administration of Puritan sympathisers and the admission of Catholic garrisons into towns and castles held in the king's name.[21] By this time Ormond had commenced the negotiations with representatives of the English

Parliament, which would lead in time to his surrender to them in June 1647. In the meantime, having received much needed military supplies from the Parliamentarians and with an expectation of further reinforcements if needed, he rejected the ultimatum.[22] At this juncture, the Catholic royalist and Ormondist supporter, Lord Clanricard, intervened seeking the agreement of the nuncio and Council to accept the peace with additional guarantees in the matter of religion. While these proposals were rejected, Preston gave his support to them and indicated that in the event of hostilities breaking out he would support Ormond. With this, O'Neill withdrew and the threat to Dublin collapsed. Preston, while still colluding with Ormond, continued to argue with the nuncio and the Council for the acceptance of the pact offered by Clanricard. However, with the threat to Dublin dissolved, Ormond was in no mind to make any further concessions and instead called on Preston to turn against the nuncio and his supporters. Having been accused of treacherous behaviour by the latter and with threats of excommunication hanging over himself and his followers, he eventually capitulated on 16 December.[23] Through the mediation of Father Oliver Darcy and on a promise to submit without reservation they were received back into favour by the nuncio and acquitted of 'any stain on their honour'.

In an army list supplied to Ormond about July or August 1646 by the Supreme Council of the Confederation, John Bellew is described as commanding the artillery, ammunition and other provisions 'gone into Connacht', a reference to Preston's expedition into that province earlier that year.[24] The train consisted of a brass cannon, a brass culverin and two quarter cannons mounted on carriages with a sledge for the cannon. It included also six score and three oxen, eight covered wagons, twenty-eight casks of powder, three thousand weight of match and three thousand weight of lead bullets. In addition he had the command of a guard company of ninety-one men, twenty pioneers, thirty-five drivers, twelve gunners, three smiths, three carpenters and one cooper. Other field artillery pieces were located elsewhere, two quarter cannons, mounted on their carriages at Ballysonan, County Kildare, and a long brass field-piece on its carriage at Tecroghan, County Meath. Later that year Bellew accompanied Preston on the march to Dublin where he is mentioned as commander of the artillery in a muster of the Leinster army taken in November.[25] In the dispute between Preston and Rinuccini, Bellew sided with the former and was one of those who signed a letter to the nuncio urging acceptance of Clanricard's proposals.[26] Bellew was among the officers received back into the favour of the Supreme Council in December, having signed the public denial issued by Preston and the commanders of the Leinster army in the previous month, in which they asserted that they had never endeavoured to withdraw from the Confederation or make peace with Ormond.[27]

When the General Assembly of the Confederation opened in January 1647, the divisions of the previous year had become institutionalised into 'Nuncioists' and 'Ormondists' and, while the former held the majority, they too were divided between the clerical party and their supporters, whose objectives were to replace the Protestant ethos of the state with a Roman Catholic one, and the others, mainly laymen, whose concern was for the maintenance of the king's prerogatives including the appointment of bishops, which the nuncio sought to reserve to himself and the Pope.[28] The Ormondist, Colonel Walter Bagnall, addressed the Assembly at length and spoke passionately of the high-handed attitude of the clergy and the risks involved in the pursuit of their extremist line:

> . . . My lords there was a time, when our ancestors, at the peril of their fortunes, and with the danger of their persons, sheltered some of you and your predecessors from the severity of the laws. They were no niggardly sharers with you in your wants; and it cannot be said that the splendour of your present condition hath added anything to the sincere and filial reverence which was then paid you. We, their posterity have, with our blood and the expense of our substance, asserted this advantage you have over them, and redeemed the exercise of your function from the penalties of the law, and your persons from the persecution to which they were subject. We are on the brink of a formidable precipice, reach forth your hand to pull us back; your zeal for the house of God will be thought no less fervent, that you preserve the Irish nation; and your judgements will not suffer for the attempt, when you give over upon better information. Rescue us we beseech you from those imminent miseries that environ us visibly; grant somewhat to the memory of our forefathers, and to the affection we bear you ourselves. Let this request find favour with you, made to prevent the violation of publick faith, and to keep the devouring sword from the throats of our wives and our children.[29]

The views expressed by Bagnall, who was of 'New English' descent from Elizabeth's famous Marshal, Sir Henry Bagnall, would have been widely shared by the Old English, including John Bellew, for whom the 'formidable precipice' was the looming victory of the rebel English Parliament while the 'devouring sword' was the imminent threat of that victory to their lives and estates. At a time when the gentry class to which they belonged depended for their very existence upon possession of a landed estate, such an outcome of their long struggle was unthinkable. For them, a compromise agreement with Ormond, followed by a union of their respective forces to oppose the common enemy was seen as the only practicable course to follow. Nearly two years were to elapse before this course was taken, by which time the king was dead and the Puritans held the upper hand in England.

John Bellew continued on active service in the Leinster army throughout the years 1647–1648 and accompanied Preston on his ill-fated campaign against the newly arrived Parliamentarian forces of Michael Jones in Dublin. He was also a participant in the ill-fated battle of Dungan's Hill in August.[30] While he himself escaped capture, he lost of his train of artillery, 'four demi-culverins each carrying a twelve pound bullet and sixty-four fair oxen attending the train'.[31] As a foretaste of what was to come, Ormond had in the previous month sequestered his lands at Willistown and Cashellstown and granted them in custodium to a Lieutenant-Colonel Bellay.[32] It is not likely that Mrs Bellew and her family were ejected from the estate, but rather that she made an arrangement to become tenant to Bellay and pay him a rental.

In the aftermath of the battle of Dungan's Hill and the equally disastrous defeat by Inchiquin of Taaffe's Munster army at Knocknanoss, outside Mallow, in November 1647, the 'Ormondists' renewed their attempts at a peace by securing a cessation with Inchiquin and by creating the conditions necessary for Ormond to be recalled as the king's lieutenant. Despite stiff resistance by the Nuncioists, a cessation was agreed with Inchiquin in April 1648, after the latter had indicated in February his intention to break with the parliamentarians and support the king. Notwithstanding the publication by Rinuccini of sentences of excommunication on all those accepting or supporting the cessation, the Supreme Council pressed ahead with its plans and appealed to Rome against the 'pretended' censures of Rinuccini. With the return of Ormond to Ireland in September, matters proceeded apace and by the following January the second Ormond Peace had been put in place by a decision of the General Assembly meeting at Kilkenny. In accordance with its terms, the Confederation was dissolved, Ormond was recognised as the king's lieutenant and commissioners of trust were appointed as an interim government.

John Bellew lost no time in shedding his rebel status. In January, with other senior officers of the former Confederate army of Leinster, he opened negotiations with the commissioners of trust for the reformation of the army, under Ormond's overall command. On 1 February 1648 he received a commission signed by Ormond appointing him as captain of a foot company of one hundred men to act as the guard of the train of artillery.[33] He was to claim later in the Restoration period that, following his commission, he laid out the sum of £100 to furnish the train of artillery in preparation for Ormond's attack on Dublin. While Ormond was to address him subsequently as lieutenant of the ordnance, he was not in fact commissioned into that rank until August 1650, suggesting that his substantive appointment prior to the latter date was as captain of the guard of the train of artillery.[34] It was in this rank that he marched with the rest of Ormond's forces out of Carlow on 1 June 1649 and joined Inchiquin's Munster army at the Curragh in County Kildare. Then the combined forces marched to Finglas, north of Dublin city, where they set up camp.[35] In August Ormond launched his long awaited attack on the city.[36] Leaving a force of 2,500 men north of the Liffey, he moved his main army to Rathmines. He also set about establishing a battery at Ringsend to deter enemy shipping entering the port of Dublin. He then commenced an encircling movement along the eastern side of the city in an attempt to capture Baggotsrath Castle near the present Baggot Street bridge, where he commenced the construction of entrenchments and a fort on which to position six field guns. Before these works could be completed, Jones launched his attack on Baggotsrath and, having routed Ormond's forces at this point, he extended his attack on the other elements of Ormond's army. In the engagement which followed, Ormond was comprehensively defeated and his army decimated. Seven field guns as well as other equipment and stores were captured, as well as John Bellew.

John Bellew did not remain a prisoner for very long. He had surrendered upon quarter and, having paid the ransom demanded, he was released on 27 September 1649. The pass given to him was signed by Michael Jones, allowing him to return to the 'Irish Quarters' with his 'horse and boy and such necessaries as he carrys for his own use, he demeaneth himself as becometh'.[37] Bellew had previously been at Ormond's headquarters at Castle Jordan, County Meath on 8 September where he was given a letter from Ormond, for delivery to Oliver Cromwell. It intimated that Bellew had been taken prisoner at Rathmines and had been sent 'to labour the ransomes of himself and the rest taken there'. It pointed out that Bellew had written twice to Jones in the matter, and was returning 'to know the certainty thereof according the contents of the articles of quarter given them, which he carries along with him'. Attached to the letter was a further note to

Cromwell empowering Bellew to negotiate 'the exchange or ransom of such prisoners as now or hereafter shall be of either side, and withal to desire your answer to my letters of the last of this August'.[38] This correspondence indicates that Jones had temporarily released Bellew, in order to negotiate the conditions of release for himself and the other prisoners taken at Rathmines and that it was not until 27 September that his actual release took place. Before the battle of Rathmines Bellew had received, on 22 July, an order from Ormond to Sir George Hamilton for the payment of the 'entertainment' due to him of fifteen shilling per diem. This had not been paid before the battle and on 22 December Ormond issued a further order, which was acted upon by the deputy muster-master Edward Birmingham. It ordered the payment of £159, less £53 15s, 'defaulked' in respect of interim payments made at Kilkenny, Finglas and Rathmines.[39] On 9 February 1650 Bellew was ordered by Ormond to 'draw the foot company' under his command to Kilkenny where the sheriffs were ordered to provide them with quarters.[40] Shortly after issuing this order, Ormond left Kilkenny for Limerick and did not again return until after the restoration of Charles II. By this time Cromwell was approaching from the south and plague had broken out in the city which was to wreak havoc, not alone among the civil population, but also in the garrison which was reduced from 1,200 to 400 men. By the time Cromwell had launched his attack on the city on 22 March, the garrison had been further reduced to 300, evidently because of desertions. The commander, Sir Walter Butler, realising the hopelessness of his situation, sued for terms, which allowed his men to march out of the city, and for the payment of £2,000 to Cromwell, on a promise that there would be no plunder of the citizenry.[41] These terms were agreed although the cathedral and other churches were unroofed and plundered.

After the fall of Kilkenny, Bellew retreated northwards to Tecroghan Castle in south Meath. A contemporary account of this strongpoint described it as having huge ditches, strong ramparts, turrets, many pieces of ordnance and garrisoned by an Ulster Irish party of 600 men under a Major Luke Guire. On Ormond's orders, they were replaced by a party of the Leinster army under Sir Robert Talbot, giving rise to resentment amongst the Ulstermen. John Reynolds, Cromwell's commissary-general, laid siege to the castle about the middle of May and the garrison, short of provisions, called upon Clanricard and Castlehaven to come to its aid. A party of 2,000 foot and 700 horse under Castlehaven set out for the castle with a train of provisions and ammunition at its rear. While crossing over a narrow causeway through a bog, the rearguard under a Captain Fox of the Ulster Irish allegedly ran away leaving the train unguarded. Meanwhile the rest of the party marched on to Tecroghan but, arriving without the necessary supplies, they had to withdraw leaving the garrison little option but to surrender to Reynolds.[42] The articles of surrender dated 25 June were negotiated by John Bellew, Captain Fiachra O'Flynn and Mr Pembroke Harbert. They provided for the entire garrison, including those of the relieving party who had remained behind after the withdrawal of the main party, to depart with their arms, bags and baggage, colours flying and drums beating.[43] No act of hostility was to be shown them until after the elapse of three days. Special provision was made for the wife of the castle owner, Sir Luke Fitzgerald, who was permitted to stay on in the castle and for the corn crop to be harvested by the local inhabitants and owners. A special provision was also made enabling Talbot to recover half of the ordnance within a period of eight weeks after the surrender. These guns were never recovered, possibly because of the lack of means to recover them. In a report by Sir Nicholas Plunkett to Ormond dated 27 June he complained that a sum of over £18 was still due to the gunners, smiths and others of the former garrison and that he had no money to pay them. In a reference to 'carriage-horses and cars taken by the Connacht forces' for which the enemy expected payment, he mentioned that John Bellew had agreed to satisfy them, he himself taking ten oxen 'in full or part payment'.[44] Later in the Restoration period, Thomas Stanley, who was one of Reynolds' commissioners involved in negotiating the surrender, testified that both Bellew and Talbot had been offered their estates in return for the surrender of the castle, provided that they undertook to 'decline the service they were then engaged in and live peaceably at home'. Both declined the offer.[45]

The Tecroghan garrison retreated to Athlone where Lord Viscount Dillon appointed Sir Robert Talbot and Sir James Dillon joint governors. At this time plague had broken out in the town, those having the infection being banished 'to the boggs', while most of the townspeople who could do so fled. Dillon was disposed to surrender to the Commonwealth forces and parleys were held with this end in view.[46] The author of the 'Aphorismical Discoverie' includes John Bellew as being one of those who engaged in these negotiations, which came to nothing.[47] The town held out against several attempts by the Commonwealth forces but, in June 1651, Sir Charles Coote invested the town and after a parley agreed articles of surrender, similar to those entered into at Tecroghan. John Bellew and a Captain Fitzgerald acted as hostages for compliance by the garrison with the terms of the surrender.[48]

Following the defeat of Ormond's royalist army at the battle of Rathmines, and even before the traumatic experience of Cromwell's violent storm of Drogheda, the Protestant British elements of the alliance making up that army fell rapidly away from their professed allegiance to the king. As Ormond himself put it:

> . . . after the defeat before Dublin, almost all those of the army that had homes of their own or their friends to go to, were retired to them, and could by no industry be gotten together again . . . and our numbers daily diminished, by the revolt of some officers and many private soldiers, the rest showing much dejection of courage, and upon all occasions of want, which are very frequently with us, venting their discontent in such dangerous words, that it was held unsafe to bring them within that distance of the enemy.[49]

After Drogheda, the desertion of the Munster Protestant army left but a rump of Protestant forces with Ormond, mainly from the remnant of the British settler forces of north-west Ulster and County Down. By April 1650 these too had left the field of battle, when the Articles of Surrender of the Protestant Party in Ireland were concluded.[50] The struggle against the English Commonwealth was continued until September 1653 by what remained of the army of the former Catholic Confederation and Owen Roe O'Neill's Ulster army bereft by the death of its commander, and badly divided by the politics of the concluding years of the Confederation. Despite the unevenness in strength and provision between the latter and the forces of the English Commonwealth, slow headway was made and as time passed, the Commonwealth began to lay down relatively soft conditions for surrender as in Tecroghan and Athlone. However, the setbacks suffered by them in the taking of Limerick in November 1651 led to the exclusion of several of the leading members of the garrison from the benefits of the articles of surrender and these were subsequently executed.[51] After this event it became evident to all but the extreme elements of the former Nuncioists that the time had come to make an honourable surrender on the best terms possible, especially in matters pertaining to life and estates. From this development came the Articles of Kilkenny, which set the principal provisions for all subsequent surrenders of what the Commonwealth authorities referred to as the 'Irish Party', a nomenclature which also included the Old English. The union of the two nations, the Old Irish and the Old English, which had eluded the Confederacy, was to be forged in the crucible of the victory of the English Commonwealth. Thenceforward the Old English ceased to exist, becoming merged with the rest as Irish Papists.

The initiative for the negotiations leading to the Articles of Kilkenny was taken by a group, mainly of leading officers of the former Leinster army, styled the Commissioners of Leinster. They were under the command of the Earl of Westmeath and consisted of Sir Walter Dungan, the commissary-general of horse, Lewes, Lord Viscount Clanmalirie, Sir Robert Talbot, Sir Richard Barnewall, Colonel Walter Bagnall, Colonel Lewes Moore, and Thomas Tyrell.[52] While all or most of these may have participated in the subsequent negotiations, it is clear also that others participated, including John Bellew, who was one of those who signed the Articles on behalf of the Irish Party. The negotiations were commenced a short time after 6 May 1652 at Gowran village, thirteen kilometres east of Kilkenny and were concluded by the signing of the Articles on 12 May in Kilkenny city.[53] They made provision for the surrender of all the forces of Leinster, as well as those in Munster under Lord Muskerry, of those in Connacht under Lord Mayo, Colonel Richard Burke, Major-General Taaffe and Colonel Garrett Moore, and of the forces of Ulster under Hugh Magennis, Viscount Iveagh, Phillip McHugh O'Reilly, Lieutenant-General Farrell and Colonel Myles O'Reilly. In fact, many of these did not surrender until much later, those of Ulster being the last to do so, under separate but similar provisions, dated 27 April 1653.[54] Provision was made for the officers to depart with pardon for life and protection for themselves and their personal estates and suitably equipped with horses and pistols according to rank. In the case of non-commissioned officers, troopers and gentlemen, horses were not allowed but those having horses were to be suitably compensated for their loss. Provision was made for those who wished to transport themselves abroad in the service of any state friendly to the English Commonwealth. In the case of individuals having real estates, they were promised equal benefit with others in the like qualification in any further offers that might be made by Parliament in this regard. The Commonwealth commissioners also promised to mediate with Parliament to ensure that such persons would also enjoy such moderate parcels of their estates as would make their lives comfortable and, in the case of those enlisting for foreign service, a similar provision was made for their families remaining behind. Amongst the additional Articles was an undertaking not to compel Roman Catholics to attend divine service against their consciences. Further explanations as to the interpretation of particular parts of the Articles were also agreed on 31 July 1652 including the implementation of the Articles in localities under the administration of Commonwealth commissioners of revenue or commissioners for the administration of Justice. Having accepted the provisions of the Articles, John Bellew was given the following pass, entitling him to return home to County Louth, and to recover, in accordance with its terms his real and personal estates – at least for the time being.

> Whereas Captain Bellew Lieutenant General of the Artillery of the Irish Party is to have the benefit of the Articles and explanation thereupon concluded at Kilkenny the 12 instant with me and others, and accordingly is to have the present possession of such estates as belong unto him as by the said Articles and explanation are set forth and in case the same or any part thereof be in custodium the profits arising thereout to pray and require the respective governors of Tredath [Drogheda] and Dundalk in whose quarters the said Lieutenant-General's estate lies to consign unto him or such as he shall appoint, the present possession of his said estate, or in case the same or any part thereof be at present in custodium, he grants [?] back him the profits arising or payable thereout as aforesaid. And the said Lieutenant-General in pursuance of the said Articles is allowed to have four horses and two cases of pistols for his proper use. Dated this 14 of May 1652.
> J. Reynolds[55]

The place appointed for John Bellew's surrender was Mullingar. His journey back to County Louth was through hostile country where roving guerrilla bands would give little quarter to a person who had submitted to the Commonwealth, hence the allowance of horses and pistols, which was equivalent to that allowed a lieutenant-colonel of horse and above that of a colonel of foot. Even on arrival in County Louth the risks were considerable because in the previous March the areas from 'Ardee to Cookstown and thence to Thomastown and Knockbridge' where some of Bellew's estates were situated had been excluded from protection by the authorities.[56] While his military career was at an end, he was to find that his skills as a lawyer would be stretched to the limit as he struggled in vain to preserve his landed estates from confiscation by the new power in Ireland, that of the English Commonwealth.

CHAPTER FIVE

'Being a people, if driven from the coast of Israel, must of necessity perish'

The county of Louth suffered very considerably during the years from 1641 to 1651. In that decade of warfare and civil disturbances, the town of Drogheda experienced four changes of occupying forces, and the county including Dundalk and Ardee, suffered five, only one of which, that of the parliamentarians in 1647 following the surrender of Ormond, was accomplished peacefully.[1] The three principal towns of Drogheda, Dundalk and Ardee had been stormed by the forces of either the Crown, or the English Commonwealth, at least once with resultant loss of life, damage and looting of property. At no time was the occupying force left without challenge, whether by opposing armies or by raiding parties from the nearby Irish Quarters in County Monaghan, a state of affairs which continued long after the occupation of the county by the English Commonwealth in September 1649. Evidence that John Bellew's estate had been plundered in the period from 1647 to 1648 is to be found in a petition made by the 'gentry and other inhabitants' of the county to Colonel Michael Jones seeking some remission of the military charges which had been imposed upon them at that time.[2] Among the places alleged to have been burned and pillaged were Drumcar, Tullydonnell, and Braganstown, as also were John Bellew's lands at Nizelrath and Lisrenny. In the early 1650s many parts of the county were described as waste, that is, without tenants. In Annaglog, in the parish of Kildemock, John Bellew had held a mortgage lease of 100 acres since 1641 from John Taaffe of Braganstown which he found lying waste upon his return in 1653.[3] Not one to lose an opportunity to enhance his rent-roll, he made an arrangement with 'the neighbours' to have 'a few acres ploughed therein', they paying him 'a consideration' for so doing. The soldiers who occupied Ardee in 1654 claimed that they found it 'altogether waste and lying in rubbish' while as late as 1667, of the three hundred and ninety-one tenements and messuages which then comprised the town of Dundalk, one hundred and fifty-one were either waste or ruinous.[4] Similar conditions existed in Drogheda, especially south of the river in the area of the Millmount and the Dales where the initial clash between Cromwell's forces and the royalist garrison took place.[5]

The form of government established in Ireland in the wake of the Commonwealth campaign was quite unlike any that had preceded it since the Norman conquest. In effect the laws, customs and usages of what was then the separate kingdom of Ireland, and which might loosely be described as its constitution, were set aside and replaced by the laws in force in the then Commonwealth of England. Control of policy was grounded in the English Parliament and council of state (and later on, in the Cromwellian Protectorate) in London, acting through Oliver Cromwell and subsequently his son-in-law, Henry Ireton, both of whom held successively the appointments of commander-in-chief and Lord Lieutenant of Ireland.[6] They in turn worked along with a group of commissioners appointed by the English Parliament whose functions in respect of the civil administration expanded as the military situation grew more secure. In the instructions given them in October 1650 they were required to 'inform themselves of the state of the ancient revenue and all the profits of the forfeited lands and to cause all forfeitures and escheats to be improved'.[7] They were also instructed to put in force all Acts etc. 'now in force in England' for 'sequestering of delinquents and papists estates' and 'to set and let such lands for terms not exceeding seven years'. An early casualty of this change was the Irish legal system including the Common Law and the Common Law Courts in Dublin. By 1651 these had been swept away and in their place Commissioners for the Administration of Justice were appointed, who in the following year were instructed to exercise their jurisdiction in accordance with the laws and constitutions of England. An important side effect of these changes was the setting aside of the Common Law as it pertained to land tenure and its replacement by English Statutes including the Adventurers Act of 1642 and the Settlement of Ireland Act 1652. Taken together, these, with other enactments of the English legislature, were to provide the legal base for the subsequent land confiscations and transplantations of the Commonwealth period.[8]

By the time the Common Law Courts were restored these massive changes in land ownership in Ireland had been substantially completed and by an Ordinance published by the Cromwellian Protectorate in

1657 the new land titles had been assured and confirmed.[9] The effects of these changes in the administration of the central government also had a local impact. The older forms of local administration were replaced by a variety of ad hoc commissions, such as the commissions for the administration of justice and the commissions of the revenue, whose functions subsumed the office of sheriff and local justices of the peace. These systems seem to have been introduced into County Louth before 1653 and continued in place until the restoration of the shrievalty and town corporations in the years 1665–66.[10] The military character of the regime is illustrated by the fact that the membership of these commissions included military personnel appointed from local garrisons. The governorships of each of the corporate towns were held by army officers, Colonel Ponsonby in Dundalk, Captain Lowe in Carlingford and, most important of all, Colonel John Fowke in Drogheda, who was the principal commissioner of the revenue in the county.[11] He was to play a leading role in the implementation of the arrangements for the sequestration of the landed estates of the forfeiting proprietors, including Protestant 'delinquents' such as Lord Moore of Mellifont and his brother Sir Garrett of Ardee.

A feature of the Commonwealth forces stationed in County Louth at this period was that they had been for the most part stationed in the county or in the nearby county of Meath long before Cromwell's coming to Ireland. These included Ponsonby who commanded a horse regiment about Athboy in County Meath in 1648, and Fowke who had come to Ireland in April 1647 as a lieutenant-colonel in Colonel Hungerford's regiment of foot. Fowke was governor of Drogheda in April 1649 when it capitulated to Inchiquin's royalist forces, after which he led only a handful of the garrison under articles to Dublin, the remainder enlisting under Inchiquin. In the wake of Cromwell's storming of Drogheda, Fowke appears as colonel of a regiment of foot of 'pre-1649' soldiers (those who had been in service in Ireland before the arrival of Cromwell in 1649) who settled about Ardee and Drogheda in the early Commonwealth period. Many of these such as Armitage of Ardee, Ruxton of County Meath, Baker of Dunmahon, the Gregory brothers of Sheepsgrange, Pierce of Dunleer, the Townleys of Ardee and Gwither of County Meath all came from families that had been settled in Ireland before 1641.[12]

The distinction made by the Lords Justices in 1641 between 'men of mean fortunes' who could be subjected to summary execution and men 'of quality' who 'could be reserved in safety' applied throughout the period of warfare. While the former had been excepted by the Act of 1652 from forfeiture of life or estate as 'husbandmen, ploughmen, labourers, artificers and others of the inferior sort', nevertheless, as a class, they were to suffer the greatest as casualties of war, famine or disease. Many of them went into exile as soldiers in foreign armies or as slaves to the West Indies. Numbered amongst these would have been many of the lower gentry who were small freeholders of land in the county or merchants in towns before the insurrection and who disappeared from the record after this time. The survivors were in the main the 'men of quality'. These constituted the middle and higher landed gentry of the county and the large merchants in towns, such as the Peppards and Deeces of Drogheda.[13] As John Bellew was to demonstrate, ability to represent and defend oneself within the complex bureaucracy of the administrative and legal processes then obtaining would also have been significant. He had been included in the list of persons named in part three of the Act for the Settlement of Ireland of August 1652 as 'excepted from pardon for life and estate' which effectively classified him as an outlaw. For a man expert in the intricate delaying tactics and deceits of the common law, Bellew, while ultimately having to transplant, must have found the system easy meat. He managed to avoid the extreme penalty of death provided by that Act, and to retain his residence in County Louth until the autumn of 1655.

It seems likely that the lands of the Old English in County Louth, whether Protestant or Roman Catholic, had been sequestered soon after the occupation of the county in the period 1649–50. Nevertheless the forfeiting proprietors, in the main, were allowed to continue in occupation, paying a tenant's rent to the commissioners of the revenue, or in some cases to individuals, who had acquired a custodium lease of their sequestered lands. The latter would have included ex-soldiers awaiting plantation in the barony of Ardee. Upon his return to Louth, John Bellew managed to secure possession of his lands and property at Willistown and elsewhere in the county, under the terms of the Kilkenny Articles and soon after embarked with others on a plan to avoid transplantation pleading the terms of the same articles.[14] Under the original plans of the English Commonwealth, the county of Louth was reserved to compensate for any deficiencies arising to adventurers in the counties reserved for them.[15] This policy was modified in July 1653, when the English Parliament accepted a recommendation from the Irish commissioners that the barony of Ardee be set aside for satisfying soldiers' arrears. The commissioners also pleaded that, as their instructions only allowed them to satisfy arrears of pay which had accrued since June 1649, they pointed out that many of the forces, which they wished to disband, 'were such as have been longest continuance in your service and have most of them interest in this nation and have most considerable arrears due to them before June 1649'. It was their desire to proceed with the early settlement of such soldiers, who by their settlement 'in those quarters where they have served and are best acquainted', would be an encouragement to those 'English as come over to plant' to have those who had 'served in arms' planted amongst them. One must suspect this argument as a self-serving plea by Fowke and others who stood to benefit by it. He had been a member of the council of officers who first mooted it and following its acceptance he was one of the seven commissioners appointed to carry it into execution in the barony of Ardee where he subsequently acquired an estate in excess of 1,600 acres Plantation Measure.

The scheme for the planting of the soldiers in the barony of Ardee proceeded at the same time as arrangements were put in train for the transplantation of the forfeiting proprietors. While the former was accomplished with comparative ease, the transplantation ran into increasing difficulties, not alone from the resistance of those ordered to transplant, but also because of the intricate bureaucracy established to give it effect. The latter consisted of a series of ad hoc commissions operating under the general direction of the deputy and council in Dublin, who in turn often had to refer to England for decision. In addition to the local commissions of the revenue and transplantation, which had their headquarters in Trim, a commission for the adjudication of claims and qualifications was established at Athlone. The transplanter had to appear before the latter, in order to defend any claim he might make against the order to transplant, or to argue for the best qualifications possible as to the amount of land to be allocated to him in Connacht or Clare. Finally a third set of commissioners was located at Loughrea in County Galway with responsibility for the issue of decrees of final settlement and the setting out of the place, and the amount of land allocated to the transplanter. At any stage it was possible for the transplanter to petition the deputy and council in Dublin against the decisions of the respective commissioners. In April 1654, for example, on foot of a letter from Colonel Fowke, as commissioner of the revenue of the precinct of Trim, the commissioners at Dublin gave him leave to delay the transplantation of the wives and children within his precinct until July, permitting them also to stay the driving of their herds and flocks towards Connacht 'until they be in condition to drive'. Evidently until weather conditions had improved. Twenty-three dispensations were subsequently promulgated by the commissioners of the revenue at Trim, in respect of County Louth transplanters. These included John Bellew, who was given until July 1654 to transplant.[16]

In February 1655 John Bellew, together with Patrick Plunkett of Carstown, Patrick Garland, Henry Gernon, Walter White and James Bellew, entered into a bond of £1,000 to stand by an award of John Aston and Patrick Tallant, attorneys in the court for the administration of justice in Dublin. This arose from a suit taken against them by Worsley Batten on foot of an alleged trespass committed by them 'in the beginning of the rebellion'.[17] Batten's deposition of September 1645 makes no reference to any such trespass nor to any of the persons named in this suit and it is therefore a matter of surprise that his complaint surfaced at this late stage.[18] Tallant was a lawyer who had County Louth connections and, although a Protestant, may have been related to the Roman Catholic Thomas Tallon, the forfeiting proprietor of the manor of Drumcar. John Aston may have been a relative of William Aston who, as major in Colonel Chidley Coote's Parliamentarian regiment, first came to County Louth in the early part of 1647. He later acquired in excess of 1,800 acres Plantation Measure including John Bellew's lands at Willistown in the planting of the soldiers in the barony of Ardee. He too was legally qualified and following the Restoration of Charles II in 1660 was knighted and appointed one of the judges of the Court of King's Bench in Dublin.[19] Having sold part of his land acquisitions in the county to another 'Cromwellian' soldier, Captain Arthur Dillon of County Meath, he obtained a grant of the residue of over 1,000 acres Plantation measure in the Restoration land settlement. Considering the background to this case, it is tempting to speculate that this was a fictional suit which, for as long as it was awaiting disposal through the commission for the administration of justice in Dublin, the defendants could plead for a delay in their transplantation to Connacht.[20]

The terms of surrender under the Kilkenny Articles provided that the submittees would receive, in respect of their real estates 'equal benefit with others in the like qualification with themselves in any offers [which] shall be hereafter held out by the Parliament of the Commonwealth of England'. A further provision was made in the Explanations of the Articles whereby the Commonwealth signatories bound themselves, 'faithfully and really to mediate with the Parliament to their uttermost endeavour concerning the real estates in the articles mentioned, that they may enjoy such moderate parcels of their estates as may make their lives comfortable amongst us'. In the interim they were to be put into the possession of their estates until 'the pleasure of

Parliament' was made known. John Bellew's pass for his return to County Louth made provision for the latter and which was subsequently put into effect, probably before the enactment of the Act for the Settlement of Ireland by the English Parliament in August 1652. As already mentioned, that Act specified Bellew by name as 'excepted from pardon for life and estate', thus excluding him from any entitlement to recover his real estates in County Louth. Clause ten of the Act did, however, contain a proviso that any such person, 'comprised within any articles', should enjoy the benefit of such articles, without prejudice to the powers of the commissioners of the Parliament in Ireland 'to transplant such persons, from the respective places of their usual habitation or residence into such other places within that nation, as shall be judged most consistent with public safety, allowing them such proportion of land or estate in the parts to which they shall be transplanted, as they had or should have enjoyed . . . had they not been so removed'. This ruling was challenged by a group of the Kilkenny submittees, led by Sir Richard Barnewall of Crickstown, County Meath, which included also John Bellew, Laurence Dowdall of Athlumney, County Meath, who was Barnewall's father-in-law and Patrick Netterville of Termonfeckin, County Louth. Almost certainly they represented a test case in which all others comprised within the Kilkenny and other cognate articles had an interest. They were all Old English, and because of their large numbers and the substantial extent of their landed interests, they must have represented a serious challenge to the policy of the English Commonwealth in regard to land confiscations and transplantations. Quoting from the Book of Samuel 2 chapter 21 verse 5, the four described their condition in a joint petition to the lord deputy and council as, 'a people concerned and reduced to that extremitie and want, as if driven, they may say, from the coast of Israel, must of necessity perish'.[21]

Barnewall and Dowdall had, like Bellew, been leading figures in the Catholic Confederation and were named in an army list of July 1646 as 'men conceived fit to be employed in the several counties'. Both sided with the Ormondist faction in the split within the Confederacy in 1646 and were included with Bellew in the Act of Settlement of 1652 as excepted for life and estate. Netterville was a captain of horse and was one of those captured at the battle of Dungan's Hill in 1647.[22] Their case was not dissimilar to that complained against Wentworth by the House of Commons in 1640, of having judicial matters determined by the deputy and council in Dublin rather than by the courts. In the time-honoured fashion of the Old English, they took their case directly to England, where a Committee for Articles had been established in the wake of Cromwell's abolition of the 'Rump' Parliament in April 1653 and its replacement by the Nominated Assembly, or as the royalists dubbed it, the Barebones Parliament, which sat from July to December of that year.[23] The function of the Committee for Articles was to adjudicate, in the absence of Parliament, on cases where the provisions of articles of surrender required a ruling by Parliament, as to what part of their forfeitable estates the submittees under such articles were to retain. Although not originally intended to deal with Irish issues, the then constitutional position of Ireland under the English Commonwealth could not preclude such an involvement.

Barnewall was particularly active in pursuit of the case, travelling to England early in 1654 where he petitioned the Committee for Articles. He returned again in June when the lord deputy Fleetwood recommended that he be arrested.[24] Subsequently, a joint petition was submitted by Messrs Barnewall, Bellew, Dowdall and Netterville, to the lord deputy and council in Dublin. Their case rested upon the provisions of the Kilkenny Articles, which had allowed the submittees to return to and recover possession of their estates and that consequently their transplantation would be a violation of the articles.[25] They further argued that the undertaking given them by the Commonwealth signatories to the articles, of 'faithfully and really' mediating with Parliament on their behalf, to secure for them the enjoyment of a moderate part of their estates, was a bar to their transplantation and that such transplantation would be a breach of trust. Since Parliament stood dissolved they argued that the exercise of the 'pleasure of Parliament' to determine what moderate part of their respective estates they were to enjoy, was a 'trust and power' settled only in Parliament, and could not be transferred for adjudication to any other. Rounding off their arguments they claimed that 'justice required that private or public faith and agreements grounded upon good considerations be performed, therefore 'what is repugnant thereunto is void'. How far these arguments would have prevailed in a Common Law Court is a matter for speculation, but where the lord deputy and council of the English Commonwealth in Ireland were concerned, they had to be rejected out of hand. Whatever about the legal niceties of interpretation that could be argued in favour of the petitioners, public policy rather than legal argument was the prime consideration, the 'delinquents' estates being then required by the state to compensate soldiers' pay arrears and adventurers' investments. Barnewall's efforts in England seems to have borne fruit as the following report by the commissioners in Dublin to Cromwell dated 18 April 1654 clearly implies:

... We make bold further to inform your Highness that we have received several Orders made by the said Committee for Articles sitting at Westminster, whereby the Irish rebels, who came in upon the Articles made at Kilkenny in May 1652, and upon other articles made since, are to have their estates until a future Parliament in England shall declare what part of their estates they shall enjoy, and that they ought not to be transplanted into Connacht. Touching which articles, upon due and serious consideration had of them and of the Act of Settlement amongst ourselves, and with most of those officers that made those articles, we conceive it our duty to declare, and accordingly have declared and published the same in print, that the said Act, being passed long after the said articles, was a signification of the Parliaments pleasure concerning their estates, and accordingly have disposed their estates, and appointed their transplantation, as we humbly conceive it to be our duty. But we find our friends the Committee for Articles at Westminster are of a contrary opinion in the case of Sir Richard Barnewall, one of the most eminent Delinquents in Ireland, and, if it be our duty in point of justice to admit him to enjoy his estate and not to be transplanted, the same rule binds us to admit all others to enjoy their estates, who have not been greater Delinquents than he, most Irishmen of estate being by articles to have the same conditions touching their estates, and consequently the satisfaction to the Adventurers and soldiers, and the transplanting of the Irish into Connacht are to be delayed until a future Parliament shall make some new declaration concerning them. And therefore we do humbly offer it to your Highness to consider whether it be not advisable, that the power of adjudication upon articles made here in Ireland be committed to such of your officers and other persons of trust in Ireland, as to your Highness shall seem fitting, because this case is of very high concernment to all your affairs in Ireland. We humbly pray that your pleasure herein be signified with what expedition your other great affairs will permit. 18 April 1654.[26]

Notwithstanding this clear-cut statement of the issues involved and the indication of how the matter should be decided, it was not until 8 January 1655 that the decision was made by the lord deputy and council to order Barnewall and 'others of the Irish party' comprehended within the Articles of Kilkenny to transplant and to receive respectively not more than one third of their confiscated real estates in the places of their transplantation.[27] Despite this explicit order to remove, the petitioners still continued to hold out and in a comprehensive review of their case published on 3 April 1655, the lord deputy and council again ordered that they transplant, not later that the 15th of that month 'or otherwise incur the penalties mentioned in the several Declarations published in that behalf' and which included the death penalty.[28] They indicated that having consulted officers of the army, including some who had been signatories to the Kilkenny Articles, they were satisfied that the order to transplant was not a violation of the articles. They further ordered the submittees to make their application to the Athlone commissioners to have their respective claims determined and also to the commissioners at Loughrea in order that their due proportions of lands in Connacht be set out to them. The submittees had evidently raised in their petition the question of the profits arising on their respective estates since 27 July 1653 and apparently withheld by the local commissioners of the revenue. The lord deputy and council agreed that they should be restored to them, less contributions and other taxes. However, as the board was not in a position to determine the extent of such profits, it ordered the various receivers of the revenues in the precincts where the estates were located to calculate the same and to notify the amounts to the receiver of the revenue at Athlone. The latter was authorised, on application made to him by the individuals concerned, to restore to them their due amounts.

The foregoing was not to be the end of the matter as the submittees lodged another joint petition raising twelve points of clarification as to the rules governing their transplantation and which was replied to on 12 April 1655'.[29] These included an instruction to the commissioners at Loughrea to 'take special care that lands and other conveniences be set out to them pursuant to the order of the lord deputy and council of the 3rd. inst'. and to set aside land surveys 'already made and returned', on the grounds that they did not 'think it safe either for the State or the petitioners to rely upon such surveys'. This appears to be a reference to either the Strafford Survey of 1636 or, more than likely, the Gross Survey of 1653–54, since neither the Civil or Down Surveys were made for County Galway. A copy of the Gross Survey for the five parishes within which John Bellew's grant was set out has survived in the Mountbellew Papers and has been published by Mr Gerry Lyne of the National Library. The latter suggests that this may have been carried out as a preliminary to a plan, subsequently cancelled, to allocate the area in question to Commonwealth ex-soldiers.[30] In place of these surveys, the Athlone commissioners were empowered to ascertain a full third of their forfeited estates, upon which the Loughrea commissioners were to set out a corresponding amount of land 'in pursuance of the order of the board dated 8 January 1655'. What may have been an important clarification of their position was that after they had settled or improved their respective proportions, they were not to be further disturbed or removed from same. While they were ordered to 'depart this city of Dublin' forthwith and to transplant not later than 1 May 1655, their wives and families were permitted to remain until the 20th of that month, 'to follow their occasions without interruption and no longer'.

In a further petition lodged by the submittees shortly after the foregoing reply, the question was raised whether 'leases and custodiums of land in Connacht' 'might not hinder the petitioners from the present possession of such lands as shall be assigned them by the council at Loughrea'.[31] While the reply was that the council would give any such grievance due consideration, the reference to 'leases and custodiums' suggests that the submittees upon their first transplantation were given temporary accommodation on such lands, *de bene esse*, before being permanently assigned lands by the Loughrea Commissioners.[32] Surviving documents dealing with John Bellew's transplantation, which took place in the autumn of 1655, as well as the subsequent orders of the Athlone and Loughrea commissioners, bear this out being dated respectively 26 March 1656 and 12 June 1656.[33] John Bellew's decree from the Athlone commissioners, setting out his title and qualifications, is based upon his County Louth estates of which he was to receive one third of his lands in Connacht. These lands are summarised hereunder together with the respective acreages as taken from the Surveyor's Book of the Down Survey for the county of Louth.

By Inheritance

In the barony of Ardee

Lisrenny	143a.0r.0p
Little Arthurstown	67a.1r.0p
Nicholastown	197a.1r.0p
Kenvickrath [Tollikeele]	311a.0r.0p

In the barony of Ferrard.

Hitchestown	91a.1r.0p
Graftonstown	89a.1r.0p

By Purchase

Willistown	141a.0r.0p
Plunkett's Land in Finvoy	40a.0r.0p
Dawestown in Braganstown [estimate]	217a.0r.0p
Adamstown	163a.0r.0p
TOTAL ACREAGE	1460a.0r.0p[34]

While the Athlone commissioners accepted, on the basis of the proofs presented by John Bellew, that the aggregate of the lands held by him in County Louth amounted to 1,460 acres Plantation Measure a slight discrepancy exists as between this figure and the aggregate acreage of 1,348 acres and 2 roods held by him as disclosed by the Down Survey. The latter does not include 'Dawestown in Braganstown' as a separate denomination but shows Dromin in the parish of Dysart barony of Ferrard consisting of 76 acres, 2 roods, as held by Bellew, which was not disclosed to the Athlone commissioners. The reconciliation set out above is based upon an estimate of the extent of Dawestown in Braganstown, which Bellew had acquired from Thomas Dawe in 1644. The annual value of the lands comprising his estate was given by John Bellew at £300 per annum or slightly over 486 acres per £100. In addition to his lands, Bellew also claimed in respect of his fishing rights in the river Dee at Willistown, Adamstown and Braganstown, which the commissioners accepted at a valuation of £50 per annum. He also claimed in respect of two statute staple bonds dated 7 December 1639 and 19 March 1639 in the aggregate sum of £1200 and due from Oliver Plunkett, Baron Louth, John Taaffe of Braganstown and George Russell of Rathmullen, County Down. The commissioners accordingly made an award of one third of the 1,460 acres of land held in County Louth. They also allocated additional lands, to the value of one third of the £50 per annum in respect of his fishing rights, and one third of the value of the incumbrance of £1,200. On the basis of these calculations the Loughrea commissioners granted Bellew a decree of 793 acres P.M., as follows:

Barony	Denomination of lands	acres profitable
Tiaquin	Clonoran, two quarters	358a.0r.0p.
	Carrowneboe one quarter	96a.0r.0p.
	Corgarrow one quarter	133a.0r.0p.
	Mullaghmore four quarters contiguous to Carrowneboe	19a.0r.0p.
	Parish of Moylagh, barony of Tiaquin, and half barony Killyhane.	
	Clonoran Oughter one quarter	67a.0r.0p.
	Iskerrowe one-third quarter	117a.0r.0p.
	Lying in the parish of Killoscobe	
Bellamoe	Knockmacskahell	3a.0r.0p.
	Lying in the parish of Ballinakilly, half barony of Belamoe	
TOTAL ACREAGE		793a.0r.0p.[35]

Given that one third of his County Louth lands amounted to 483 acres, the compensation for the loss of his fishing rights and incumbrances of £1,200 was 310 acres, not an excessive amount considering that at that time the value placed on lands in County Louth was £600 per 1,000 acres. One third of the incumbrance would therefore be worth over 664 acres of County Louth land, suggesting that its full value of £400 was not allowed. John Bellew appears to have transplanted by 1 May 1655, the date appointed by the lord deputy and council. The transplantation of his wife and children, which was to have been accomplished by 20 May, may have been delayed, as permission was given him on 16 June to reap his crop of corn in County Louth. This was confirmed in a subsequent order to the sheriff dated 23 August 1655.[36] Mrs Bellew and her family may have remained in Louth until this had been accomplished, after which she departed for Galway together with her children, household goods, farm animals and corn, making the long and perhaps hazardous journey to Athlone and thence into Connacht to join her husband. It is likely that she travelled in convoy with other women whose husbands also awaited their arrival. One such would have been Mary, the wife of Patrick Netterville of Termonfeckin, who was to be settled in the barony of Killian in County Galway adjacent to the lands of Corgarrow, which had been allocated to Bellew.[37] Another such family was that of Patrick and Joan Gernon of Gernonstown who were allocated 480 acres in the nearby barony of Ballintober, County Roscommon.[38]

The resistance to transplantation put up by John Bellew and his other colleagues was, almost certainly, a forlorn hope from the very beginning. Nevertheless, through their petitions and representations in England as well as in Ireland, they caused a considerable delay in the implementation of the Commonwealth plantation and transplantation policies; to the former by the delay in vacating their estates, to the latter by failing to transplant until mid-1655. When eventually they arrived in Connacht, a formidable task was to confront the Loughrea commissioners in setting out to them their respective estates, which was not accomplished until the summer months of 1656. The orders given by the Council to the commissioners on 12 April 1655 regarding the Kilkenny submittees to 'take special care that lands and other conveniences be set out to them pursuant to the order of the lord deputy and council' also conveyed a series of concessions to them, which suggest that their concerns were dealt with in a careful, even a generous fashion, according to their respective titles and qualifications. The Act of Settlement of 1652 provided that most of them were excepted from pardon, for life and estate, and therefore not entitled to be reckoned for lands in Connacht. The recognition of the protection afforded them by their articles made it necessary, however, for such a provision to be made, thus adding to the pressures on the already depleted stock of lands in Connacht available for the transplantation. By December 1655 a warning had been given of 'a great falling short' of lands for transplanters. In a probable reference to the preliminary settlement of the Kilkenny submittees earlier that year, it was complained that 'divers Irish' had acquired considerable quantities of forfeited lands, 'de bene esse', who had no legal right to them under the Act and to the prejudice of those who had.[39] Another contributory factor was the withdrawal of the counties of Sligo, Leitrim and a part of Mayo from the transplantation scheme in the period 1654–55.[40] This had been done at the behest of the officers of Sir Charles Coote's regiment, who sought to have these areas reallocated, as compensation for the pay arrears of the troops who had served under their command, many of whom had been settled in north Connacht before 1641.[41] In November 1656 the Loughrea commissioners complained that the available land was falling short in satisfying decrees and that many persons had obtained grants who had been excepted from pardon.[42] The situation was then reported by the Council to the Lord Deputy Fleetwood, complaining that the Loughrea commissioners had set out 'great stopes of land' to such as had been adjudged as comprehended under the first qualification of the Act, who ought not to have had any land grants 'by which means others . . . fall short of satisfaction'. Almost certainly this situation arose directly from the decision of the lord deputy and council to admit individuals, such as John Bellew and his colleagues who, although excepted from pardon under the Act, had acquired prior rights under their articles of submission, enabling them to recover some portion of their forfeited estates through allocation of lands in Connacht. Compared with the rather modest estate of 793 acres acquired by Bellew, Sir Richard Barnewall got an estate of 2,500 acres, Patrick Netterville, 1,407 acres and Laurence Dowdall, 4,858 acres. Other like beneficiaries of articles were Richard Nugent, Earl of Westmeath, 11,574 acres, Edward Butler, Lord Galmoy, 4,600 acres, Sir Luke Fitzgerald of Tecroghan Castle, 2,034 acres, Lieutenant-Colonel James Barnewall, County Meath, 2667 acres, Sir Robert Talbot, County Meath, 6,030 acres and Colonel John Fitzpatrick, Queen's County, 4,000 acres.[43] These comprised the 'great stopes' of land complained about by the Council who, considering its role in the affair, was more than a little disingenuous in placing the blame on the Loughrea commissioners. It is likely that its desire to obtain the vacant possession of the forfeited estates of the submittees in Leinster, overcame its scruples in dealing with the transplanters in Connacht, where the losers were those least able to defend their interests by string-pulling in England, special pleadings or legal argument. Many of them were said to have left 'fine estates' and 'left unaccommodated', were 'reduced to little better than a starving condition'.[44]

John Bellew was about fifty years of age upon his transplantation to Connacht and had been married some twenty-two years. At least three of his children, Patrick the eldest, Thomas and Christopher, were by this time either young adults or in their teenage years and therefore capable of being of service and support to their parents. Despite the several upheavals that the family suffered throughout the decade of the 1640s, their education seems not to have been neglected. Patrick and Christopher are referred to frequently in the 1660s as assisting their father in the conduct of his business affairs and some part of their education included legal training. John Bellew's wife, Mary, seems to have been a capable woman and in difficult times managed to see to the upbringing of her children, very often without the support of her husband, whose involvement in political or military affairs took him away from his family at critical times. That he was a competent lawyer, skilled in the presentation and pleading of cases, and in negotiating in difficult circumstances is suggested by the frequency with which he was involved, at first in parliamentary affairs and later in negotiating articles of surrender on behalf of colleagues more senior than himself. His success can also be measured by the fact that he was able to increase by purchase, his land owning interests in County Louth from 718 acres to 1,460 acres in the years 1627 to 1641 and to lend very substantial sums of money in the period 1638–39. Throughout the war years he also seemed to have had ready cash; to buy out Thomas Dawe's interests in Braganstown; to expend £100 in 1648 on the maintenance of the train of artillery; to raise cash to buy his release after the battle of Rathmines and to satisfy the demands of the Commonwealth forces following the surrender of Tecroghan Castle. All of this suggests that the war did not unduly impair his legal practice, which would have been a major source of his income.

Bellew seems to have discharged his duties as lieutenant-general of artillery in a competent fashion and on many occasions rendered signal service to the Leinster army in the reduction of forts and other strongholds. Although a devout Roman Catholic, his refusal to bow the knee to the papal nuncio in 1648 was a mark of his loyalty to the crown. Like many others of the 'Ormondist' faction he saw the need for a compromise solution, which would enable him to remain loyal to his religious beliefs while at the same time fulfilling his obligations of loyalty to a Protestant monarch. It was also a recognition by him that his survival, as a landed proprietor and gentleman, depended upon that loyalty. This was only to recognise the reality that the alternative was the precipice, which his colleague Walter Bagnall warned of, in the crisis precipitated by the nuncio and the clerical party in 1646–47. He seems to have been punctilious in his dealings with others, as evidenced by his refusal to depart from his brief at the behest of the Earl of Nithsdale in the Wentworth affair in 1640. In a letter to Preston in 1647, he explained his refusal to take orders from Colonel Warren's major, arguing that he had 'an ample patent' for his place and that hitherto 'left-colonels have taken their orders from me'.[45] While this characteristic may have been derived from his legal training, it has also to be remembered that in an age when family lineage and 'gentry' status was of immense importance, he would have been conscious of his own pedigree and standing in society. Consequently he would not have suffered lightly any apparent infringements on his dignity and would have reacted haughtily towards anyone appearing to do so.

Following the death of Oliver Cromwell in September 1658 and the resignation of his son Henry as lord lieutenant of Ireland in the following June a period of great political uncertainty was ushered in. Henry's replacement was a commission of five men, republican-military and Baptist in character, led by the Welshman Colonel John Jones. They were totally out of sympathy with the aspirations of the Protestant gentry, who had given their support to the English Commonwealth in the period after the storming of Drogheda in 1649, and who had come to a prominence in affairs in the period of Cromwell's lieutenancy. Principal amongst these were Lord Broghill and Sir Charles Coote, lord presidents of Munster and Connacht respectively.[46] These belonged to the 'Old Protestant' faction who had been long settled in Ireland before the English Commonwealth and who, with the encouragement of the Cromwells, distanced themselves from the republican militarists whom Henry Cromwell replaced in the latter part of the Commonwealth decade in Ireland. Watching and waiting at a discreet distance were their Protestant kindred who had sided with the king and had never given up hope of his restoration. Principal amongst these was the royalist faction in County Down led by Viscount Montgomery of the Ardes and Colonel Mark Trevor of Rose Trevor and latterly of Dundalk, where he acquired a lease of the former corporation property of about 5,000 acres from Henry Cromwell shortly before his resignation. He was to claim that he attempted to subvert Cromwell, offering him an army of 5,000 men if he were to declare for the king.[47]

In August 1659 Lieutenant-General Ludlow was ordered to arrest 'the principal and leading men within the county of Galway as shall be conceived active or dangerous persons'. Whether this was a case of 'rounding up all the usual suspects' or whether the Old English transplanters in County Galway had also entered into the conspiracy cannot now be determined but considering Coote's position in Connacht the latter cannot be ruled out. Included in the list to be arrested was John Bellew described as 'the late lieutenant-general of the ordinance', the Earl of Westmeath, Sir Richard Barnewall, Laurence Dowdall, George Fitzgerald, the son of Luke of Tecroghan Castle and Lieutenant-Colonel Barnewall, all of whom had been submittees under the Kilkenny articles.[48] On 13 November Jones reported the possibility of a plot by the County Down royalists following which Viscount Montgomery was arrested and brought to Dublin castle.[49] On 13 December Sir Theophilus Jones and Colonel Hardress Waller, both of whom were Old Protestants, led a coup d'état in Dublin where they captured the Castle and released Montgomery. Following this they issued a declaration calling for the restoration of the parliament in London. Subsequently Broghill and Coote backed this up, by securing the garrisons in their respective presidencies and in February 1660 a Convention was established in Dublin ostensibly to secure the restoration of the Irish Parliament. The underlying motive was however, to provide a front for the Protestant Episcopalian gentry to secure their return to power in Ireland. On the 15 February Hardress Waller, realising the crypto-royalist nature of the movement, together with other like-minded army officers, seized Dublin Castle but were subsequently overcome and sent under arrest to Athlone. Some days later Broghill and Coote issued separate declarations, calling for a freely elected parliament, and each sent an emissary to meet the king at Brussels. It was a case of getting aboard the 'bandwagon' of the king's Restoration, which was accomplished by the following June. For the Connacht transplanters, the Philistines had been defeated and, their loyalty to the king undimmed, their hopes were raised that they would yet see the 'coast of Israel' again.

CHAPTER SIX

'It being repugnant to all reason that the estates of such as served his majesty, should now be the reward of those who fought against him'

The Dublin Convention of February 1660 gave to the 'Old Protestants' who had supported the English Commonwealth in Ireland an instrument by which they were able to seize control of government, in the wake of the collapsing Commonwealth. By providing them with a forum for debate and a unified policy, their leadership was enabled to move forward with some degree of confidence in a period of otherwise great uncertainty.[1] Notable amongst this leadership was Sir Charles Coote, who had been appointed by General Monck, along with Roger Boyle, Lord Broghill of Munster, and the Presbyterian, Major William Bury, as commissioners for Ireland in January 1660. In the following month Coote despatched Sir Arthur Forbes to Brussels with an unconditional offer of loyalty to the king. For Coote this was to be a profitable embassy, as the king in reply commended him for his new-found loyalty and promised him an earldom as well as other favours. His colleague, Lord Broghill, did likewise, sending his brother Francis with a similar message of loyalty to the king and then hastened himself to England, where in April he found a seat in the Convention Parliament, which was to oversee the Restoration settlement in that kingdom.[2] With the proclamation of Charles II as King of Ireland on 14 May both he and Coote, as part of a delegation of thirteen commissioners appointed by the Dublin Convention, were despatched to London to attend on the king as representatives of the Protestant interest in Ireland. Included amongst them were Colonel Arthur Hill and Major George Rawdon, former leading members of the Commonwealth administration in Ulster. The delegation brought with them a gift of £20,000 for the king, £4,000 for his brother, the Duke of York, and £2,000 for his younger brother, Richard, the Duke of Gloucester.[3] The instructions given them by the Convention, dated 12 May 1660, included the securing of agreement for the early holding of a parliament and the appointment of a chief governor and council.[4] They were to seek a general pardon, indemnity and oblivion for 'all Protestants whatsoever in Ireland'. They were to seek also for the enactment of an Act of Attainder, 'in such manner as the next parliament will agree', no doubt with the intention of securing a confirmation of existing attainders of Roman Catholics, thus debarring them from recovering their forfeited estates. They were also to secure the agreement of the king for the introduction of legislation confirming adventurers and soldiers in the estates acquired by them during the Commonwealth period as well as a confirmation of the Connacht Transplantation. That they had made some progress is suggested by a draft of a Proclamation, sent by the king to the chairman of the Convention, but which for some reason was never promulgated. It indicated a willingness on the part of the king to grant a free and general pardon to 'all our subjects of that kingdom who have been bred and brought up in the Protestant religion or who have been Protestants since the 23 October 1641'.[5] In the case of the Roman Catholics, the pardon was to extend only to those 'who had proved their constant good affection' to the English interest, a phrase taken directly out of Clause eight of the Act for the Settling of Ireland.

By the end of the year Broghill, now Earl of Orrery, and Coote, now Earl of Mountrath were, with Sir Maurice Eustace as Lord Chancellor, appointed Lords Justices, to act in the place of General Monck the newly appointed but absentee Lord Lieutenant. If in the period prior to the king's Restoration all the initiatives seem to have been taken by the de facto government of Coote and Broghill, those other Old Protestants who had remained loyal to the king during the Commonwealth were, if surreptitiously, not less active. As William Montgomery of County Down put it, it was a time when 'every party minded their own knitting to work the best for themselves respectively'.[6] The influential County Down royalists, to whom he belonged, led by Viscount Montgomery of the Ardes, maintained contact with developments through the agency of Theophilus Jones, whom William Montgomery described as his 'great friend in usurping times'. The more pro-active Colonel Mark Trevor maintained a direct correspondence with his friend Ormond in Brussels.[7] When the Irish Privy Council was re-established in December 1660, its membership was revealed as a coalition between those Old Protestants who had exercised the 'usurped power' of the English Commonwealth on the one hand, and on the other, those of their kindred who had remained loyal to the king.[8] Although many of the latter had suffered sequestration of their estates and the imposition of composition fines at the hands of the former, their common concern to secure hegemony in Ireland for the Protestant interest soon overcame any lingering antipathy that may have existed between them. With the restoration of the Episcopalian Church Establishment, the Protestant ethos of the state had also been secured, albeit to the chagrin of the Presbyterians of Ulster, whose preference was for a non-Episcopalian establishment.

With a few rare exceptions, the Protestant interest in Ireland could not boast, any more than the Old English, of an unfailing loyalty to the king throughout the years of war. Even Ormond's loyalty had been tarnished by the treaty he made with the rebel Parliamentary commissioners in Dublin in 1647. His directions to all the garrisons under his command to transfer their allegiance from the king to Parliament was followed by his departure to mainland Europe, fortified by a substantial grant of money, which he had received from the Parliamentarians.[9] The prime concern of the Old Protestants, in the first months of the king's Restoration, was therefore to secure a general pardon and indemnity for themselves, in like manner as that introduced into the Convention Parliament in England in May 1660. With the exception of the regicides, those who had any connection with the execution of Charles I, the legislation had provided for a general pardon for all transgressions committed during the wars. In addition they also sought to ensure that the Catholic interest in Ireland would be excluded. In this they were substantially successful in that the legislation excluded any Catholic who had participated in the 'plotting, contriving or designing' of the insurrection of 1641, excepting only those who might subsequently be named in an Act for the Settlement of Ireland.[10] This exclusion also extended to a prohibition of the restoration of their estates.

Unlike the Old Protestants, who held the major part of the power and most of the land in Ireland in the later Commonwealth period, the Roman Catholic or Irish Party had been dispersed. Those who had elected to remain at home were in internal exile in Connacht, while the remainder were in exile abroad, many of them serving in the king's army in mainland Europe. Less able to engage in concerted action and excluded from any participation in government, their only recourse would be that of petition. To prevent such an approach, the agents of the Irish Protestants in London secured the publication of a royal proclamation on 29 May, pronouncing that the insurrection of 1641 had not as yet been suppressed and ordering the arrest of all 'Irish rebels' then in England or travelling thereto.[11] A party of twenty-one 'Irish nobility and gentry' had already arrived in London by this date from where they addressed a petition dated 6 May to Ormond, then at Breda in Belgium.[12] In a reference to the changes taking place in London, 'whereby those impediments which stood in our sovereign's way to his Kingdoms are laid aside', they averred that they had come there to witness 'what in their greatest extremities they had always hoped and prayed for'. It was their desire to 'behold this admirable work and to reap, with the first in this twilight of a coming settlement, the advantage now denied to the rest of their poor countrymen of enjoying and manifesting the excess of their gladness and consolation'. Coming to the point of their petition they asked Ormond, who they claimed had been principally instrumental 'in diffusing this good spirit of union and peace now spreading throughout the three nations' to represent to the king their faithful good affection towards him, and their sufferings for him. They also asked him 'to stand between the king and the misrepresentations of them, by malicious persons, and thereby do a just and charitable act that would redound to his majesty's honour'. Rather than expose the king's clemency 'to the malignancy of any jealous eye', they had refrained from making a direct approach to him and instead threw themselves 'wholly upon your excellencies goodness', whose knowledge of their contributions during the years of war could not be bettered by anyone else. This was a reference to the Ormond Peace of 1648/9, which had been concluded 'for and on behalf of his most excellent majesty' Charles II. Its terms, which they now sought to have implemented, had provided for an act of oblivion for all Acts, ordinances and orders made by both or either Houses of Parliament, 'to the blemish, dishonour or prejudice of his majesty's Roman Catholic subjects'. It had also provided for the removal of attainders and outlawries, the restoration of their estates and the removal of any bar to participation in the 'next intended parliament'.[13] It is not known what action Ormond took on foot of this petition. The reality was, however, that the king, even if he had a mind to do so, was in no position to deliver on the undertakings given by him in 1649. His Restoration had been procured, not by the defeat of the enemy but by a caucus of officers of the former army of the

Commonwealth, acting in alliance with the conservative elements of the Protestant Episcopalian landed gentry. Most of these had expectations of a confirmation of title of the land acquisitions that they had made in Ireland during the period of the Commonwealth and would be opposed to any concessions being made to the Irish or Catholic Party.

When eventually the king promulgated his decisions for the settlement of the land question in Ireland, it was clear that he intended to support the Protestant interest and renege on the promises solemnly made on his behalf by Ormond in 1648. His 'Gracious Declaration' of 30 November 1660 carried a clear message to the new Protestant establishment in Ireland that there would not be any undoing of the settlements made by the English Commonwealth in respect of the adventurers and soldiers. This was in flat contradiction of an acknowledgement, contained in the Declaration, that 'their present estates and possessions', if examined 'by the strict term of the law would prove very defective and invalid'.[14] The Declaration acknowledged the existence of 'difficulties in the providing for and complying with the several interests and pretences there'. This included the Irish Catholic interest which, as the price of their loyalty to him, had lost all to his erstwhile enemies now, as the Declaration put it, 'returned to their duty and obedience to us'. It referred to the Acts of Parliament by which these settlements had been effected, on the basis of which the adventurers and soldiers were now 'in possession of a great part of the lands of that our kingdom'. The Declaration ignored the fact that this legislation had been enacted by an English parliament, and in the case of the Act of 1652, was an act of the 'usurped power', whose constitutional validity could be called into question. Nonetheless, assurances were given that the king would be 'very careful' of the interests of the soldiers and adventurers. No such assurances were given to the Catholic interest whose lands had been taken from them. This was consistent with the policy, which had prevailed throughout the whole Stuart era, of denying Catholics statutory recognition of their landed interests, forcing them instead to depend on the dubious grace and favour of the crown.

Wrapped in hypocritical humbug, the king acknowledged the loyal service given by the 'Irish subjects of that our kingdom', especially those who had served in his army 'during the time of our being overseas', his description of the period of his banishment by the Commonwealth. Much more to the point of the Declaration was the statement, in clause eleven, of his 'remembrance of the Cessation', which his father was 'forced' to make with the 'Irish', 'during the late troubles', and by which 'he was compelled to give them a full pardon for what they had before done amiss'. Neither could he forget that 'Peace' which he was 'necessitated to make with our said subjects', in the time of the usurped power. Acknowledging that he could not but hold himself obliged 'to perform what we owe by that Peace', he added the heavy qualification that, 'we and they were miserably disappointed by the effect of those promises, by an unhappy part of them [presumably the Nuncioists], which foolishly forfeited all the grace which they might have expected of us'. The Instructions to the commissioners appointed to carry the Declaration into effect, promulgated in February 1661, evidently relying on these provisions in the Declaration, heavily circumscribed the categories of Roman Catholics who were to be restored as 'innocent' as to render almost nugatory the value of the king's remembrances of the services done by them as a class.[15] Excluded from the category of 'innocent papist' were inter alia, all those, who before the cessation of September 1643 were of the 'rebel party', or who resided in the 'rebel quarters', or who had entered into the 'Roman Catholick Confederacy at any time before the Peace of 1648'. These provisions were aimed at excluding a whole swathe of loyal subjects of the crown, including John Bellew, from a recovery of their estates on the grounds of innocence. The bias towards the Protestant interest was further reinforced when the provisions made on behalf of those army officers who had served the king before 5 June 1649 and had not been paid their arrears were confined only to Protestants.[16]

Unlike the Protestant interest, which had been able to present a united front and had command of most of the organs of power, the Roman Catholic interest was hopelessly divided. In the first place there were differing expectations between those who had been transplanted and those who had served in the king's army abroad. The Connacht transplanters had high hopes of their full restoration to their forfeited estates, the loss of which they directly attributed to their struggle on behalf of the king in the years 1648 to 1652. The main thrust of the Gracious Declaration, with its emphasis on the principle of non-disturbance of the Commonwealth Settlement, was continued into the Instructions. The latter severely limited the possibilities for Catholics to secure a restoration of their estates, notwithstanding that their loyalty to the king was demonstrably better than those who had ousted him in the period of the 'usurped power'.[17] The divide between those of the former nuncio's party and those who supported Ormond still lingered, with the latter inclined towards his mediation and which the former opposed. After the initial approach to Ormond, this channel of intercession was not further pursued, and they turned instead to Richard Talbot of Carton, County Kildare, gentleman of the bedchamber of James, Duke of York, the king's brother. Sir Nicholas Plunkett, who was one of the Kilkenny submittees and a signatory to the petition to Ormond was also approached. He was later to be banished from the court when the Earl of Orrery produced a letter in March 1662, which had been signed by Plunkett in 1647, offering Ireland to various Catholic powers on the continent in return for military aid.[18] In addition to his banishment, the king prohibited further representations by the Catholic agents.

John Bellew was in London in the early months of 1661, during which time he may have become associated with the agents of the Irish Party then in the capital. This could explain the existence of two documents in the Mountbellew Papers dealing with the implications of the Gracious Declaration. They appear to have been composed by Bellew in the period after the publication of the Instructions of February 1661, and before the enactment of the Act of Settlement of 1662. They are entitled respectively, 'A brief of the difference betwixt his majesty's subjects of Ireland claiming to be restored to their former estates and those who now possess them' and, 'Reasons enforcing the performance of his majesty's peace made in Ireland in 1648'.[19] The documents are copied in Appendix V. The first document pointed out that those who claimed restoration were either innocent persons, or those, who, having adhered to the peace of 1648–9, had fought under the king's authority against the 'usurper' until the 'interruption of that authority' when the usurper ousted them from their estates. Turning to the state of things then existing, and drawing a distinction between 'those who now possess their estates', and those 'from whom their said former estates are yet detained', it asked, 'was it not without precedent and repugnant to all reason and justice that the estates of such as served his majesty should now be the reward of those that fought against him and his royal father'. It further questioned why the matter of religion should admit so much inconvenience to fall on the one side, namely the Catholic Irish, and advantage only to the other, namely the Protestant British. It asked why the Catholics, a considerable number of whom were of English extraction, and had preserved the interest of the crown of England there for five hundred years, must now be destroyed for a new sort of people who made it their work, ever since they had a power in Ireland, to destroy monarchy, church, nobility and gentry. Rather stiffly it argued that it should be duly weighted, how inconsistent it would be with his majesty's public faith, honour, interest and safety to give away his subjects' estates, that suffered so much and served so faithfully, unto such persons, and how inconsistent it would be, to turn the Declaration and Instructions into a law in which there were so many ambiguities and contradictory expressions inserted, that it could not be put in execution before it be well explained. It further argued, 'how unreasonable it would be to enact the Bill into law, considering the aspersions cast in the Preamble on all of the nation, but such as were of Cromwell's party; making the dispossessions, sequestrations, transplantations and seizures of Cromwell the ground work of the forfeiture of estates in Ireland'.

The second document continued in a similar vein but not without a considerable degree of emotion. It argued that the Peace of 1648/9 was not injurious or unjust for the king to grant, considering that he granted 'to the Irish' nothing 'but their own or what was formerly theirs'. Two paragraphs in the document graphically express feelings of despair and disillusionment at the way matters had transpired for their party:

> Is it worthy [of] consideration if that peace had been in itself unreasonable as it is not, whether the blame should not altogether be imputed to those who would now (right or wrong) hold the estates of the Irish; were not those the men who put this necessity in part on his majesty, were not they the men who adhered to all interests and resolutions to serve their own turns those eighteen years past and not his majesty's; were not those the men who with hearts and hands enjoyed with the regicides and approved and justified the murder of the king, were not those the people who moved and voted the perpetual extirpation and banishment of the royal family and cried down Church and Nobility. It is to be considered for what services they will keep his majesty's subjects' estates; is it not for their rebellion and service under Cromwell since the murder of our king; O God what an impudence it is for the greatest of rebels (if the Act of Indemnity had not interposed) to dare open their mouths, to keep ones subjects' estates in recompense of such treachery and rebellion, if they be not blinded with too much self interests, would not they have thought themselves to have met the most gracious and indulgent crime that ever was, to confer honours and offices of profit and trust both in military and civil employments upon them and to give a general pardon for all their offences and such of them as had estates formerly to let them enjoy them, such as had not, it were pity to reward their rebellion with granting them other mens' estates.

While these documents reflect an understandable attitude of deep frustration and even of despair at the turn of events, it is arguable whether the hardline tactics adopted by the Irish party in their dealings with the king were, considering the circumstances of their position, in their own best interests. By their condemnation of the Protestant party, they provided the latter with a pretext of denouncing their attitudes as offensive and arrogant, accusing them, as Ormond described it, of habitually 'instructing the king and his council in what was good for them and recriminating others'. Whatever justification they could claim for the high moral ground, their attitude cut little ice with a monarch like Charles II, who hardly welcomed reminders of past obligations and who, like his father before him, was unwilling to do anything that might be construed as undermining the Protestant ethos of the State. As the Restoration of the king was by Protestant effort alone, owing nothing to the services of his Roman Catholic subjects in Ireland or abroad, then the land settlement was also to be Protestant in character. Such Roman Catholics as might eventually be permitted to participate would be allowed to do so, not by statutory right as a class, but on an individual basis after humble petition, and then only through the grace and favour of the crown.[20]

While a commission had been appointed to implement the various provisions of the Gracious Declaration and the Instructions that accompanied it, this did not debar the exercise of the ancient right of petition to the king. At this period a network of patronage existed which facilitated the exercise of this right, the apex of which was the king himself acting by the royal prerogative. This network, in turn, permeated downwards throughout all levels of the landed nobility and gentry, and at times was even capable of transcending agreements made at the political level. Apart from those in the most privileged position of having direct access to the king, a friendship or the acquaintance of a highly placed courtier, based upon some family or marriage connection, educational establishment or professional occupation such as the law or the army, often facilitated a successful conclusion to a 'humble petition'. Nor was the highly placed courtier above the acceptance of a bribe for the favour of his assistance. The Gracious Declaration had already made provision for many of those in the highest category, granting them special favour for the 'eminent services' rendered by them. These included the royalists Ormond and Inchiquin, and the former agents of the 'usurped power' George Monck, newly created Duke of Albemarle, Roger Boyle, Earl of Orrery, Charles Coote, Earl of Mountrath and Sir Theophilus Jones. Amongst the Old Englishry, most of whom were Roman Catholics and former submittees under the Kilkenny Articles were the Earls of Clanricard, Westmeath, Fingal, and Clancarthy, Viscounts Gormanston, Mountgarrett, Dillon, Taaffe, Ikerrin, Netterville, Galmoy and Mayo, the Barons Dunboyne, Trimleston and Dunsany; while amongst the gentry were Sir Richard Barnewall, Sir Valentine Browne, George Fitzgerald of Tecroghan and Bernard Talbot of Rathdown, all of whom were ordered to be restored to their former estates. Almost certainly these were people, many of whom had held prominent leadership positions in the former Catholic Confederacy, who had the ear and patronage of Ormond. Following these was a long list of those who had served the 'king's ensigns beyond the seas' who were also to be restored but not before the disturbed adventurer or soldier was first reprised elsewhere with an estate of equal worth and value.

John Bellew was not sufficiently influential to gain a mention in the Gracious Declaration. Nonetheless, thanks to his connections in the court, he was able to secure the king's favour on foot of a humble petition submitted by him at Whitehall in London on 19 February 1661.[21] He based his request for restoration, not on innocence, but on the fact that he adhered to the Ormond Peace of 1648–9 and thereafter served as lieutenant-general of the ordnance and captain of a foot company, until he was compelled under pain of death to transplant into Connacht. Aware of the limitations imposed by the Gracious Declaration, he sought only that such part of his estate as lay in the king's hands be restored to him. With regard to that part 'in the hands of adventurers or soldiers', he sought that reprisals be made to him of such other lands in the county as were in the king's hands. This was but one of scores of petitions lodged with the king at this period. While most of them, like Bellew's, sought the restoration of lands forfeited in the time of the Commonwealth, others were submitted by Old Protestant loyalists, seeking land in recompense of arrears of pay, and by minor courtiers claiming land in return for services rendered to the king. Some of these petitions would have been bogus in character, relying on the quality of the patron rather than on the quality of the evidence.

Because of the large numbers of petitions received, an ad hoc arrangement was made by which committees were established to examine the content of each petition and to recommend accordingly to the king.[22] In the case of John Bellew, the committee consisted of Arthur Chichester, Earl of Donegal, Thomas Roper, Lord Viscount Baltinglass and John King, Baron Kingston, all of whom were Old Protestants and of the Irish peerage. Their report, dated 2 March

1661, contained a summary of the evidence submitted by Bellew in support of his petition, which included letters from Ormond, who confirmed his record of service, and that he had 'suffered much in that behalf and otherwise on behalf of his majesty'. There was another from Theobald Taaffe, Viscount Corren, who confirmed that Bellew had served under his command as lieutenant of the ordnance and had contributed £100 to the furnishing of the artillery 'upon the expedition then to Dublin' in 1649. Sir Thomas Stanley, who had been one of Commissary-General Reynolds' commissioners at the surrender of Tecroghan Castle, also confirmed that Bellew had been offered, and had refused, the return of his estates, if he should decline further service with the king. In face of this evidence the committee made as ample a recommendation for the restoration of John Bellew as he could have wished.

> For as upon the whole matter we are humbly of opinion that in regard of the said Mr. Bellew's timely and constant adherence to your majesty as aforesaid and his integrity manifested by the trust reposed in him by the said lord marquis of Ormond by conferring the aforesaid employments upon him, as by his commissions in that behalf appeareth, and his good affections in laying out his own monies as aforesaid and his zeal to your majesty's service, his losses and sufferings by several imprisonments and by the ransom paid by him as aforesaid, the acquittance whereof hath been produced before us, his refusal to accept of his estate from the usurped power upon terms of declining of your majesty's service and the particular enforcement put upon him to transplant into and take lands in Connacht which manifestly the same not to be his own act, we hold him a very fit object both in honour and justice of your majesty's particular favour and regard which your majesty may be pleased to extend towards him as a reward of his sufferings and merits in your majesty's behalf, by giving order to repossess him of such part of his estate as is in you majesty's hands. And for so much thereof as is in the hands of reprisable adventurers and soldiers, that they be forthwith reprised and he settled in the possession thereof as by his petition is requested, the rather that he refused to accept the same upon terms of declining your majesty's service as aforesaid.[23]

Apart from the merits of his case, the fact that John Bellew had the patronage of such eminent courtiers as the Marquis of Ormond and Viscount Corren, both of whom were intimates of the king, would have weighed heavily with the committee, whose recommendations the king accepted. On 7 March 1661 he issued a letter in favour of Bellew, which was duly entered at the Signet Office in London on 1 April next following, ordering his restoration in the following terms:

Charles R:

Having taken into our consideration the report made by the earl of Donegal, the Lord Baltinglass and the Lord Kingstowne upon our order of reference of the 19 February last on the petition of John Bellew Esq., who served us as lieutenant of our ordnance in our kingdom of Ireland and having weighed the same and being fully satisfied of the said John Bellew's good affections towards us, his timely submission and constant adherence to our peace therein mentioned his sufferings and merits on our behalf and the particular enforcement put upon him to transplant into and apply himself unto the several Judicatures at Athlone and Loughreagh for lands in Connacht which manifest the same not to be his own act. And therefore and for several other motives and reasons both in honour and justice inducing us we hold ourself engaged and accordingly do by these our Royal Mandate order and adjudge that the said John Bellew is not by such his acceptance of lands in Connacht debarred by our Declaration and Royal Intentions therein, from having his own estate and that accordingly the said John Bellew shall forthwith be put into the present possession of such of the ensuing lands and towns as are in our possession viz., Lisrenny, Little Arthurstown, Nicholstown, Kenvickrath, Daweslands, Willistown, Adamstown, Plunkettslands, Graftonstown, Hitchestown, Reynoldstown and Garvagh, together with all such lands, tenements and hereditaments, mills, waters, watercourses, fishings, fishing weirs, mortgages and leases whatsoever, which did or anyway ought to belong unto him the said John Bellew which are in our hands, together with the rents, issues and profits, payable thereout by the occupiers thereof for this present half year determining the 25 inst., or at Easter or May next. And for such of the premises as are in the hands of reprisable adventurers or soldiers or in the hands of any other person or persons during any interest or estate from or under them or any of them, We do hereby require that forthwith reprisals be without delay made unto them and he the said John Bellew or his assignees put into the present possession thereof and in case any difficulty should arise by reason of improvements or any other matter whereby present reprisals may not be had or made for such as now possesses the said John Bellew's estate, We are graciously pleased and do by these our Royal Mandate order and adjudge that forthwith reprisals be without delay made unto him the said John Bellew in lieu of his estate, or unto such whom he shall appoint of such lands, tenements and other hereditaments as he shall fix on which are in our hands in the same county where his said estate lyeth with the rents, issues or profits thereof as aforesaid which he is to have and enjoy unto him, his heirs and assigns in lieu of his estate or any part thereof, and he the said John Bellew thereupon put into the quiet and peaceable possession of his said estate and of every part and parcel thereof. And if any rent or rents or other sum or sums of money do remain in charge on the premises or any part thereof in our court of exchequer in that our kingdom which was put in charge since October 1641, the barons of our said court and every of them and every other officer there whom it may concern are forthwith to cause the same to be put out of charge. And we do by this our Royal Mandate, will and require our Justices of that our kingdom of Ireland and all other our Governor or Governors for the time being our Attorney-General and all officers and others in their several respective employments whom it shall or may concern to cause this our order and judgement in each particular to be as full put in due and present execution, any directions, letter, Declaration, Order or Instructions, Act or Acts or other matter or thing be it of fact or record to the contrary notwithstanding for which this shall be unto them and every of them a sufficient warrant and discharge. And all and every person or persons now possessing any of the premises of other the said John Bellew's estate, or such lands, tenements, or other hereditaments as he shall fix on as aforesaid are in pursuance of these our orders to yield up and deliver the quiet and peaceable possession of the same unto the said John Bellew or unto such whom he shall appoint as they and every of them will answer the contrary at their perils. Given at our court at Whitehall this 7 day of March in the 13rh., year of our reign.

By his majesty's command,
Will'm Morice.

Entered at the Signet Office 1 April 1661.
John Nicholas.[24]

At this early stage of the restoration land settlement, a king's letter of this kind was as much as Bellew could have wished for. It held forth an expectation for a full restoration of his estates in County Louth, notwithstanding the provisions of the Gracious Declaration and its accompanying Instructions and which were ordered to be set aside in his particular case. As only the barony of Ardee had been the subject of plantation in that county and then only by soldiers, the rest of the county had been withheld from plantation as a security for adventurers not satisfied elsewhere. As these lands, estimated at about 45,000 acres profitable, had not been planted by the end of the Commonwealth, they passed at the restoration into the hands of the court of exchequer as agent for the crown.[25] As 'forfeited lands' the court was empowered to let the same in short-term leases or custodiums, pending a final decision as to their disposal. A king's letter was a prerogative act of the crown, directed for execution by the king's representatives in Ireland, at this time the Lords Justices, while its entry in the Signet Office was a recognition of it as an act of state and in accordance with the instructions issued by the king following the Bellew-Cashell petition of November 1640. On this basis, Bellew might not therefore have to wait upon the further consideration of his case by the commissioners appointed to implement the Gracious Declaration.

In the light of subsequent events there is no doubt that it was the patronage of Theobald Taaffe, Viscount Corren, which won the grace and favour of the king for John Bellew. It is clear that a close bond of friendship had existed between them for many years and in Taaffe's letters to Bellew he frequently addressed him as, 'Dear Cousin' probably on the basis of his grandfather's second wife Ismay, who was a daughter of John Bellew's grand-uncle, Sir Christopher Bellew of Castletown-Dundalk.[26] This friendship, based on family connection, would have been further strengthened by their common service in the Parliament of 1640–1 and in the army, especially after the Ormond Peace. Taaffe was the eldest son of Sir John Taaffe who had been created Baron Ballymote and Viscount Corren in Sligo in 1628 and grandson of Sir William Taaffe, the second son of John Taaffe of Braganstown County Louth, who served in the Nine Years War against O'Neill. He later succeeded Sir James Fullerton in Sligo and in the 'freeholding' of Sligo in 1617, Sir William acquired the manor of Ballymote as well as the reversion of the lands of the McDonaghs of Corren. Theobald's sister Ismay had married Brian Og McDonagh who died without heir in the battle of Manorhamilton in 1643 and his estates in Collooney passed in reversion to Theobald.[27] Theobald Taaffe had been the only Roman Catholic appointed a regimental commander in the force raised by Wentworth for service against the Scots and was subsequently appointed to transport a regiment abroad after its disbandment. After the insurrection, he was one of those appointed by Parliament along with John Bellew to negotiate with the insurrectionists but there is no evidence that he ever acted in that capacity. He subsequently participated in the affairs of the Catholic Confederacy, as general for the province of Munster until the first Ormond Peace of 1646. After the peace of 1649 he was appointed master of the ordnance and Bellew's superior officer, in succession to Sir Thomas Lucas.[28] His career as a soldier in this period was as indifferent as his effectiveness in the political arena where he was perceived as a tool of Ormond and, by the Nuncioist faction, as a person not to be trusted. He was vilified by the author of the 'Aphorismical Discoverie', who described him as 'a comon, cogginge gamester, a route banke and a temporizer fit for any stampe'.[29] Yet for those who knew him otherwise, theirs was a different opinion. When, in January 1649, a suggestion was made that Taaffe might be sent to Spain with a party of troops, possibly as a compromise to the Nuncioist faction, who would have had no wish to see him serve under the commission of trust, a strong objection was lodged against such a move by a party of officers of the former Leinster army including John Bellew. They referred to him as a person of 'soe much honor and galantrie', that they could not discharge the duty which they owed to a person of his merits, especially having regard to the role he played in securing the [Ormond] peace, without making representations against his departure from Ireland at that time.[30]

In 1651 Taaffe was involved in the diplomatic mission, appointed to treat with the Duke of Lorraine, for aid to be sent to Ireland in the struggle against the Commonwealth forces. While the mission was not successful, it did give Taaffe access to the European diplomatic and political scene, which may have been of some use when he later joined the exiled court of Charles II in Flanders. Like Bellew, he was exempted from pardon for life or estate. After his departure from Ireland, provision was made for his wife Mary under the articles of Ballymote in June 1652, granting her 'liberty with her family to reside at Ballymote in the protection of the State of England'.[31] This suggests the possibility that she may not have joined her husband in exile. She may therefore have been spared the humiliations of his scandalous behaviour in the Court of Charles II where his dissolute lifestyle was notorious. He managed to establish, a close friendly relationship with the king, whose own lifestyle was not much different to that of Taaffe's. He was of particular service to the king in the management of his relationships with his several mistresses, notably Lucy Walters whose first child by the king was adopted by Taaffe and whose second may have been his own.[32] After the Restoration he continued as a close intimate of the king, whose patronage was to be of prime service to him in the Restoration Land Settlement.

As one of those mentioned in the Gracious Declaration as, meriting 'in a special manner', the 'grace and favour' of the king, Taaffe became entitled to the restoration of his forfeited estates in Ireland, 'without being put to any further proof'. Unfortunately for him, however, his estates in Sligo had all been planted by Commonwealth ex-soldiers including Sir Charles Coote and his brother Richard, while the ancestral estates in Smarmore in County Louth were all in the barony of Ardee where they too had been planted by ex-soldiers.

The brothers Coote, by now respectively the Earl of Mountrath and the Lord Baron of Collooney, were also mentioned in the Gracious Declaration, which preserved their titles to any lands held by them 'by virtue of any grant, order or disposition of the late usurped powers'. This included Richard's occupation of the McDonagh estates of Collooney to which Taaffe had also a valid claim for restoration. This was to be but one of the many contradictions contained in the Gracious Declaration, which would have to be resolved by the Act of Settlement and its successor, the Act of Explanation. As Taaffe intended to remain on in the court at London it became necessary for him to appoint an agent to manage his affairs in Ireland including the conduct of representations and negotiations with the executive agencies of government in Dublin. These included the Lords Justices and the barons of the Court of Exchequer, all of whom would be involved in giving effect to the decisions of the king made on his behalf in London. Considering his political affiliations and general reputation, Taaffe would have needed an agent in Ireland who was knowledgeable of the law, skilled in the arts of negotiation and networking and above all loyal and discreet. In April 1661, probably while he was still in London, he asked John Bellew to accept the position. John accepted the agency, which he continued to hold for the next seven years.[33] During this period their respective pretensions in what was to become the lottery of the restoration land settlement, would be brought to a relatively successful conclusion for both. While the king's favour was crucial, the conduct by Bellew of the intricate business and legal activities associated with the settlement, in the hostile environment of the Dublin administrative and legal establishments, was a considerable feat in itself. It may also have been significant for his success that John had the active involvement of his wife Mary and their two sons, Patrick and Christopher, in the conduct of the business.

John Bellew was back in Ireland by the middle of April 1661. He brought with him a copy of the king's letter of 7 March, as well as a copy of another from the king's brother, James, Duke of York, recommending him to the favour and protection of the Lords Justices 'as often as his occasions shall require'.[34] Thus armed, he lodged a petition with the Lords Justices seeking the implementation of the decisions made on his behalf and in particular, restoration to his former lands 'now in the king's hands' i.e., not held by soldiers, and located in the barony of Ferrard.[35] These were Graftonstown, Hitchestown, Reynoldstown and Garvagh [Garralough]. Taking no chances against a legal challenge to his claim, he submitted a certificate from Thomas

Kennedy of the Court of Chief Place, to the effect that, while he had been indicted for high treason in 1642, he had not been outlawed and was therefore qualified to hold lands from the king.[36] Recognising that the rest of his former estate could not be 'conveniently restored', he requested reprisals, as he was entitled to do by virtue of the king's letter. The lands specified by him were High and Low Disart, Barmeath, Haynstown and Dromin, Walshestown, Baggotstown, Kiltallaght, Drumgooter and Ardbollis, Parsonstown, Painestown, Cruicestown, Labinstown and Nicholastown. The decision of the Lords Justices, was promulgated by Eustace, Orrery and Mountrath on 20 June 1661. They found that it would take time for the due observance of the king's instructions to be accomplished, but that in the meantime, Bellew was to have a custodium lease of the lands mentioned in his petition, at an annual rent of £50 'during his majesty's pleasure'. Instructions to that effect were issued to the barons of the Court of Exchequer to seal the same.[37] The issue of the latter would also have been accompanied by an injunction to the high sheriff of County Louth to put Bellew into the peaceable possession of the lands mentioned in the lease. John Bellew was in County Louth later that year possibly arranging for the taking over of the lands and the leasing of the same to tenants.[38] He had at last returned to his 'coast of Israel' but without the surrender of the lands allotted to him by the 'usurped power' in Connacht.

Sometime after his return from London, John Bellew established himself in an office 'at the widow Humphrie's house at Cook Street in Dublin' adjacent to the Four Courts, the Parliament House and Dublin Castle.[39] From this place he conducted his business on behalf of Taaffe for the next seven years and kept a detailed account of his transactions on his behalf including the costs incurred.[40] As agent, he had power of attorney for things done in Taaffe's name in Ireland and also to take responsibility for his debts. In default of some of the latter, Bellew may have spent some time in prison. By the time he relinquished his agency he was about sixty-three years of age and remained still active until his death in 1679, some eleven years later. Throughout 1661 Taaffe was the recipient of four king's letters conveying him grants of lands in Ireland. The first of these is dated 16 March and was in respect of the forfeited estate of the regicide Sir Hardress Waller in and about the city of Limerick. The second is dated 9 April and conveyed a grant of custodium lands in County Louth in reprisal for the Collooney estate in County Sligo, his claim to which Taaffe was prepared to forgo in return for the lands in Louth. The third was dated 13 May and confirmed the reversion of the estates of Christopher Taaffe of Braganstown and

Theophilus Taaffe of Cookstown, which Taaffe claimed had been entailed on his ancestors. The fourth was dated 30 August and conveyed the restoration to him of the manor of Ballymote, County Sligo, then occupied by ex-soldiers and which was an inheritance of Taaffe's from his father.[41] While Taaffe, who had been created Earl of Carlingford in June, was negotiating these deals with the king and his council in London, Bellew was busy in Dublin seeking to make them effective through the legal processes of the courts, notably the Court of Exchequer. He also had dealings with the respective high sheriffs in the counties in which they were situated.[42] There was little he could do about the last two letters. The Taaffes of Braganstown and Cookstown were still alive and had, in their own right, king's letters providing for their restoration, albeit that their respective estates lay in the barony of Ardee and, like the manor of Ballymote, were in the hands of ex-soldiers.[43] The latter issue was referred by the Lords Justices to the commissioners set up under the Gracious Declaration and with which Bellew had some dealings. The business in the Court of Exchequer and the various offices associated with it involved the formal entering of copies of the king's letters, searching the records for particulars of estates such as rentals etc., securing custodium orders from the barons of the exchequer as well as injunctions for service on the relevant sheriffs to obtain freehold possession of the lands in question. Bellew encountered considerable difficulties in his dealings with the legal bureaucracy in Dublin. He also had to pay the necessary fees and petty bribes for the services rendered by officials of the court. These included the payment of from two shillings and sixpence to three shillings to the doorkeeper at Lord Orrery's office; ten shillings to Sir James Ware the surveyor-general in the Court of Exchequer; three pounds to the lord chief baron's man 'to assist the speedy carrying both the custodiums and to dispatch the same'; to Mr Burniston, two pounds to get the chief baron to sign an order which the latter 'was slow to do'; and to Sir William Domvile, the attorney general, 'a piece of gold of £3.04s.0d', 'to befriend my lord' [Orrery] 'when I brought him the said reference'. In addition, Bellew had to regularly employ attorneys and counsel for legal opinions, the drawing up of legal documents and representational work at the courts.[44]

The acquisition of Sir Hardress Waller's estate on behalf of Taaffe seems to have been substantially accomplished by John Bellew by the end of 1661. Waller was an Englishman born in Kent who settled in Ireland where, upon his marriage in 1629 to the second daughter of Sir John Dowdall of Kilkenny, he acquired on foot of the marriage settlement the seignory of Castletown in County Limerick consisting of 7,139 acres.[45] He was a Member of Parliament for Limerick in 1640–41 and was one of those who signed the petitions to the king and the English House of Commons in November 1640. He later served in Inchiquin's Parliamentarian forces in Munster and later in the West Country of England during the English Civil war, under his cousin Sir William Waller. He was one of the judges in the trial of Charles I whose death warrant he signed. He returned to Ireland in Cromwell's army in 1649 and was later a supporter of Henry Cromwell against Fleetwood and Ludlow. After his failed coup d'état early in 1660 he was arrested and sent over to England to stand trial as a regicide and was executed. His estates in Ireland were duly sequestrated. On the basis of the king's letter in favour of Taaffe, the Lords Justices on 25 August 1661 ordered the chief baron to grant a custodium lease of the estate to Taaffe, 'a particular of which' was annexed to the order; excepting lands lying in the King's County which had been granted to Lord Angier as well a lease of lands in Limerick made to Michael Boyle the bishop of Cork.[46] The custodium was for a period of one year commencing 1 May 1661. Having acquired the custodium, Bellew had then to travel to Limerick to make arrangements with the sheriffs for the taking over of the estate. He found that the rental due on the estate in 1661 was £820 per annum, the moiety of which was due in May and which he was entitled to collect. The demesne lands at the time of Waller's imprisonment, including the rent of the tenant living thereon, were worth £239, a moiety of which was also due in the May gale. Having taken over the estate, Bellew appointed a Captain Pope and a Gerald Og Fitzgerald to let the estate and collect the rents. His son Patrick described as 'of Clonoran County Galway' accompanied him and was later appointed receiver of the rents from the estate on behalf of Taaffe.[47] He continued as such for many years thereafter and was evidently his father's representative in Limerick. That the work was not accomplished without some local trouble is evidenced in the bill of costs, which Bellew incurred as follows:

First to the sheriff of the county of Limerick for delivering the possession of the lands in the county-at-large.	£40 0s. 0d.
To the sheriffs of the city of Limerick for the possession delivered by them.	£21 0s. 0d.
Given to a counsel upon the dispute what the sheriff's fees might be and spent then in that trouble.	£1 16s. 0d.

Given to several messengers and such as assisted during the time of getting the possessions and taking up the rent.	£2 9s. 9d.
Spent in my journey into Munster, being five weeks and in coming hither to Dublin.	£8 17s. 0d.
Disbursed in getting bills of exchange to secure the monies hither to Dublin, the ways being dangerous.	£4 9s. 0d.
For the expenses of such as I employed whilst I was making out that of Dromroe and Castletroy and the sending of letters and orders then to the sheriff and others in Munster and the getting of the orders which was in the former government touching Drumroe.	£3 17s. 0d.
Allowed the gardener and sergeants.	£4 0s. 0d.[48]

In November 1660 Richard Coote, Baron Collooney, submitted a petition to the king, in which he referred to the town and lands of Collooney, as formerly owned by Bryan McDonagh and which had been secured to the petitioner, by the king's favour. He also stated that he had spent £400 in buildings and improvements to the estate. He referred to Theobald Lord Taaffe's claim to these lands, and pointed out that he had made an agreement with him that, on foot of the improvements made by Coote, Taaffe was willing to forgo his rights to restoration, provided he could recover reprisals elsewhere in lieu thereof. This arrangement was approved by way of a king's letter dated 9 April 1661. On 20 October following, Taaffe sent a letter to John Bellew from London, informing him that he had procured new letters from the king. These confirmed all his former grants together with an annual payment of £800, as well as a grant of the forfeited incumbrances on the Collooney estate in Sligo from which he was entitled to a chief rent. The letters were directed to Bellew and conveyed to Ireland by Lord Kingston.[49] Taaffe assured Bellew that if anything was found wanting in any of the king's letters, it would be his own fault; 'for I could insert what words I pleased, it being his intention I should not be disturbed in anything I possess, yet if any new thing be necessary, send me in writing what it is and I believe I shall obtain it'. In a reference to the Lords Justices, he assured Bellew that there was none of them but were his friends and would do justice to his case. As to Bellew's own situation he felt that little would be done, 'there being a general rule resolved on for the whole nation, which I hope will appear more clement and just that is reported'. He did however assure him that he would, nonetheless, use his influence to secure his estate. Carlingford's trust in the king's benevolence was not misplaced although it was to take eight years and the direct intervention of the king before his pretensions were finally settled. His difficulties may have arisen from an over reliance on those responsible in the Irish administration, many of whom were by no means 'his friends'. In the event the 'general rule decided upon for the whole nation' was also applied to himself in the form of the Act of Settlement 1662 and the further Explanatory Act of 1655.

John Bellew's 'Account' suggests than he commenced proceedings in County Louth for the reprisal lands granted to Taaffe in lieu of the Collooney estate shortly after the issued of the king's letter of 9 April 1661. However, the work of acquiring lands in Louth at this period was of a different order of difficulty than the acquisition of Waller's estate in Limerick. In the latter case only one estate was involved, the former owner was dead and his lands sequestered as one of the hated regicides. In Louth, not alone was more than one estate involved, but many of the former proprietors would already have commenced proceedings for their recovery, aided by king's letters no less valid than Taaffe's. There were also the Connacht transplanters, including John Bellew himself, who entertained legitimate pretensions for a recovery of their estates. To complicate matters further, the king had also issued letters containing grants of land in the county to other court favourites. These included Ormond's friend, Colonel Mark Trevor, who had a grant of the corporation lands and tenements of Dundalk and Carlingford, and Sir Henry Tichborne, who was seeking title to the Plunkett lands at Beaulieu, the forfeiting proprietor of which, Thomas Plunkett, also had a king's letter for restoration. Incoming claimants to County Louth lands included Major Nicholas Bayly and Captain Read who had a king's letter for some 5,000 acres in County Louth; Colonel William Legge who had a lease of forty years for lands in the baronies of Ardee, Ferrard and Cooley; Erasmus Smith seeking 'satisfaction of his adventures for land in Ireland', by means of a grant of land in the barony of Ferrard and Lord Massarene seeking reprisals for an estate in County Antrim which he was required to yield up to the king's favourite, Daniel O'Neill.[50] As there was not sufficient land available to the crown to satisfy all of these demands, great pressure was brought to bear by the various parties on the Court of Exchequer, where the deployment of legal skills, financial resources, to meet the costs of fees and petty bribes, and above all attention to legal niceties and procedural detail would be as important as the king's favour.

Bellew's problems were further exacerbated by the fact that it was envisaged that the only lands that Taaffe would be allowed to reckon as reprisals for the loss of the Collooney estate were those of which he had a custodium of before 1 August 1661. In fact Bellew was not able to complete this task until September by which time he had acquired nearly 4,500 acres, yielding an annual rental of £720.[51] In addition to the custodium lands, which had been part of Bellew's own grant, the lands of Henry Gernon of Milltown Dromiskin consisting of 1,728 acres had also been included in Taaffe's custodium. These were in turn leased by Bellew to Gernon's son Nicholas, who recovered the estate subsequently under a decree of innocence granted under the Act of Settlement.[52]

The granting away of lands by means of king's letters acting through the royal prerogative gave rise to widespread unease and discontent especially amongst the ex-soldiers and adventurers still awaiting confirmation of their land's titles. The commission established under the Gracious Declaration had functioned only fitfully and ineffectually. The Commissioners held their first meeting on 20 March 1661 and, as might have been expected, they subsequently approved the passing of letters patent in respect of land grants made by the king to favoured men, such as Colonel Mark Trevor, whose claim to the lands of Dundalk and Carlingford was the subject of dispute between him and local Commonwealth ex-soldiers. Viscount Montgomery of the Ardes, who had a king's letter granting him the Allen estate of St Wolstons in County Kildare and to which Sir Thomas Allen had a legitimate claim, also got letters patent from the commission.[53] That the king may have envisaged a similar service being performed on behalf of Taaffe is suggested by his letter of 5 March 1661 ordering Taaffe's restoration. In it he stated that it was 'a step in which the Commissioners employed by us by the General Convention of Ireland concur'. However while Taaffe's case was submitted to the commissioners of the Gracious Declaration, nothing came of it. On 20 August 1661 the commissioners issued a proclamation requiring soldier grantees to submit particulars of their respective estates. These were to include details of the debentures on the basis of which the lands had been allocated to them; the extents and location of the lands themselves with the names of the former proprietors and such other relevant information as would enable the commissioners to make a decision.[54] They were later required to attend the commissioners to verify under oath the particulars submitted and that the claimant had been in actual possession of the lands mentioned in the claim on

7 May 1659. The objectives were twofold, firstly to verify the facts of the claim so that the necessary fiant or certificate could be issued, to enable the grantee to take out letters patent, and secondly to discover lands held in concealment, being lands held in excess of the value of the debentures issued. Notwithstanding nothing further was done by the commissioners to enable the soldiers to secure legal title to the grants made to them during the time of the Commonwealth. The commission on behalf of the Trust for the '49 officers, established under the Gracious Declaration, had also become active by mid-year 1661 acquiring lands and properties assigned to the Trust under the terms of the Declaration. Much of these were in the walled towns where many of the ex-soldiers had acquired properties in concealment during the period of the Commonwealth. These they were now being required to yield up to the Trust, the benefit of which would pass in due course to their former enemies, the Protestant officers who had supported the king in the period 1649–1650.[55] The Trust was also in conflict with grantees of king's letters whose grants entrenched on lands specifically assigned to the Trust under the terms of Declaration.[56] The general confusion created by these many anomalies and contradictions created local problems for sheriffs seeking to give effect to mandates issued by the court of exchequer. These mandates began to be questioned in the courts. Eventually, a ruling was given by the judges that the procedures were 'no warrantable rule to walk by in the disposing of mens' estates'. This was all the more evident by the fact that the Declaration itself envisaged the enactment of legislation to give it effect.

The Irish Parliament, which was intended to deal with the legislation, assembled on 8 May 1661 and while Roman Catholics had not been excluded from election, control of the freeholds had passed so completely to the Protestant interest in the period of the English Commonwealth that only one Roman Catholic, Geoffrey Browne of Galway was elected. The Gracious Declaration was considered and adopted and while complete agreement was not reached between the Lords and Commons as to the final content of the Bill of Settlement, the latter was subsequently brought over to England by the agents of the Lords Justices.[57] There the respective interested parties, including the Roman Catholics, began their representations on the Bill in discussions with the English Privy Council. After the exclusion of the Roman Catholics in March 1662, on foot of the revelations of Sir Nicholas Plunkett's dealings with the continental powers in 1647, approval was given for it to be prepared for transmission to the Irish Parliament in accordance with Poynings' Law. There it was read for the first time on the 6 May and after much debate, including a call for an Explanatory Bill, it had passed all stages by the 30th of that month.[58] Ormond, the newly appointed Lord Lieutenant, arrived in July and on the last day of that month he gave royal assent to the Bill in the House of Lords.

As might have been expected from a Protestant-dominated Parliament, the preamble to the Act of Settlement was strongly anti-Catholic in character, placing all the responsibility for what had happened in Ireland in the years following the insurrection of 1641 on the 'Irish Papists', whose 'Supreme Council did first assume, usurp and exercise the power of life and death, make peace and war, levy and coin money and many other acts of sovereign authority . . . disowning and rejecting your royal father and your Majesty's undoubted right to this kingdom'.[59] In a massive rewrite of history, it asserted that, with the help the Almighty had given his majesty, 'by and through your said English and Protestant subjects, absolute victory and conquest over the said Irish popish rebels and enemies', was achieved, 'so as they, their lives liberties and estates are now wholly at your majesty's disposition'. The message and the expectation were clear, the fruits of that victory, namely the estates of the Irish, should pass to the Protestants, an expectation that was in large measure to be accomplished. To facilitate this, all lands which had been forfeited since 1641 'upon account of the said rebellion or war', including the forfeitures of the period of the Commonwealth were vested in the king. Only excepted were such lands, whether of Protestant or Catholic proprietors, which were found subsequently, by a court, authorised for that purpose, to have been held by a person innocent of having participated in the rebellion. This provision included any decisions to that effect made by the commissioners appointed under the Gracious Declaration. The court authorised for the purpose of making the determinations was set up, as a court of claims, under clause 74 of the Act, the members of which were required to take an oath of impartiality in respect of their dealings. The qualifications for innocence as originally set out in the Instructions were retained and additional provisions made for the '49 Officers Trust. An important feature of the Act of Settlement was the provisions, or provisos, for named individuals of high standing, most of whom had already been the recipients of king's letters. In addition to such grandees as the Dukes of Ormond and York and the former rebels Mountrath and Orrery, others included Ormond's former secretary, George Lane, Erasmus Smith, Lord Castlehaven, Colonel William Legge, Viscount

Massarene and John Bellew of Castletown-Dundalk who was John Bellew's cousin. The purpose of a proviso was to enable the holder to proceed to the Court of Claims where upon pleading the terms of the proviso, he would obtain a favourable decision on his petition.

Taaffe was one of those who was granted a proviso in the Act of Settlement. In a letter to John Bellew dated April 1662 he mentioned that he had 'arrived at a conclusion' in his business. He had obtained a proviso for all the lands set out to him by way of custodium in the county of Louth, including the estates of Taaffes of Braganstown and Cookstown, but wherein he met with more difficulties than he had expected.[60] 'Had not the king positively appeared' in his concernments he declared, 'he would not have prevailed'. His main difficulties arose from the agents of the Duke of York, who had succeeded in having Hardress Waller's estate in Limerick included in the duke's proviso, thus debarring Taaffe of the opportunity of acquiring the freehold of that estate. He complained to Bellew that the duke had been 'severe' on him, affording him only £600 a year rent charge out of the estate, 'though it be worth more'. The proviso which Taaffe had sought included Waller's estate, his own former estate in Ballymote, his 'antient' estate in County Louth, including those of Braganstown and Cookstown and the custodium lands in County Louth, in lieu of Collooney. As it transpired Taaffe obtained two provisos, one under clause 189 of the Act of Settlement, which restored to him all lands held by him on 22 October 1641. The second under clause 215, confirmed the grant of such of the custodium lands in Louth as was held by him on 1 August 1661, together with the reversion of the lands of Braganstown and Cookstown.[61] The next stage in the achievement of Taaffe's pretensions now swung back to Ireland and especially to John Bellew, who would carry the major burden of the work in steering them to a comparatively successful conclusion.

It is impossible at this remove to be certain as to the circumstances and purpose of John Bellew's commentaries on the proposed restoration land settlement in Ireland. However, the time and place of their composition strongly suggest that they were briefing documents, prepared by him on behalf of the Irish party, then in discussions with the king. There cannot be any doubt however that they also represent his inner feelings and fears at the trend in the events then unfolding, and which must inevitably conclude in a settlement prejudicial to the Irish interest. While his worst fears were to transpire, it is doubtful if the hard-line approach, so evident in the second document, would have cut much ice with the king or his immediate advisers. However, considering the strength and political influence of the Protestant British delegation, it is doubtful if a more conciliatory approach had been adopted by the Irish Party, the outcome would have been any different. For John Bellew himself this was a watershed period. The proposals in the Bill of Settlement carried no great assurance that his landed interests would be protected. It must also have been clear to him that if he and his family were to survive, as landed gentry, the changes in land ownership foreshadowed by the proposed legislation, it would require of him the maximum use of patronage at the highest level of political influence and a single-mindedness of purpose in the pursuit of his objectives. If Theobald Taaffe was to provide the former, Taaffe himself was also to be a beneficiary of Bellew's single-mindedness which played such an important part in ensuring their survival.

CHAPTER SEVEN

Agent to Theobald Taaffe, Earl of Carlingford

As Carlingford's agent in Ireland, Bellew had to steer the way through the legal and administrative maze of the Dublin bureaucracy, making friends with and, where necessary, paying the fees and bribes to the officials involved. By these means he sought to ensure that the king's favour in London was translated into reality in Dublin and in the various localities where their respective landed interests were located. He also had to negotiate at the highest levels of government administration, including the Lords Justices and subsequently the Lord Lieutenant Ormond, seeking to overcome legal obstacles and conflicts of interests with others.[1] This involved a constant attendance at the courts, particularly the exchequer and the successive courts of claims set up under the land settlement legislation. In addition to his dealings in the courts, he also had to conduct research into the land titles, family particulars and even the discrimination records of individuals whose forfeited lands had been included in the custodium leases which he and Carlingford had acquired in County Louth. Any such lands, not recovered by the former proprietors under the provisions of the Act of Settlement, would revert to the crown and thus become available for regrant to Carlingford under the terms of his provisos in the Acts of Settlement and Explanation. The importance of maintaining a regular attendance in Dublin was testified by James Jones, Colonel William Legge's agent in Ireland.[2] In his rummaging through the legal records in Dublin, Jones had discovered a defective title in a lease held by Lord Louth of the former Knights Templars estates in Kilsaran and Cooley and thus enabled Legge through the king's patronage to acquire a ninety-ninety year's lease of the property. This was subsequently converted for Legge into a freehold estate of 2,400 acres in accordance with a proviso contained in the Act of Explanation 1655. In May 1666 Jones complained of his need to constantly attend the Court of Claims, 'fearing surprises' and of being unable 'to go into the country to bustle about this years setting of the acres, lest in that time you should lose them all'. John Bellew also had to attend to the management of the newly found estates in Louth and Limerick, ensuring that the rent rolls were maximised and the rents duly returned and accounted for. In this he was supported by his son Patrick in Limerick and by Carlingford's cousin Christopher of Braganstown in Louth. A Captain Webb and another Carlingford relation, George Taaffe, supported him in Sligo, where some recovery of former Taaffe lands had taken place, even before Carlingford was restored to his ancestral estates in that county under the Act of Settlement. Nor was Bellew based exclusively in Dublin. Where necessary he had to travel into the country from time to time to collect rents and attend to local legal and other business. In the period December to February 1664 for example, he had to journey to Louth and Sligo in connection with Carlingford's decree from the Court of Claims as well as to collect rents in Louth.[3] He travelled from Dublin to Louth on horseback on 18 December where he stayed a few days and then, hiring fresh horses, he travelled to Athlone. There he sent a man back to Louth with the horses he had hired there and journeyed on to his house in Clonoran, County Galway. From there he travelled to Sligo and then back to Galway on 25 January, returning thence through the county of Louth to Dublin where he arrived about 5 February, all of which was accomplished on horseback. Such a mid-winter journey made by a man who was almost sixty years of age suggests that he had very considerable physical strength and endurance.

At this period Bellew was much dependent on his family for support. In addition to the help given by Patrick in the management of affairs in Limerick, his wife Mary seems to have had the responsibility of managing the Bellew estates at Clonoran, County Galway. His son Christopher was also employed by him but not before he completed some form of legal training, either with Oliver Keating, the clerk of the crown and peace for Connacht, or John Keating, who held a similar office in Ulster. A letter from Mary Bellew to her husband, dated 22 June 1662 dealing with Christopher and with estate matters at Clonoran seems to show her as a person with her own mind and strongly held opinion, and evidently happy with the opportunity of running affairs at Clonoran:

> Dear Heart,
> Doe not you beleeve Vines; nor doe not relie upon him at all, for hee is married to a Galway woman for I assure you the Quaker toald mee the

oxen were not booked. Mall Esmay and I can swere the same. I will doe all things according your derection. I am glad that you have preferred Christopher to Mr. Keating, but am troubled that you do not writt mee what promises you have of him as concerning his religion. I refer all other concernaments to the relation of the bearer, I am,

Your faithful wife and servant,
Mary Bellew.
Clonoran, the 22th., of June 1662.

Post:
My opinnion of the sheriefe is that he is a knave and doth but deceave you as Henry Roe did. Patrick will tell you of a letter which he writt to the subsheriefe Blacke wherein is mentioned that all the fines will fall upon himself, which Blacke was made subsheriefe by Redmond Burke himself and is bound for him to the sheriefe in the house now six score pounds of which there belongs to Patrick foure and forty pounds the which hee got in Limmerick one way or another and fourteen pounds of . . . I layed out fifteen pounds upon an advantagious bargain this oxen and my muttons I hope will make [an] other hundred pounds soe your business cannot starve for want of money but would advise you to be very scircomspect how [you] dispose of it, for I fear all will com to [naught] as the king's orders did remember something of the selling of the wool for 'it bears noe prise heer and look after those that look after his [care] . . . Farewell Mary Bellew.

This letter was written at a time when Bellew was heavily engaged in Dublin in securing the custodium lands in Louth and in connection with which he employed Mr Keating in legal business connected with the Carlingford agency. Mrs Bellew's prejudice against Galway women is all the more remarkable, since she herself was a Galway woman, unless of course the Galway women she was referring to were native Irish born as against her own Old English ancestry.[4]

The decision to incorporate Hardress Waller's estate in Limerick into the Duke of York's proviso under clause 194 of the Act of settlement represented a severe set-back for Carlingford. The situation was further compounded by the fact that the same estate had been included in two other provisos in the Act, that of the bishop of Cork under clause 100 and of Sir Richard Ingoldsby under clause 161.[5] Carlingford's failure to have the estate included in his own proviso placed him entirely at the mercy of the duke and his agents. At the same time he found himself in dispute with the other proviso holders as well as with the tenants on the estate, who, as John Bellew described them, had become 'refractory hearing that the Duke of York was to have that estate again'.[6] Bellew made three separate journeys to Limerick in connection with his attempts to get in the May gale of 1662 during which he had to distrain for the rent at 'Innish McCoony', Killonan and Castletroy. He had to hire a boat to get to Innish McCoony accompanied by the sheriff and a party of soldiers. Not being able to get any rent he levied a distress by seizing a flock of sheep, which had to be ferried back from the island. It had been a violent mission during which Bellew was wounded and had to receive treatment from a surgeon.[7] Later in the year the dispute with Ingoldsby took a serious turn when the latter, taking advantage of his parliamentary immunities, had Bellew's son, Patrick and his local assistant in Limerick, Garrett Oge Fitzgerald, arrested by the sergeant-at-arms of the House of Commons, probably on a charge that he had entrenched on his proviso estates around Limerick. This took place at a time when John Bellew was busy with affairs in Dublin and with the arrest under similar circumstances in County Louth of two other Carlingford servants, Jenico Taaffe and George Warren. On Carlingford's directions Bellew's son Christopher took his place in Dublin and Louth while John travelled to Limerick. After the arrests of Patrick Bellew and Garrett Fitzgerald, a conference was held in the House of Commons in Dublin on 10 December 1662 at which agreement was reached with Ingoldsby and the prisoners were ordered to be released.[8] Part of the agreement was the relinquishment of Innish McCoony to Ingoldsby, which Bellew was ordered by Carlingford to effect while he was still in Limerick. In September 1662 Carlingford's position in Limerick had been regularised by way of an agreement, made with the Duke of York's commissioners, providing for the grant of a lease of Waller's estate in Limerick to Carlingford for a term of 31 years at an annual rent of £400, a rent charge of £600 to be recovered from the rent roll of the estate.[9] The agreement also provided for the grant of reprisal lands, out of the duke's estates, in respect of a recovery of any part of the Waller estates under the Act of Settlement. This situation continued until December 1669 when Carlingford relinquished the lease in favour of another agreement he made with the duke.

In December 1661 Carlingford asked John Bellew to hire a house for him in Dublin which 'if delayed will be difficult to find and dearer than now'.[10] This was at the beginning of a period during which a great influx of people flowed into the city of Dublin, many of them from the neighbouring island of Britain. In addition to those seeking recovery of their forfeited estates, others sought legal title to acquisitions made by them, either as adventurers or as Commonwealth ex-soldiers in the period of the usurped power, while still more sought the conversion of their king's grants into real estates in Ireland. This state of affairs was to continue for many years, during which a strong social and even elegant life style developed, including the theatre, where the Earl of Orrery, for example, was able to give full vent to his literary pretensions.[11] In response to Carlingford's request Bellew procured a house of six hearths in Winetavern Street in the parish of St John's.[12] In April 1662 Carlingford advised him of his expected arrival in the following month when he was 'to have a good house for me, well furnished and provision for horse meat and corn'.[13] The great man arrived with his entourage in July, the previous two months having been spent in getting the house ready.[14] In addition to his wife Mary and their sons (Captain) Francis and 'young' Johnny, the party also included a Mr Nicholas Browne, the earl's man, 'my Lady's gentlewoman', a Mrs Mottam, the cook, Mr Vicoure, the coachman as well as sundry footmen, grooms and a postillion, then essential support staff for a 'noble earl'. Carlingford did not intend a permanent residence in Dublin and when his business had been concluded at the Court of Claims set up under the Act of Settlement, he returned to England early in 1665, leaving the management of his Irish affairs in the hands of John Bellew and Taaffe's son Nicholas. During his time in Ireland, John Bellew had the added responsibility of providing funds for the management of the household in Dublin, principally to Lady Carlingford for provisions and entertainment for visitors including wine and acquavitae. Other household expenses included 'young' Johnny's clothing and education, periodic payments to Captain Francis, while the coachmen and their horses had to be regularly provided for. In September 1663, for example, Bellew had to provide the coachman Mr Vicoure on Carlingford's instructions with £38, 'when his lordship was going to Kilkenny with my Lord Lieutenant'. This was an occasion when Ormond had convened a privy council meeting at Kilkenny thus providing a pretext for the gathered nobility and gentry including Carlingford, then a member of the House of Lords, to engage in a bout of hunting, coursing and hawking in the locality.[15] On another occasion Bellew had to pay the sum of £17 to the 'gentleman of the lord lieutenant's wine cellar' and ten shillings to Mrs Hales for 'a barrel of beer that was drunk by the soldiers before the wars when his lordship was made prisoner'.[16] In time Bellew was to claim with evident justification that Carlingford was never out of his debt.

The principal business that brought Carlingford to Ireland was his petition to the Court of Claims set up under the Act of Settlement. This seven-man court took up office on 20 September 1662, but for a variety of reasons did not commence hearings until January 1663. By the following August, when the Court was closed down, it had made decisions on 829 petitions, but leaving perhaps thousands of others unattended, including Connacht transplanters such as John Bellew.[17] The Court of Claims was essentially an administrative tribunal. It was responsive to decisions taken by the Lord Lieutenant and council in Dublin, or by the king in London, and was constrained to act within the provisions of the Act of Settlement and its successor, the Act of Explanation of 1655, and without prejudice to rights under the common law.[18] The individual members of the court, all of whom were English were frequently approached by or on behalf of plaintiffs or defendants and some were held to favour one side more than another. The political balance was not however one-sided, and considering the legal and socio-political pressures brought to bear upon them, they appear to have done their work with a remarkable degree of fairness. The procedures of the court required the plaintiff, i.e., the claimant, to submit beforehand a petition setting out the qualifications of the petitioner seeking the decree, accompanied by a claim or schedule(s) describing the lands and other properties involved. Individuals opposing the application, which invariably included the attorney-general on behalf of the state, and those occupying the lands in dispute, were described as defendants. In cases of pleas of innocence, the defendants had access to the outlawry and other criminal records, including the depositions of 1641–54, which they could use to discover records discriminatory of the plaintiff and which they could use in the court.[19]

Carlingford's petition was submitted to the Court of Claims on 6 November 1662 and consisted of four schedules as follows:[20]

> *First schedule*
>
> *Part one*: The Taaffe ancestral estates in Ballymote County Sligo.
>
> *Part two*: The Taaffe ancestral estates in County Louth.
>
> This part of the claim was advanced, on the basis of the proviso contained in clause 189 of the Act of Settlement, which provided for the restoration to Carlingford of the estates in Sligo and Louth held by him, or in trust for him, on 22 October 1641 and for the reprise of all persons disturbed in consequence with lands elsewhere in Connacht or in County Clare.

Second Schedule

> The claim in respect of the second schedule was based upon the proviso in clause 215 of the Act, enabling Carlingford to acquire a grant of the custodium lands in County Louth, in reprisal for the loss of the McDonagh lands in Collooney County Sligo, provided that such lands were seized and possessed by him on 1 August 1661. Some at least of the former proprietors of these lands who had suffered forfeiture in 1653 were named, such as Henry Gernon of Milltown Dromiskin, John Babe of Newtowndarver and Newry, James Plunkett of Carstown, Patrick White of Dundalk, Michael Barnewall of Drogheda and Patrick Gernon of Gernonstown.

Third and Fourth Schedule

> The lands in the third and fourth schedules were those of the Taaffes of Braganstown and Cookstown. The former was the senior branch of the family, the proprietor of which in October 1641 was John Taaffe who had succeeded to the estate in 1632 when he was described as being thirty-five years of age and married. He was described as having died in 1649 and was succeeded by his son Christopher who was subsequently 'expulsed by the late usurper'. He, together with his cousin Theophilus Taaffe of Cookstown, had been the subject of a king's letter dated 31 May 1661, ordering their restoration to their respective estates, but being in the hands of Commonwealth ex-soldiers it had not been acted upon.[21] The letter recognised that these estates had been the subject of settlements and entails the effects of which were that, in the absence of heirs male, which was the case for both Christopher and Theophilus, these estates would pass in remainder to their cousin Theobald Taaffe Earl of Carlingford.

The claim did not come to a hearing by the court until 5 August 1663, a delay of nine months since the date of lodgement. In the interim the basis of the claim came under close scrutiny, not alone by the officials of the Court of Claims, but also by the privy council in Dublin. The latter became involved by virtue of the powers conferred by clause 226 of the Act upon the Lord Lieutenant and council. These allowed them to suspend the execution of any proviso, and following examination, 'in their full latitude', to alter or change the same, or determine, 'how far and in what manner the same shall be executed or observed'. While this was a power that was intended to expire on 1 December 1662, that is less than a month after Carlingford's claim had been lodged, Bellew's 'Account' reveals that it was exercised in respect of Carlingford's proviso and that Bellew submitted a petition in respect of the same. This was the subject of hearings with the council and Lord Lieutenant on a number of occasions the outcome of which was promulgated on 10 June 1663 as follows:

> That they did not think fit to suspend the execution of the said first mentioned proviso or clause concerning the said Theobald Lord Viscount Taaffe earl of Carlingford nor to retrench, alter, change or disallow of the same so far as concerns the said earl otherwise than in manner and form as follows:–
>
> That the said Theobald earl of Carlingford, shall be restored unto and vested in all and singular the messuages, manors, lands, tenements and hereditaments whereof he the said Theobald earl of Carlingford, or John Viscount Taaffe, deceased father to the said earl, or either of them or any other person or persons, to the use of or in trust for them or either of them were seized or possessed upon the 22 October 1641, And that such persons their heirs or assigns to whom any of the said lands have been set out and who are by the said Act of Settlement reprisable for the same be forthwith reprised for the said lands and improvements thereupon out of the first lands that shall come into his majesty in the province of Connacht or county of Clare, by the restoring of any persons to their estates who were formerly transplanted, in such and the same manner as reprisals are to be set out to such persons, as are or shall be removed from the estates of innocent persons and that the said earl, the now claimant, do pay such rent out of the premises as he is liable unto by the said Act of Settlement.[22]

This decision had a twofold effect; firstly it conferred on Carlingford all the benefits applicable to an innocent person under the provisions of the Act of Settlement, without putting him to the necessity of proving the same which could have been difficult. Secondly, it deferred a decision on the other provisos connected with the remaining schedules of his petition. All of these pertained to lands that were the subject of claims, whether by former proprietors or their heirs, Commonwealth ex-soldiers in Braganstown and Cookstown, or the holders of provisos and king's letters (letterees). These would therefore be in competition with Carlingford for the possession of the lands held by him in County Louth, under custodium leases. They were subsequently joined by the Duke of York, who began to entrench upon the 'forfeited' lands of County Louth at this time, in reprise for lands allegedly lost elsewhere.

At the hearing of Carlingford's petition by the Court of Claims on 15 August 1663, Sir Edward Dering, a member of the court, noted that Carlingford claimed as an innocent as well as under his proviso giving rise to a debate as to whether he should, 'go on upon his innocence and waive his proviso, or upon his proviso and waive his innocence'.[23] Considering the decision of the Lord Lieutenant and council, which effectively adjudged him innocent and ordered his restoration, it is difficult to understand why such a question should have arisen unless the court, on the basis of some legal technicality, required him to make such an election. In the event he elected to rely upon his proviso and the court found in accordance with the directions given it, subject to a saving for an incumbrancer Patrick French in respect of the lands of Killina, County Sligo. Dering noted that Carlingford 'did not go on for any part of his new estate', and the decision of the court was to 'except' these from their order and decree. It declared that it would not 'proceed to the adjudication thereof until the proper time and order for the hearing, the like concessions or grants made by the said Act'.

After this decision the court set up a sub-commission whose task appears to have been to verify the particulars of the lands to which Carlingford was to be restored. This process took some time to complete and was not without dispute.[24] A Roger Gregory had laid a claim to the lands of Clintonsrath in the barony of Ardee, which had been included in Carlingford's claim. The matter was referred to the sub-commissioners who found in favour of the latter. John Bellew's 'Account' reveals that a good deal of negotiation and compliance with legal requirements had to be undertaken, before the final decree was issued on the October 1663. This included, in the later stages, dealings with Sir Richard Rainsford's 'man' (Rainsford being a member of the court), who was paid nineteen shillings by Bellew for going with the decree to the sub-commissioners, 'for he would not trust me with the same'. He was subsequently paid one pound, 'when he got Sir Richard's hand to the said decree and the rest of the commissioners who were then going away'. He also had to pay the sum of ten pounds to Mr Kennedy, the clerk of the court, for the decree itself. Carlingford must have been reasonably satisfied with the outcome, marking the occasion with a dinner on 23 October, at which the guests included the Earl of Arran, Lord Inchiquin and two members of the Court of Claims, Colonel Winston Churchill and Sir Allen Broderick. As well as the slaughter of an ox for the dinner, a sum of £1.16.00 was expended on wine and one shilling on pipes and tobacco. The next month John Bellew paid Churchill £113.18s.00d., 'acreages monies', presumably the fee of one penny per acre due to the court under clause 58 of the Act.

With the exception of the townland of Garralaugh in the barony of Ferrard in County Louth, all of the lands restored to Carlingford by his decree in the counties of Louth and Sligo were in the hands of Commonwealth ex-soldiers for whom reprises had to be obtained before Carlingford could obtain freehold possession. The surviving evidence suggests that this was accomplished in the period after the enactment of the Act of Explanation in 1655, and may have taken some years to complete.[25] Bellew's 'Account' reveals that legal proceedings had to be taken against Townley and Gregory in respect of Clintonrath where they had 'troubled the tenants' in December 1664. In October 1663 it was reported that Captain John Chambers had come with a party of soldiers to Tullykeel in the parish of Clonkeen and, breaking into the house of Christopher Taaffe the earl's cousin, threw Mrs Taaffe and her daughter out of the house, the former onto the dunghill.[26] Sir William Aston also gave difficulties in respect of 514 acres in the townlands of Harristown, Hoathestown, Richardstown, Mullacurrin and Roestown, all of which were in the barony of Ardee. In a letter to John Bellew in February 1664 Carlingford referred to Aston, Captain King and others, averring that they 'may live to repent their injustice to me'. In the following month he reported that Aston 'employs some considerable friends here [London] to persuade me to an agreement with him and to use him favourably, but for ought I find he will not deserve it, but until my arrival my tenants and myself must suffer'. Whatever agreement was concluded between them, it is clear from the Carlingford Book of Survey and Distribution that succeeded in recovering the lands in dispute and that Aston was reprised elsewhere.[27] The lands recovered by him in County Sligo amounted to 9,839 acres and in County Louth to 2,045 acres.[28]

The decision of the Lord Lieutenant and council and, subsequently the Court of Claims, to postpone action on the other provisos was a severe setback to Carlingford. John Bellew, acting on his behalf, was forced into a continued contention in the courts with the other grantees of County Louth custodium lands, whose grants encroached upon the custodium lands held by Taaffe. Bysse, who was the chief baron of the Court of Exchequer, and a former recorder of the Drogheda Corporation, was no friend of either Carlingford or Bellew and frequently gave the latter difficulties, or 'rubs' as he described them, in the grant or renewal of custodium orders.[29] Considering the pressures brought to bear on the court by the various parties involved, Bysse may not have been any more prejudicial towards Carlingford than he might have been to any other, in seeking to hold the ring in as impartial a manner as possible. In effect it was a situation where all the contending parties were engaged in a scramble for the available lands, using whatever means were to hand, political or legal including in particular, the loopholes and tricks notoriously associated with the Common Law Courts. In the lead up to the proceedings of the Court of Claims many of the former proprietors were mentioned in legal proceedings, men such as the Gernons of Killencoole, Kilcroney and Milltown, Plunkett of Carstown, Clinton of Clintonstown, Dowdall of Killaly and Babe of Darver.[30] In a search for evidence, John Bellew accessed the records of the Discrimination Office, for details of the indictments standing against such persons as White of Richardstown, Taaffe of Cookstown, Plunkett of Bawn, Gernon of Killencoole, St Laurence of Cruicestown and Taaffe of Braganstown. His searches were subsequently extended to include the entire county. Bearing in mind that the proceedings of the Court of Claims were largely concerned with claims of innocence by the forfeiting proprietors of the Commonwealth era, it is not surprising that the court demurred from hearing Carlingford's claim to the custodium lands. A substantial section of these lands were already included in claims coming before the court, some of which were successful. These included Nicholas Gernon of Milltown who recovered an estate of 1,728 acres, all of which had been in Taaffe's custodium, John Babe of Darver who recovered an estate of 615 acres and Thomas Clinton of Clintonstown [Charleville] who recovered an estate of 828 acres.[31]

CHAPTER EIGHT

'The Earl of Carlingford is the most powerful man in the county'

The termination of the proceedings of the Court of Claims in August 1663 effectively brought to an end all claims based upon innocence and with the enactment of the Act of Explanation in December 1655, the forfeiting proprietors including Bellew were eliminated from the contest for their former estates. This left the field open to the other claimants, consisting of the adventurers and soldiers who were confirmed in their estates (with a cut-back or retrenchment of one third of the lands held by them under the Commonwealth); the proviso-men and nominees under the Acts, and letterees and ensign-men, in the actual occupation of an estate on 22 August 1663. As in the case of the Act of 1662 the Act of 1655 vested all the forfeited lands, not already restored, in the crown, for reallocation in accordance with its provisions and by means of a Court of claims established for the purpose.[1] Additional powers were conferred on the executive in Dublin and on the Courts, thus limiting the exercise of the prerogative by the king.

John Bellew's 'Account' reveals a variety of disputes which were ventilated in the Courts between Carlingford and others, such as Mark Trevor the Viscount Dungannon, Erasmus Smith, Lord Massarene, Nicholas Bayly and, most important of all from 1664 onwards, with Dr Gorge and the commissioners of the revenue of the Duke of York.[2] Of these, the disputes with Bayly and York were the most persistent and were settled only after protracted legal and other proceedings. Bayly's only claim to the king's favour was that he brought the news to the exiled king in Brussels of Monck's decision to march on London and to restore Parliament in 1659.[3] For this signal service he was rewarded in 1661 with a lease of approximately 5,600 acres in County Louth. These comprised the forfeited estates of

Patrick Bellew of Verdonstown Dundalk, who was a distant cousin of John Bellew's and had served with distinction in Preston's Leinster army during the wars; those of Jenico and Stephen Taaffe of Athclare near Dunleer and of John White of Ballriggan Dundalk. Bayly's problem was that much of this land was already in the hands of others, such as Sir Robert Reynolds, Cromwell's former commissary-general, who held White's lands at Balriggan, and Taaffe's of Athclare, part held by Commonwealth ex-soldiers. Inevitably encroachments arose between Carlingford and Bayly, involving Athclare lands in the barony of Ferrard, the former lands of John Plunkett of Bawn and Mullahullagh and William Moore's lands at Barmeath, all in the barony of Ferrard, the former lands of Peter Clinton in Derrycammagh, and Taaffe's of Braganstown lands in Mansfieldstown all in the barony of Louth.[4] The aggregate of these various holdings was 1,306 acres, and with the exception of Barmeath, over which a bitter legal battle took place between Bayly and Carlingford, the remainder may have been held by Bayly prior to 1662 as they are not included in the Carlingford's rent-roll of that year. However, the outcome of the Court of Claims, including the decrees of innocence granted to Gernon, Clinton and Babe put pressure on John Bellew to seek the expansion of Carlingford's custodium lands elsewhere in the county. The clash with Bayly must have been an outcome of that pressure.

Carlingford and Bayly had already clashed in the autumn of 1662, probably in respect of the former Taaffe lands of Athclare, causing Bayly to petition the House of Commons, of which he was a Member for Newry, in December 1662. He sought the attachment of George Warren and Peter Taaffe for 'disquieting' him in his possessions, evidently by their encroachment, on behalf of the Earl of Carlingford, on some of Bayly's custodium lands.[5] Warren was living at Darver near Dromiskin, while Taaffe, (whose tower house still stands at Athclare), was one of the forfeiting proprietors of Athclare, and had been transplanted to the barony of Ballintober in County Roscommon, along with Patrick Warren of Warrenstown, who may have been either father or brother to George.[6] While Taaffe may have evaded arrest, Warren was apprehended at Darver, 'with a fowling piece on his shoulder', by William Tisdell the deputy to the sergeant-at-arms of the House of Commons on Wednesday 10 December, who conveyed him to Dublin on the following Friday. Tisdell subsequently deposed that along the way Warren asked leave to call 'at a friend's house in Cook Street, which he suffered and went in with him, where was one Bellew', who he was informed was the Earl of Carlingford's steward.

At Bellew's suggestion Tisdell agreed that Warren should meet the Earl of Carlingford who was then in a nearby house, because, as Tisdell explained, he had been asked by the sergeant-at-arms 'to be very civil to Warren'. During the meeting with Carlingford the latter identified Warren as his servant and refused to allow him to go with Tisdell as his prisoner. The latter protested that, as in all civility he had allowed Warren to call on him, he should not now keep him from him against the wishes of the sergeant-at-arms. Carlingford refused to relent and Tisdell then left without Warren. Having reported to the sergeant-at-arms what had transpired he was instructed to return to the Earl of Carlingford, bringing with him an assistant named William Dobbin to demand the release of Warren into his custody. Again Carlingford refused to release Warren saying three times that he was rescuing him and would answer before Parliament for his actions. Tisdell also reported that during all these proceedings Bellew was present.

If Nicholas Bayly's parliamentary privileges has been invaded by Warren and Taaffe justifying their arrest by the sergeant-at-arms, they, as the Earl of Carlingford's servants were also entitled to immunity from arrest, as part of Carlingford's privileges as a member of the House of Lords. On 12 December a message was conveyed by the House of Lords to the House of Commons referring to the attachment issued against these men, seeking that if it had not been executed that it be suspended, but if executed that the men be released. On 20 December in the course of some conferences had between committees of both Houses Carlingford protested that he did not intend any disrespect to the House of Commons and offered to bring Warren before the bar of the House. Sometime after this Warren must have been rearrested and imprisoned and thus remained while the houses, standing upon their respective dignities, debated the matter through committees of both Houses. On 27 February the Commons declared that 'so high a breach of privilege' had taken place, as the like had never before been attempted by any subject whatever, and was calculated 'to be of very great and dangerous consequence to this Kingdom'. Warren was not set at liberty until 5 March 1663 when both Houses agreed to a scheme of registration for the menial servants of the members of both Houses 'thereby avoiding proceedings against them' in the future.[7]

The clash with Dr Robert Gorge, the agent of the Duke of York, was much more serious. In addition to the influence he could deploy, Gorge was also a totally unscrupulous land-grabber, whose success in securing an estate of 100,653 acres for the Duke of York in Ireland, not one acre of which had been held by him before the restoration, was a major disruptive influence on the whole land settlement.[8] In June 1664 Bellew records a meeting attended by him with the duke's commissioners 'touching the lands in Louth upon the letter sent by his royal highness for having all lands in his majesty's hands, by way of custodium or otherwise'.[9] This must have been the opening round of the duke's encroachment into County Louth in search of reprisal lands, allegedly in compensation for 'regicide lands' granted away to others by decrees under the Act of Settlement, a move subsequently regularised by clause 49 of the Act of Explanation, which provided for the grant of reprisal lands of an equivalent amount in the counties of Louth, Dublin, Kildare and Cork. Several letters patent were passed on foot of certificates from the Court of Claims between April 1668 and May 1669, conveying an aggregate of 6,559 acres to the duke in the baronies of Dundalk, Ferrard and Louth.[10] The proviso included in clause 90 of the Act of Explanation, on behalf of Carlingford, merely confirmed the earlier provisos, without 'any retrenchment, change or other alteration thereof, made by the lord lieutenant and council of Ireland and any other matter or thing in the said former Act or this present Act contained to the contrary thereof in any wise notwithstanding'. This failed to correct the deficiency in the earlier proviso, which limited Carlingford to the custodium lands held by him on 1 August 1661. The Duke of York's commissioners soon took advantage of this deficiency. In May 1665 Bellew had to retain a counsel, 'to follow my lord's business when the news came that his royal highness was to have all the custodium lands in Ireland and all other lands that patents were not passed for'.[11] In March of the following year Bellew made arrangements to join Carlingford in England who was then making arrangements for his departure to Vienna as the English ambassador to the Court of the Emperor Leopold.[12] In May Bellew was advised that the duke's commissioners were in England 'with power to settle my concerns' and instructed him 'to repair hither'. Nevertheless Bellew had not gone over before Carlingford left for Vienna as the following letter to Bellew, dated 8 July at Vienna indicates:

> Sir,
> Yours of April 13 from Dublin I received last night by which I find that my provisos in the Act of Settlement did not afford me the advantage the king intended, from whom only I can hope for reparation, all others have been severe to me in their proceedings and in regard that

my stay here is unavoidable, preferring the loss of all my fortune to the disobeying my king. You must supply my place and solicit his majesty for such necessary orders as may restore me to what the commissioners have severely adjudged against me, wherein I presume, you will meet no difficulty or delay, considering the assistance my Lord Arlington will afford you, who I am sure is my friend. You must likewise make application to his royal highness and my lord chancellor to both whom I have written and am persuaded neither of them will countenance any unjust or rigorous proceedings of Doctor Gorge. You are to wait on Sir Heneage Finch his majesty's attorney-general who drew my proviso, being my friend and councel he will direct and assist you to obtain from the king what may supply the deficiencies therein, as also on my Lord Arlington, to whom I recommend your concernments as the likeliest to be able to do you good. Mr. Williamson will convey what letters you write unto.

Your affectionate kinsman to serve you,
Carlingford.

I have recommended your own business to Sir Heneage Finch as the most able to direct you what to procure from the king for your advantage. I have remitted my interest in Munster to what my lord chancellor and my Lord Ormond will adjudge, 800 I was to have had; I hope his R.H., will command restitution of my possession.[13]

Bellew arrived in England about the time this letter was written. He had a further letter from Carlingford dated 11 July in which he expressed the hope that Bellew would 'meet with more favour in my concerns than in Ireland' and expressed the hope he would 'live to reproach some that have wanted friendship for me'. His return to England would depend on the king's pleasure. Rounding off the letter he assured Bellew that he 'doubted not his industry' and that if ever he had the power it would 'be requited'. During his absence in Vienna, from where he did not return until January 1667, John Bellew remained in London at lodgings 'next door to the sign of the Frying Pan near Charing Cross on the Strand', while Carlingford's eldest son Nicholas took care of affairs in Ireland.[14] John's wife Mary was also involved in the conduct of Carlingford's business at this period.[15]

The 'some that wanted friendship' for Carlingford at this time may have included Ormond and his particular faction in the Dublin administration. This is suggested from the correspondence that passed from Nicholas Taaffe to Bellew in which he advised him to depend on the friendship of the secretary of state, Henry Bennett, Earl of

Arlington, whose particular sphere of influence was foreign affairs. He may have been responsible for the appointment of Carlingford to Vienna.[16] The Mr Williamson mentioned in the correspondence was Sir Joseph Williamson, the head of Arlington's secretariat and a close confidant of Colonel Richard Talbot. The latter was a Gentleman of the Bedchamber of the Duke of York and leading broker for Catholic and Irish interests at the Court in London. He also acted as counsel before the Court of Claims in Dublin. That Carlingford employed him in his affairs is suggested by a statute staple bond in the sum of £200, which he gave to Henry and Richard Talbot in May 1665.[17] Another influential circle in which the Taaffes curried favour included the Boyles, Roger, Earl of Orrery and his younger brother Michael. The latter had been the Bishop of Cork in the period 1660 to 1663 before his appointment as Archbishop of Dublin, where he became lord chancellor in July 1665 in succession to Eustace.[18] The bishop was also one of those who had an interest in Waller's estate in Limerick on foot of a grant made to him by the king in 1661. In a letter from Nicholas Taaffe to Bellew in July 1666 dealing with the Limerick estate he mentioned that Gorge's proceedings were 'very contrary to my lord of Cork's discourse with me'.[19] This was a reference to the acquisition of the estate by Dr Gorge on behalf of the Duke of York who had received a certificate and an injunction from the Court of claims a short time before to be put into possession. The connection with the Boyles is further borne out when in July 1667 the Earl of Carlingford solicited the Earl of Orrery's help on behalf of John Bellew probably in connection with his business then before the Court of claims seeking a certificate for his Connacht estate.[20]

In his letter of July 1666 Nicholas Taaffe urged Bellew to acquaint the king of the situation and to ask him to speak to the Duke of York, 'at whose mercy we now are' and to point out how disadvantaged his family was because of the absence of his father.[21] He referred particularly to Sir Allen Broderick who was both a member of the Court of Claims and a commissioner of the revenue of the Duke of York whom he described as the 'chief instrument against us' and of whom he was 'to take no notice'. In October he reported to Bellew that Gorge had summonsed him to make out the Taaffe title to the Collooney estate by 8 November and that the duke had put all Carlingford's lands in County Louth into his claim. He also urged him to let Arlington know how destructive the king's last letter had been to his father's interests.[22] One of the contentions between Carlingford and Gorge was the rent charge of £600 on the Duke of

York's newly acquired Limerick estate. Later that year Nicholas Taaffe, in a letter to Bellew, referred to a suggestion, that the Earl of Carlingford might accept lands in Louth, held by the Duke of York, in exchange for his rent charge on the Limerick estate. In the light of subsequent events this must have been the beginning of the solution of this particular dispute.[23] He also referred to a letter, which Bellew had, providing for reprisals for the ex-soldiers disturbed in Sligo and Louth by virtue of Carlingford's decree of 1663. On 6 December Nicholas Taaffe gave the following substantial report on affairs in Ireland including some references to legal tricks then in vogue:

> Cousin Bellew,
> I received yours of the 17th. First I will give you an account of what I have done as to our custodium lands. I have by the friendship of some of the commissioners [of the Court of claims] put off our hearing on the 9 January, though I was very much opposed. I have as well prevailed for the second custodium as the first, and as for Alexanders telling you of a feoffement produced in Court the day of our trial, he lies like an arrant knave, for there was not a paper shewed of either side which the whole Court can justify, but it is by such false suggestions that such villains as Gorge and he ingratiate themselves. As for our concerns in Munster, I admire my lord of Cork should think my father well dealt withal to have £600 a year without any consideration for his lease when Dr. Gorge before Colonel Richard Talbot at his first offer, told the colonel we should have £800 a year in Louth of maintenance [?] for our interest in Munster. As for my particular I know not what to advise you, nor did [sic] I, were it safe for me, without my father's consent; but this I know, the duke's orders came over to use all diligence for the possession of that estate. They cannot remove a tenant by order of the Court, which I got put in and withal the tenants have six years lease to come from my father, which I sent them purposely to give them more trouble, upon which I am assured they cannot dispossess them 'till that time be expired . . . I think your petition to the king is very well. I am assured, by several letters of my lord, being on his way which I hope will put an end to all our trouble.[24]

The petition to the king referred to in this letter may have been that lodged in the name of Carlingford's eldest son William in January 1667.[25] In this petition, reference was made to a decision by the Court of Claims on Carlingford's proviso regarding the Braganstown and Cookstown estates. Having heard the case put by Garstin (Braganstown) and the other ex-soldiers, the Court had ruled that the latter were entitled to prior reprisals before being removed. The petition also referred to the claim by the Duke of York for precedence over Carlingford in regard to the custodium lands. Following this petition, the king sent a letter to the Court of Claims asking the Court, to take 'for a certain ground that the clauses inserted in the said Acts were and still are intended by us and should be taken and construed in the most large and beneficial sense for the earl's good profit and avail'. This was indeed a timely intervention by the king and may have provided the pretext for the agreement subsequently made between the earl and the duke.

Upon his return from Vienna Carlingford, following on from this decision by the king, entered into negotiations with the duke and his commissioners the outcome of which was an agreement the terms of which were conveyed in a letter to Dr Gorge dated 2 April 1667.[26] In it the duke observed that the lands in Taaffe's custodium had not been vested in him on 1 August 1661, as was required by his proviso. In consequence, the grant made to him in September 1661 was not supported by that proviso and consequently not secured by the second (Explanatory) Act. Nonetheless, despite this 'inadvertency or want of diligence in those who were trusted by him', he recognised Carlingford's service to the king in 'attending him during the greater part of the time he was beyond the seas', and was resolved 'not to take that advantage of him, which in the strictness of the law he was entitled to do'. Accordingly he ordered Gorge not to entrench on Carlingford's custodium in Louth, which he estimated to be between 4,000 and 5,000 acres. He also advised Gorge that having consulted with his commissioners, he was prepared to set out such lands held by him in County Louth to be assigned to Carlingford as a valuable recompense for the £600 a year granted out of the Waller estate in Limerick. On 12 April the king moved to have this agreement implemented in Ireland by issuing a direction to Ormond to secure that all the lands and tenements claimed by Carlingford in County Louth not exceeding 5,000 acres be granted to him by letters patent.[27] He further ordered that Carlingford was not to suffer in any respect for his attendances upon the king, or his concerns, and that the king's letter of the previous February, concerning the Braganstown and Cookstown estates, be acted upon and that the reprisals in exchange for the restoration to him of 'his antient estates' be observed 'in all the particulars thereof'.

Despite the peremptory nature of the king's letter to Ormond, the issues between the Duke of York and Carlingford were not fully resolved until December of that year. It was not until 13 July 1668 that the Court of Claims issued the necessary certificate to enable letters patent to be passed. In a letter, dated 14 September, to his attorney Jeffrey Browne, Carlingford reported that he had reached an agreement with the Duke of York, regarding the custodium land in Louth, who had also agreed to issue a command to his agents, 'not to pretend upon any account unto them or any of them'.[28] The delay in bringing Carlingford's affairs to a conclusion at this time may also have been in part due to his continuing dispute with Bayly. The latter had been reduced in his expectations in County Louth by the Duke of York's acquisition of Michael Bellew's estate in Verdonstown leaving a residue consisting of the lands of Bawn, Mullahullagh, Mansfieldstown and Barmeath, all of which had been included in Carlingford's custodium claim. Of these Barmeath had been the subject of claim and counter-claim in the Courts with the hapless former Commonwealth tenant Wetherall caught up in the actions.[29] The dispute came at length to the Court of Claims probably in July 1668 the proceedings of which are recorded in a minute kept by Sir Edward Dering, a member of the Court.[30] The Court found that the lands in dispute had not been included in Carlingford's custodium, albeit that Mansfieldstown, being part of the estate of Taaffe of Cookstown, should nevertheless pass to the earl. Leave was given to the parties to place adventurers' deficiencies upon the remaining lands, with Bawn and Mullahullagh passing to Bayly and Barmeath to Carlingford. Clause 5 of the Act of Explanation defined adventurers' deficiencies as 'adventurers who never had any lands set out to them in satisfaction of their adventures, or were never fully satisfied for the same'. As with soldiers' debentures, these were saleable commodities in Restoration Ireland, of interest to speculators in Irish land who having purchased them at a discounted price were subsequently sold on by them to third parties for use in the Court of claims to correct a defective title. Clause 10 of the Act of Explanation enabled any soldier or adventurer who having more lands in his possession than was required to satisfy the two-thirds part of his former Commonwealth estate, could 'place' such adventurers' deficiencies on the 'over-plus lands' and thereby obtain title to them. A similar arrangement was made in respect of individuals in their provisos. This concession was evidently granted to Carlingford by the Court of Claims in respect of the lands of Barmeath, the acquisition of which might otherwise breach the limit of 5,000 acres which Carlingford was permitted to acquire.

The negotiations to secure adventurers' deficiencies on behalf of Carlingford were conducted by John Bellew through the brokerage of

Sir George Rawdon. On 28 November 1668 the latter entered into an agreement allowing the Earl of Carlingford 'to apply unto the lands of Barmeath in the county of Louth and the barony of Ferrard, 398a.1r.00p., for part satisfaction of two thirds of the total and original adventure of Sir William Strickland Kt., amounting to £600'.[31] Two days later Bellew confirmed by deed that Strickland would receive in return, a rent charge of £20 per annum out of Barmeath.[32] On 30 November Mr Samuel Bull, 'one of the attorneys of the Court', certified that Strickland was a deficient adventurer for £600, that he had not been heard before the Court, had not received satisfaction for his adventure and that 'the said adventurer was a good adventure'. On foot of this certification Strickland was allowed a 'total and original deficient adventure of £600, unless cause be shown to the Court to the contrary by this day fortnight'. On 3 December Rawdon, 'at the instance of Mr. John Bellew' confirmed to Sir Edward Dering, the agreement made for the payment of the rent charge to Strickland, thus clearing the way for the matter to be brought before the Court. While some doubt can be entertained as to the correctness of Bull's certificate that Strickland was a 'deficient adventurer', the Court issued a certificate on 17 December confirming that his deficiencies be applied to the said lands of Barmeath at the request of Rawdon and Bull.[33] Rawdon had been summoned as a witness to attend the Court but in a letter he apologised for his non-attendance, confirmed that he had written to Dering and advised that 'Captain Bellew was acquainted with the cause'. On the day prior to the issue of this decree John Bellew entered into a bond vesting the lands of Barmeath in the Earl of Carlingford subject to Strickland's rent charge of £24 per annum. With these preliminaries completed, the Court issued a final certificate on the following day. It allowed Carlingford to place Strickland's deficiencies on Barmeath, 'the said earl having contracted for the same; the lands having been sequestered by reason of the rebellion' and decreed that 'the said earl shall hold and enjoy the said lands'. On the basis of this certificate the Lord Deputy, Ossory, issued a fiant, dated 22 December, allowing Carlingford to pass letters patent on 2 January 1669 for his custodium, and other lands in County Louth including Barmeath. It provided, however, that the parts of the Braganstown and Cookstown estates lying in the barony of Ardee and in the hands of the ex-soldiers should not be confirmed to him until after the latter had been reprised. As it transpired they were never reprised and the lands in question remained with the ex-soldiers, their heirs and assigns.[34]

The agreement reached between Carlingford and the Duke of York in July 1667 for the relinquishment of the rent charge on the Limerick estate in return for lands acquired by the duke in Louth was not completed until 1669–1670 as the following letter from Carlingford to John Bellew dated 7 December 1669 indicates:

> His royal highness is sending an authority to his commissioners there to set out the 4,000 acres long since promised and I find that I must attempt of them in the county of Louth contiguous to Carlingford or any other part of my estate in that county. I shall appoint my son and you to treat with them and if you shall differ upon the land and signify to me the cause of it and send me a list of the lands you shall fix upon, I am confident I shall prevail with his royal highness to grant them to me.[35]

Clause 194 of the Act of Settlement provided that all the lands acquired by the Duke of York should vest in the duke and be therefore free of all rents etc., as were chargeable on other lands by virtue of the Act. Accordingly where any such lands were subsequently alienated by the duke, the grantee was required to pay the appropriate rent to the exchequer and probably pass letters patent accordingly. The summary of the letters patent conveying lands in the county of Louth to the Duke of York refers to an aggregate of 6,134 acres situated in the baronies of Louth, Dundalk and Ferrard.[36] This figure cannot, however, be reconciled with the information contained in the BSD, which shows an aggregate of 6,664 acres held by the duke including the lands of Lisdarragh, Betaghsrath and Monksland in the parish of Carlingford. The details of the negotiations, conducted by Bellew and Carlingford's son Nicholas with the duke's agents in Ireland have not survived. However, on the basis of a rent-roll of the Taaffe's estates of 1677 and the BSD,[37] it is possible to identify lands held by the estate, in the Carlingford peninsula barony of Dundalk, consisting of 3,735 acres, formerly held by the Duke of York.

The gross total of the lands decreed to Carlingford in the county of Louth by the successive Courts of claims was 12,016 acres. Of these, 3,566 acres were included in the Braganstown and Cookstown estates, which were subject to reprisals which were never provided, leaving a net figure of 8,450 acres. These consisted of Taaffe's 'antient estate' of Smarmore amounting to 2,045 acres in the barony of Ardee, 5,154 acres, formerly the 'custodium lands' and 1,251 acres, formerly of the Braganstown and Cookstown estates outside the barony of Ardee. Of the net figure, a total of 832 acres were 'Saved' to individuals named in the letters patent and who on the strength of their 'Savings' recovered the lands in question from Carlingford. In addition, a total of 2,722 acres were subsequently disposed of by the Taaffes, 1,505 acres to John Bellew and his son Patrick, 643 acres to Hugh Gernon son of Patrick Gernon of Killencoole, 472 acres to John Keating of Castlering and 100 acres to Matthew Plunkett Lord Louth. These together with the 'Savings', when taken from the net figure of 8,450 acres, left a residue with Taaffe of 4,896 acres which, when added to the acreage acquired from the Duke of York, amounted to 8,631 acres. The rent-roll of this estate in 1677 amounted to £1,812 per annum. Of the other lands then included in the estate, Sligo yielded £688, Tipperary £469 and Meath £218 per annum. The lands in Slane were those of Baitestown parish of Siddan and Killruffan parish of Dromconrah, part of the Taffes of Braganstown estates, while those in Tipperary had been acquired originally as custodium leases of lands in the counties of Tipperary, Wexford and Kilkenny.[38]

Before Carlingford's departure from Ireland in 1665 he made arrangements through John Bellew to lease the tower-house and 'the plot about it', on the lands of Warrenstown (now Dillonstown) parish of Drumcar.[39] This estate and house had formerly belonged to Patrick Warren and was part of the lands acquired by William Aston in the Commonwealth plantation of the barony of Ardee. Aston subsequently sold part of his estate, including Warrenstown, to a Captain Arthur Dillon of County Meath, with whom the lease was entered into by John Bellew on behalf of Carlingford. Carlingford's purpose was to find accommodation for his wife Mary whom he evidently did not wish to accompany him to London. In the light of subsequent events, it seems clear that his intention was to desert her, as the following letter from Lady Carlingford to John Bellew graphically portrays:

Kruston (Cruicetown) the eight of May (1665).
'Tis heare reported in the contr [country?] that my lord has gone to London again with my lord Duck [duke of Ormond?] which trobles me very much. Pray let me know the truth of it if you have not already written to him to furnish me with some muny, pray do it out of hand, for I am come to a runey littel [sic] house as ever was seen. Here is not a penny of muny to be had, here the tenants of Klintenrath are stolen away with three cattel and owe two gales of rent and good part of the third. The oxen I took for the rent of this place are strade home to their oner; they disput with me and will not pay me a penny, others pay in their rent in malt and wheat. This is my condition, lett me here from you soone and you may command'
Your affectionate friend Mary Carlingford.[40]

In the previous April Bellew had sent several sums of money to Lady Carlingford whom he described as 'being in want of monies' and probably in early May he gave Jenico Taaffe 'on assignment to receive £105', 'to supply my lady and settle her in Warrenstown'.[41] For the next three or four years she was to continue in the same want, with John Bellew providing her with funds on a number of occasions and at the same time paying the rent on the property to Dillon. While he was in England the rent does not appear to have been paid, resulting in Dillon taking an action for recovery against Bellew. Nicholas Taaffe seems to have lived at Warrenstown for some of the period 1669 and in his letter to Bellew of 6 December 1666 he referred to debts owing by the Earl of Carlingford to Lord Meath (gambling debts) and Captain Dillon. He blamed Captain Webb of Sligo 'for I never yet had one penny out of the estate in Connacht'. He also advised Bellew that Dillon, not hearing from him was planning to 'show him to an outlawry' and which he could prevent by writing to him and to 'Webb to make payment'. In an undated part of the Bellew 'Account', which appears to relate to the period 1667–1668, there is a reference to several bills outstanding against Carlingford including the gambling debt due to Lord Meath and the rent of Warrenstown due to Dillon amounting in all to £219. Referring to this Bellew recorded, 'I am now to be clapt in prison if the same be not satisfied by his lordship.'[42] While Bellew seems to have escaped imprisonment, Carlingford still owed John Bellew £100 on the Dillon account in January 1688.

In his letter to John Bellew of 7 December 1669 Carlingford indicated his intention to return to Ireland. In the previous year it was reported that his brother, the Franciscan friar James Taaffe, had departed from London to Ireland in the company of Carlingford's mistress where 'she will remain in Ireland with the earl whose wife is still living'.[43] Oliver Plunkett, the newly appointed Roman Catholic Archbishop of Armagh, in his first report on the diocese of Armagh compiled early in 1670, described Taaffe as the most powerful man in the county, which would seem to suggest that he might have been resident there at that time.[44] He confirmed the king's role in the acquisition by him of his estates in the county and described the possessions given him as having belonged to Catholics before the war adding lamely, 'it is better that a Catholic should have them rather than Protestants'. While the death of Carlingford's wife Mary is not recorded, it is known that Carlinford married secondly, Anne daughter of Sir William Pershall, who survived his death at Ballymote, County Sligo in December

5. All that remained in the 1920s of the 'runey littel [sic] house' to which Lady Carlingford was consigned in May 1665 after her husband returned to the Court in London.

1687. His third son, Nicholas, succeeded him. His two elder sons, William and Robert, predeceased him. Although Old English in family background and an Irish Roman Catholic in upbringing, Theobald Taaffe's career displayed all the characteristics of the cavalier class that emerged in England and Wales in the closing decade of the reign of Charles I. Its class was to emerge as the dominant political force in the Restoration era of Charles II. Its reputation as a hard-drinking, reckless and often dissolute class could easily be exemplified in Taaffe's personal lifestyle. Bellicose and irresponsible, he served Charles II in his banishment period, mainly as an intermediary between him and his mistresses, and his involvement in duels claimed at least one death and caused him for a time to be excluded from the exiled Court.[45] As with many other cavaliers, his reputation as a soldier was at best indifferent and uncaring of the troops under his command. He displayed a similar indifference for the rights of others in his land acquisitions in the restoration period. He readily relinquished his claim to the Collooney estate in Sligo in return for a free hand in County Louth, where he acquired an extensive estate of lands, formerly belonging to his own kind. This marks him out as a person not fundamentally different from those other British predators for Irish land in the Restoration period. These included in County Louth such men as the Duke of York, Nicholas Bayly, Mark Trevor and William Legge, none of whom had held any land in the county prior to the insurrection of 1641. All had however served as cavaliers and had a ready access to the king's ear and hand.

CHAPTER NINE

'It were hard that your petitioner, who showed his affections to his majesty's interest, should now, himself and his family perish'

The decision to 'postpone', and thus effectively exclude Connacht transplanters from access to the Court of Claims, in pursuit of their claims of innocence, must have come as a severe blow to John Bellew's expectations, especially since the king's letter of 7 March 1661 would have been of material use to him in making his case. Nor was his patron Carlingford much use, because his influence evidently did not extend to securing for him a proviso in the Act of Explanation of 1665 or his inclusion in the list of nominees mentioned in that Act. In all probability his appointment of Bellew as his agent was the best service he could have rendered him, by placing him at the centre of the legal and administrative proceedings in Dublin by which the restoration land settlement was effected. Bellew's training and experience as a lawyer would have enabled him to acquire an intimate knowledge of the statute law governing that settlement, as well as its application within the current constraints of the common law and the influences of the administrative and political processes, in England as well as in Ireland. This would have enabled him to take a realistic view both of his limitations as well as of his opportunities and to use whatever means were to hand to further his interests. These would have included his connections with Carlingford who, despite his limitations, was sincere in his expectations that he would eventually secure Bellew in his estate.

The Act of Explanation made no provision for dealing with the Connacht transplanters whose anomalous position under the Act of Settlement was that, while it was recognised that some had been 'dispossessed of their estates meerly for being papists', their subsequent transplantation to Connacht or Clare was deemed to be, (without any foundation in fact), an 'act of their own' and for which the crown 'might without any injustice deny to relieve them'.[1] Nonetheless, the Act of Settlement did provide that upon establishing their innocence they were to be restored to their former estates, yielding up their lands in Connacht to the crown. No attempt was made in the second Act to 'explain' this anomaly, which was further compounded by the fact that the transplanters were forced to continue reliance for their land titles on the grants made them by the 'usurped powers' of the Athlone and Loughrea commissioners. This carried the implication that any inquisition held in respect of a transplanter's estate could result in a judgement of defective title and escheat to the crown. Bearing in mind that the Protestant interest had as an objective the confirmation of the Connacht transplantation, the omission of any 'explanation' in the Act for such transplanters must have been deliberate and calculated, in order to continue the Connacht transplanters in their former 'rebel' status.

No evidence has been traced as to the reason why John Bellew included the custodium lands, granted him by the Lords Justices in June 1661, in Carlingford's custodium lands. It may have been that at that time he had an optimistic expectation of making a full recovery of his forfeited estates, in which event he would have had to relinquish them to the crown or, realising the time limit laid down by which the custodium lands had to be acquired by Carlingford, he included them in Carlingford's first of his two custodium leases. Nor can it be ruled out that it was done by way of an arrangement agreed upon with Carlingford with the intent that he would subsequently recover them from him after the latter had passed letters patent in accordance with the provisions of the Acts.

Whatever the reasons for excluding the Connacht transplanters from access to the first Court of Claims and barring claims of innocence under the Act of Explanation, John Bellew was left virtually bereft of any means of recovery of his former estates. Clause 148 of the Act of Explanation provided a saving for the thirty-eight persons specified in the first Act, who were to be restored on the basis of the 'eminent services' rendered by them, but for whom no provision had as yet been made. A further sixteen names were added to this list and styled the nominees. They were to be restored to their 'principal seats' and not more than two thousand acres. Those to be removed for the purpose of effecting this arrangement were to be first reprised with lands of equal worth and value elsewhere. Numbered amongst these nominees were such Connacht transplanters as the Earl of Westmeath,

Sir Richard Barnewall, and Sir Lucas Dowdall, the son of Laurence Dowdall of Athlumney, both of whom had been former comrades of John Bellew in Preston's Leinster army. Evidently these were persons who could deploy a heavier weight of influence, and probably with Ormond, than either Bellew or Carlingford. Provision was also made in clause 157 of the Act for recipients of king's letters, such as Bellew, to enable them to be restored to lands held by them on 22 October 1641, provided that they were in actual possession of such lands on 22 August 1663. In such cases it was provided that the process of restoration to such lands should be the same as that applicable to the nominees. This included an upper limit of 2,000 acres of restorable lands and a requirement that the recipient pass letters patent on foot of a certificate awarded by the Court of Claims. The implication of the latter was that the recipients were not restored as innocents, but rather, their lands were re-granted to them under the terms and conditions provided for in the Acts of Settlement and Explanation. This was the only loophole in the Act by which Bellew could recover his former estates in County Louth. While still in England on the business of the Earl of Carlingford in the early part of 1667 and probably after consultation with him he obtained a legal opinion from an English counsel as to his position under the Act of Explanation, the text of which is as follows:

> The case of John Bellew Esq., concerning his right to be restored to his lands by virtue of the Act of Explanation in Ireland.
>
> John Bellew Esq., the 22nd., October 1641 was seized of and rightfully entitled unto a capital messuage and the lands belonging thereunto called Willistown and Adamstown, Plunkett's lands, Woodtown, Dawes Freehold in Braganstown, Lisrenny, Little Arthurstown, Nicholstown, Kenvickrath, Hitchestown, Graftonstown, Reynoldstown and Garborgh in the county of Louth.
>
> The king by his royal mandate bearing date 7 March in the 13th., year of his reign did order and adjudge that the said John Bellew should be put into the present possession of such of the said lands as were then in his majesty's possession and as to such as were in the hands of reprisable adventurers and soldiers, they to be reprised without delay and the said John to be put into the present possession thereof.
>
> In pursuance of those letters mandatory the said John Bellew was put into possession of Graftonstown, Reynoldstown and Garvaugh the rest being then set out to soldiers, and the said John continued the possession thereof the 22nd., August 1663.

In the Act of Explanation it is enacted that those who were in possession of any lands or houses upon the 22nd. August 1663, to which they were restored by virtue of any his majesty's letters, if they or any in trust for them, were thereof seized and possessed upon the 22nd., October 1641 and thereunto rightfully and are not otherwise provided for by that Act, should be restored unto and put into possession of such houses and so much of the lands lying contiguous and thereunto adjoining and shall not exceed the quantity of 2,000 acres, in the doing whereof the commissioners are to proceed by the same rules orders and directions and in like manner and form as they ought to proceed in the settlement and restitution of any the four and fifty persons in that Act before named and not otherwise.

The said John Bellew is not otherwise provided for by the said Act.

The question is whether the said John Bellew by this clause ought to be restored to his mansion house and two thousand acres or unto so much only whereof he was in possession the 22 August 1663.

I conceive the very probable opinion to be upon the case that a mere possession in 1663 under a rightful title in 1641, without regard to quantity, capacities a man to be restored to 2,000 acres or to all his lands not exceeding that quantity.

1. For the intention of the Act I conceive is to give great favour in this particular to persons whom his majesty had culled out of the rest to be sharers of his favour, especially for that the king in this case was the supreme judge whose order and determination was to be observed without appeal or resort to the Act of Parliament.
2. Because many had letters but few were restored to possession by virtue thereof, so that the design of Settlement by the Act could not be so much retarded by admission of a few to full restitution as the . . .
3. All the nominees are restored to 2,000 acres upon seizen only in 1641 and the same Rules and Directions are to be observed in this case as in the case of the nominees.
4. A possession of any lands 22nd., August 1663 by virtue of the king's letters is but a description of the persons to be restored and a necessary condition precedent to the restitution, not a limitation or qualification of that restitution, for if he were possessed of any lands in 1663 etc., he shall be restored to such houses and so much of the lands contiguous without any regard that the contiguous lands were also possessed or not in 1663.

So that upon the whole matter, though I acknowledge the penning of the Act in this and the other clauses to which it relates to be very obscure and intricate, yet I conceive t'is more for the king's honour and the benefit of the grantee that a possession in 1663, by virtue of the king's letters of any land, how little soever the parcel was, (because

It were hard that your petitioner 127

t'was an evidence of his majesty's judgement and favour) which without some possession pursuant the commissioners could not take notice of though de facto his majesty did write (sic) shall give a title to be restored to 2,000 acres if the quantity of the letterees lands extended to so much.

Joseph Ayloffe [?].[2]

March 19 1667

At this period in the restoration land settlement, except for cases in dispute, the adventurers and soldiers has already received their certificates enabling them to pass letters patent for the lands granted them by the Court of claims. The stock of reprisal lands had also been substantially diminished making difficulties for nominees and letterees, such as John Bellew, to secure possession of lands 'contiguous and thereunto adjoining' and not already in their hands on 22 August 1663. This was true especially in cases where adventurers or soldiers in possession would have had to be displaced. The legal opinion obtained by Bellew was itself seriously flawed in that it placed great reliance on the mandatory nature of the king's letter. However much this argument might have prevailed in England or in Ireland in the period before the enactment of the Act of Settlement, a prerogative act after that time would only have been advisory, since the forfeited lands had all been vested for the purposes of the Acts. They could not, therefore, be granted away without a certificate from the Court of Claims. Bellew's counsel observed that the Act was both obscure and intricate, nonetheless, he expressed the opinion that it permitted the grant of the additional lands, as he put it 'without any regard that the contiguous lands were also possessed or not in 1663'. In John Bellew's case the lands in question were all in the hands of the ex-soldiers, including men such as Sir William Aston, who would resist any attempt to displace them. The next following clause in the Act did empower the Lord Lieutenant and council to direct the Court of Claims to set out and allot so much of the forfeited lands as shall remain undisposed, after 'the several Protestant interests herein' shall be provided for. This provision was applicable only where the merits of the person in question would have warranted such a course. As the custodium lands awarded to Bellew by virtue of the king's letter were 'forfeited lands' for the purposes of that clause, it is surprising that John Bellew did not seek this course as a solution for his problems. It may have been, however, that by this time Carlingford had a prior claim to the lands, by virtue of their inclusion in his custodium leases.

The Court of Claims apparently decided to deal with the nominee and letteree petitions in the period 1666–1667 when Bellew was in England dealing with the business connected with Carlingford's dispute with the Duke of York. He was, therefore, in the same dilemma as Carlingford, whose embassy to Vienna at that time presented the risk that because of his absence he would lose all his fortune by obeying the king. However, while Carlingford had the favour of the king in the protection of his interests, no such assurances were available to Bellew other than what favour his patron could deploy on his behalf. He followed up the legal opinion by the lodgement of a petition to the king in the same month.[3] In it he claimed that, 'he was one of those whose ancestors for so many ages, by the effusion of their blood and loss of their substance, maintained the English interest in Ireland since the first conquest thereof'. He referred to the king's letter of March 1661, stating that he had been partially restored to his former estate by 22 August 1663. He sought the grant to him of 'his mansion house [at Willistown] with 600 or 700 acres adjoining', as well as a parcel of his estate near the same, 'called Dawe's freehold in Braganstown, about 100 acres by the survey'. He offered the lands held by him in Connacht as 'reprisals for so much of his own estate as those lands extend unto'. Alternatively, he sought that he should 'be settled and established' in his Connacht lands until he was 'wholly restored'. In conclusion he requested that these arrangements be included (as savings) in the Earl of Carlingford's patent 'now to be passed', and that because of his attendance in London on the earl's concerns, that he be protected from any prejudice arising from his absence from Ireland. His petition was referred to Arthur Annesley, the Earl of Anglesey and member of the English Privy Council who reported on 13 April 1667 as follows:

> In obedience to your majesty's reference bearing date April the 1st., 1667 I have considered of the case of Mr. John Bellew and by the papers annexed to his petition and your majesty's letter of the 7 March in the 13th., year of your reign in his behalf. I do find him well meriting a particular regard from you and as your majesty in a just consideration thereof did pass your royal judgement and give several directions for his restitution, which have yet been but in part effectual for his relief. I am therefore humbly of opinion that you majesty may be pleased by your royal letters to the lord lieutenant of Ireland to reinforce and confirm your majesty's said judgement and directions therein, expressing your will and pleasure to be as much as in you lies or the Authority of the Act of Settlement and Explanation will bear, that the same be made

effectual for the restitution and relief of the said John Bellew, and that therein be further signified your majesty's pleasure to your commissioners in Ireland [the Court of claims] to execute such power, as the said Acts do give unto them for those ends, and that the said John Bellew may be in equal condition with the Nominees, as by the Act of Explanation is intended and until he be wholly restored, the lands he enjoys in Connacht may be continued unto him. All which nevertheless I humbly submit to your majesty's great judgement.
April the 13 1667
                              Anglesey.[4]

Anglesey had been one of those involved in the construction of the Act of Explanation and would therefore have had some competence in making his recommendations on behalf of Bellew. He appeared to recognise the limitations imposed upon the exercise of the royal prerogative by virtue of the legislation. Whereas the king's letter of March 1661 was mandatory in character, whatever letter he might issue on foot of this recommendation would be limited to a recommendation that the Court of Claims accept Bellew 'in equal condition to the nominees'. As this was already provided for under clause 157 of the Act it did not push Bellew's case much further than that.

The success of the nominees and letterees under the provisions made for them in the Act of Explanation was patchy. In Louth, Oliver Plunkett, the sixth Baron Louth and former Nuncioist, as a letteree, recovered an estate of 1,142 acres mostly in the barony of Louth where no ex-soldier complications existed. This was in addition to the lands recovered by his son Matthew under his decree of innocence.[5] In County Down, Arthur Magennis, the third Viscount Iveagh, had been a captain of a foot company in the king's brother, the Duke of Gloucester's regiment on the continent and had been the recipient of a king's letter ordering his restoration.[6] However, as his former estates were all in the hands of adventurers and soldiers, this could not be effected. While other County Down Magennises succeeded in obtaining decrees of innocence, there is no record of Viscount Iveagh having appeared before the Court of Claims nor was he subsequently included in the list of nominees. He did, however, seek the benefits of clause 157 of the Act of Explanation and elected for 2,000 acres in the Kilmore or northern section of his former estate and an attempt was made to secure Ormond's backing for his case. In September 1667, in a letter to George Rawdon, Viscount Conway informed him that it was expected that the Court of Claims would terminate in the following January and that Sir Edward Dering had told him that their important business at that time was that of the nominees.[7] He expressed the view that their restitution would only be partial, as they could only obtain the favour of the Lord Lieutenant Ormond, but that no general rule would be applied to them. Revealing Rawdon's particular interest in Iveagh's case, he went on, 'I doubt not but your being in Dublin may easily prevent Lord Iveagh.' Iveagh never did recover his 2,000 acres in Kilmore, having to make do instead with an estate of 1,200 acres in Ballintober, County Roscommon.[8] Conway's reference to the 'lord lieutenant's favour' reinforces the probability that only those nominees and letterees who could curry favour with Ormond would be successful.

The king does not appear to have issued any letters on foot of John Bellew's petition. Instead, in his letter of 12 April 1667 to Ormond on behalf of Carlingford, he referred to a request by the latter and by Bellew 'who has been in attendance on us concerning matters relating to his lordship'. He directed that he should suffer nothing in respect of his claim, by virtue of his absence from Ireland.[9] On Bellew's return, he acted upon this decision by way of a petition to the Court of Claims. In it he referred to an earlier decision by the Court to hear his case, in conjunction with Carlingford's case, as soon as some members of the Court had returned from England. He followed this up with a further petition in which he outlined the background to his case including the grant to him by the 'late usurped power' of a much reduced estate in Connacht the details of which were set out in a schedule attached.[10] He sought a decree from the Court that he be settled therein 'until he be fully and entirely restored unto his former estate'. Evidently he did not pursue further his claims under clause 157 as a letteree. This turn of events must have arisen on foot of an understanding reached with Carlingford, which provided for the transfer to Bellew of part of his former custodium lands, which had been granted away to Carlingford in his letters patent. The implementation of this agreement took place in the period between February 1669 and February 1671 but not without opposition from the earl's son, Nicholas.

It is clear from the correspondence between Bellew and the Taaffes in the latter part of the 1660s that the earl's son had acquired a considerable influence over his father's affairs in County Louth and that by 1668 he had virtually replaced Bellew as the earl's agent. As this developed, the relationships between the two progressively deteriorated, with Nicholas Taaffe becoming more and more disenchanted with his father's agent. This may have had its origins in the hiatus which arose over the custodium lands in County Louth and the failure to recover in full the Taaffe lands in Braganstown and Cookstown, which Churchill had claimed should have been the subject of separate proceedings before the Court of Claims. The differences came to a head in August 1669 in an intemperate letter sent by Bellew to Taaffe as follows:

> My Lord,
> Mr Stephen Taaffe hath been with me several times about Dysart and Dromin and at last showed me a letter of your lordship's conferring the same. Upon which I told him of your father's command in that behalf. Truly I have been several times told that your lordship intend me a prejudice and that even by strangers, but would never believe it until now. And if your lordship be of such an account, I cannot but signify (and sorry to give me cause to say it) that if it not to the value of Dysart and Dromin, were I so minded, that I could prejudice your lordship, nor are they of half the yearly value of the forbearance of what monies I disbursed in your father's occasions. Your lordship hath been pleased to say that had you gotten as much by serving your father, as I have done, his business should not [want?] for £20. His lordship's business did never suffer in the least in my hands through want of monies or pains and I left them and all things in very good order for your lordship's management. And if his occasions did suffer for want of £20, I was not in this province when such happened and do now find, it was well I was not; for had I disbursed all I have I see by your lordship's expressions what a hard way you would endeavour to see me satisfied. And if your occasions be carried hand over head blame no one for it but yourself for you never sent or spoke unto me concerning them; but on the contrary have several times said that you would not have me concern myself in your father's occasions and as for my geting [?] by his lordship, I defy any man's master in that kind and believe it those things are beneath me and had I disbursed £800 and odd pounds (besides eight years labour) for any person, as I have done in your father's concerns, for which I am owing at this present to others £140 and odd pounds, such I am confident would not be the thanks or forbearance should be returned me. As for your lordship's bidding me to sue your father if he owes me any monies, I know it is far from his honourable to put me to any such, but if his lordship should be wrought on in that kind [as] in other things he hath been and that believe [?], if not for his advantage or yours, your lordship may be confident that I will receive the same, every penny. And for that expression of forcing your father; I honour your father as much as I do any man but I was never servant to him nor to any other and your

lordship might use those expressions to your dependants or followers, and so I rest.

           Yours servant.
           John Bellew.

23 August 1669.[11]

Taaffe's reply of 28 August was no less intemperate and threatening:

> Sir,
> I received your of the 23rd., this morning which was very impertinent to say you could prejudice my father to a high degree. To my knowledge he values not what you can do and as for any forbearance as you writt, I never heard of any to be allowed. Where there is no debt acknowledged, which is your case, for my father absolutely disowned it at his departure. You are dissatisfied that I writt you of serving my lord of Carlingford, truly I could wish I had done it at the rate you did, it would not offend me at all, though you say you never had but labour and expense in his business, others and many, some persons of great quality, will affirm you got £400 and £500 a year by my father in Munster for some years and yet you say he owes you money. Our comfort is nobody will believe you; I can assure it is so little in my father's that you will find the contrary at his arrival and were you not ungrateful, you and yours ought to own your being from him, upon this last settlement. To conclude law must decide more things than you can imagine between my lord and you, which shall appear to the world very sudden.
>   I am your humble servant,
>   Taaffe.[12]

A disagreement as to the cost and worth of the services rendered by a lawyer was as common in the seventeenth century as it is today. In his time, John Bellew was not less a lawyer than his colleagues, whose profession was frequently complained against for their cumbersome and arcane procedures, delays and above all, the cost of their services.[13] There is some evidence that the Taaffes were slow to pay their debts and when he might have been able to assist Bellew avoid financial embarrassment over the payment of the rental on the Taaffe lease of Warrenstown, Nicholas Taaffe did nothing other than to warn Bellew of his predicament. It seems evident that John Bellew's 'Account' was prepared in connection with this dispute with the Taaffes and represents a statement as to the costs incurred by him during the period he was Carlingford's agent from April 1661 to 4 March 1669. The 'Account' indicates that, taking into account receipts from rentals etc., an estimated sum of £783 was outstanding and unpaid by Carlingford. The 'Account' describes this amount as, 'what monies I have expected since the said 25 January [1669] to this present, being the 4 March 1669 in my attendance and otherwise on his lordship's occasions, as in passing his patents and all other his concerns here in Dublin and elsewhere'.[14] It is clear from the correspondence that Nicholas Taaffe was aware of the extent of Bellew's claim and was determined not to meet it, asserting that had he been paid at the rate Bellew was claiming, he would not object to being called somebody's servant, a riposte to Bellew's denial that he was ever Carlingford's servant. In his 'Account' Bellew claimed that from the time he first became Carlingford's agent (in April 1661) he did not receive any payment until the following November and that thereafter Carlingford had never been out of his debt. Since going to England in 1666, he had to meet the financial demands arising from the dispute with the Duke of York and his agent Dr Gorge as well as other debts including the rental arrears on Warrenstown out of his own resources and what he could borrow from his friends. He claimed that Carlingford rightly understood the situation and that 'his occasions were never one hour at a stand for want of being supplied with monies'. Coming to the point he asserted that were it not for 'the unexpected malicious endeavours that were used to cross his lordship' he would never have gainsaid 'in the least the 300 acres which I desire of him, having dearly bought the same'. As the aggregate extent of the lands of Disart and Dromin mentioned in Nicholas Taaffe's letter was 286 acres, these would appear to have been the lands Bellew had in mind and which Taaffe was evidently granting away to his cousin Stephen Taaffe.

Carlingford did not share his son's opinion of Bellew as evidenced by the fact that he appointed Bellew in December 1669, together with Nicholas, to negotiate with the Duke of York's representatives regarding the 4,000 acres in County Louth which he was to receive from the latter. In his letter conveying this suggestion, he referred to a previous letter which he had received from Bellew in which he found 'my son and you', 'at some distance'. He assured him that he would, 'not only labour to reconcile but will appear in all things to be your affectionate kinsman and servant'. That a clear understanding had already existed between them, allowing Bellew to acquire certain lands included in Carlingford's letters patent, is suggested by an indentured agreement, which they entered into on 19 February 1669. This transaction took place less than one month after the passing of the letters patent, and conveyed 'the town, village, hamlet and lands of Barmeath containing 398 acres' to Bellew, subject to the payment of the rent charge of £24 per annum to Strickland.[15] This transaction also suggests that the original acquisition of Barmeath by Carlingford was but a prelude to Bellew's subsequent acquisition. On 24 February 1671 another indentured agreement was entered into between them, whereby Carlingford sold to John Bellew the towns, villages, hamlets and lands of Barmeath, Disart, Graftonstown, Hitchestown, Reynoldstown and Garvagh in the barony of Ferrard. The consideration was 'the said John's pains, care and loss of time from his occasions in the said earl's affairs and concerns' and that 'Graftonstown, Hitchestown, Reynoldstown and Garvagh sometimes belonged to the said John'.[16] A further consideration was a sum of £745 'paid down to the said earl' and which may have been accomplished by the discharge of the debt of £783 due by Carlingford to Bellew. Another transaction entered into at this time was a 'concord made in the King's Court' on 11 April 1669, between Theobald Taaffe, Earl of Carlingford, Mary his wife and William, Lord Taaffe, their son and heir on the one part, and John Thomlinson of Walshestown on the other, whereby the former conveyed to the latter 'ten messuages, ten tofts, 100 cottages, one mill, twenty gardens, 122 acres of land, twenty acres of meadow, 400 acres of pasture, fifty acres of heath and twenty acres of moor in Walshestown, Baggotstown, Kiltallaght and Drumgooter', the consideration not mentioned.[17] While the reasons why this conveyance was made are not given, subsequent proceedings in the Court of Chancery in 1681 suggest that it was in fact a mortgage lease, entered into by Carlingford, he being then 'necessitated' for money. These lands had all formed part of John Bellew's custodium lands and were to be the subject of a further dispute between Nicholas Taaffe and John Bellew's son Patrick, after John's death, the outcome of which was that the lands passed to Patrick after proceedings in the Court of Chancery.[18]

The aggregate of the lands acquired by John Bellew from Carlingford was 1,081 acres.[19] Evidence that he had obtained freehold possesion of this estate by 1671 is contained in an award of arbitrators in June 1671. This arose from a dispute as to land boundaries between certain intermixed lands in Upper and Lower Disart in the ownership of Patrick Levins of Dysart who won a decree of innocence from the Court of Claims in 1663.[20] Levins had been restored to 108 acres in Dysart, Painstown, Dundalk and Carrigine in the parish of Drumcar. The agreed arbitrators were Theobald Verdon and Patrick Warren, both of whom were the sons of the forfeiting proprietors of Clonmore and Warrenstown respectively, the latter having also been a Connacht transplanter. When the award was issued it was signed and sealed by Bellew and Levins, Verdon and Warren and witnessed by Messrs Gerald Alymer, Christopher Bellew, Oliver Luttrell and Thomas Fitzgerald. As might be expected from a process of settling land disputes in County Louth dating back to the middle ages, the disputant parties delivered possession to each other by means of a 'clodd of earth'.

John Bellew's petition to the Court of claims concerning the lands held by him in Connacht came to nothing and when the Court was wound up on 2 January 1669 the case of the Connacht transplanters had been left unattended. Despite the high hopes he may have entertained on foot of the king's letter of April 1661, the restoration land settlement had left John Bellew and many others of the Connacht transplantation unrequited, although many of the higher gentry, whether letterees or nominees, fared a lot better. Many of them managed to recover a portion of their former estates while still retaining the lands allotted to them in Connacht. Examples of these were the Earl of Westmeath, Sir Luke Dowdall of Athlumney County Meath, Sir Richard Barnewall of Crickstown County Meath and Conly Geoghegan of Donore County Westmeath.[21] Whether by accident or design, the higher levels of the Old English landed gentry fared better in the restoration land settlement than those at the middle or lower levels. This can be demonstrated in County Louth where the two leading gentry families the Plunketts of Louth and the Bellew of Castletown-Dundalk were fully restored along with Nicholas Gernon of Milltown, Thomas Clinton of Clintonstown, and Theobald Taaffe, Earl of Carlingford in respect of the Smarmore estate.[22] It was as if a minority, albeit a representative number, of the former gentry class had been allowed to return to their former estates to merge with the newly emerging gentry class of the British ascendancy. This pattern of settlement might have been a reflection of the policies pursued by Ormond who had a dislike for the former soldiery of the English Commonwealth while at the same time favouring some restoration of their estates for the Old English gentry families. In any selection process concerning the latter it would have been affected by the pecking order in vogue, taking account of such matters as rank or title, size of estate, level of indebtedness, leading family as against a collateral branch, or even availability of heir. One or more of these factors could explain the non-recovery of their estates by John Bellew and his distant cousin, Michael Bellew of Verdonstown, Theobald Verdon of Clonmore, Thomas Plunkett of Beaulieu and Andrew Dowdall of Killaly and Castletown Cooley. All of these were letterees and, with the exception of John Bellew, had their estates outside the barony of Ardee.[23]

The period following the closing down of the Court of Claims, and the replacement of Ormond by a succession of short-lived lord lieutenantcies, Robartes in 1669, Berkeley in 1670, Capel, Earl of Essex in 1672 until Ormond's reappointment in 1677, was one of intense political intrigue. During this period the Irish Catholic gentry sought to revive their claims and in a petition to the king dated November 1670 they sought the establishment of an 'impartial tribunal' to hear their grievances and that meantime no further grants of undisposed lands be made.[24] Their case was presented by Richard Talbot and was considered by a committee of thirteen including Ormond, who also heard a rebuttal of it by the attorney-general, Sir Heneage Finch. The outcome was inconclusive. A second committee was established under the chairmanship of Prince Rupert but, because of Protestant reaction in the English House of Commons to what appeared to them to be a policy of appeasement to the Catholic party, this committee was withdrawn in April 1673. This was followed by a proclamation confirming the land settlement. It may have been because of these political manoeuvres that the position of the Connacht transplanters was left unattended until 1675 when a commission was appointed to deal with Connacht land titles, including the transplanters.

In 1676 John Bellew lodged his petition to the 'commissioners for the hearing and determining the claims of the transplanted persons in the Province of Connacht and county of Clare'.[25] In it he outlined his case, reciting the lands which he had forfeited in County Louth, as well as the details of the decree of the 'pretended commissioners at Loughrea' dated 12 June 1656, which allocated 793 acres to him in the barony of Tiaquin and the half baronies of Tiaquin and Bellamoe. He excepted from his claim the 'quarter of Corgarrow' 133 acres, which he had demised to Sir Nicholas Plunkett of Dublin and his fourth son, Nicholas Bellew of Barmeath, in trust for his third son, Christopher, and in respect of which the latter had submitted a separate petition.[26] At the same time it would appear that his eldest son, Patrick, had also submitted a petition, probably because his father may have been in ill health and who was to die in 1679. The outcome was the issue of letters patent to Patrick in March 1678 providing for the grant of the following lands to John Bellew for life, remainder to Patrick and his heirs, with a jointure of £80 per annum to Patrick's wife Elisabeth alias Barnewall:

It were hard that your petitioner 137

In the barony of Tiaquin County Galway:

Clooncallige Qr.	172 acres	£1.14s.09,1/2d.
Carrownecreggie Qr.	29 acres	£ 0.05s.10,1/4d.
In the same	19 acres	£ 0 3s.10d.
Clonoraneoughter Qr.	8 acres	£ 0 1s.09,1/4d.
Carrownecreggie Qr.	32 acres	£ 0. 6s.05,1/2d.
In the same	9 acres	£ 0 5s.10,1/2d.
In the same	17 acres	£ 0 3s.05,1/2d.
In the same	56 acres	£ 0.11s.04d.

This last to the use of Sisly Bourke als Concannan and her heirs

Clonoran 2 Qrs.	358 acres	£3.12s.05,1/2d.*
The third part of		
Iskerrow als Killdoone	117 acres	£1.03s.08d.*
Clonoraneoughter Qr.	67 acres	13s.06,3/4d.*
Carrownaboe	96 acres	19s.05,1/4d.*
Mullaghmore	19 acres	03s.10d.*
Net total acreage in Tiaquin	1,019 acres	

In the barony of Dunkellyn County Galway:

Ballingarrie &		
Cloghmoyle 2 Qrs.	165 acres	£1.13s.04,1/2d.

In the half barony of Killyan County Galway:

Carrownegappell Qr.	20 acres	£ 04s.00,1/2d.
Ballinlassy 3 cartons	03 acres	£ 7,1/4d.
Corgarragh	133 acres	£1. 06s.11,3/4d.*
Ballynekill & Creggan	40 acres	£ 08s.01,1/4d.

In the half barony of Bellamoe County Galway:

Knocknenantekahell al		
Knocknankskahell	3 acres	£7,1/4d.*

Total acreage in County Galway 1,455 acres.

In the barony of Moycarnan County Roscommon:

Fadane & Glantane	116 acres.	£1.03s.06d.
Killnimullrugen 2Qrs.	35 acres.	£ 07s.01d.
Shanballyhugh	22 acres	£ 04s.05,1/2d.
Total acreage in Roscommon	173 acres.	
Grand total acreage	1,628 acres.[27]	

The discrepancy between the 793 acres contained in John Bellew's petition to the commissioners and the 1,628 acres contained in the letters patent granted to his son Patrick can be explained as land purchases made by Patrick in the period following the settlement of the Bellews in Connacht. The Roscommon lands had been purchased from William Brabson and the Galway lands from Sir Samuel Foxon, Edward Butler, Sir Henry Slingsby, William Manning, Laughlen Kelly, George Thornton, Nicholas Sutton and Daniel Morrisy and were estimated to be worth £270 per annum in 1686.[28] Of these William Brabson, William Manning, Laughlen Kelly and Daniel Morrisy appear to have been of internal transplanter families, while the remainder were of transplanter families from outside Connacht i.e., Slingsby from Cork, Butler from Waterford, Sutton from Kildare and Thornton whose county of origin has not been traced.[29]

John Bellew's petition of 1676 also dealt with the case of another Connacht transplanter named Katherine Dillon alias Wogan. Her claim was that, having suffered forfeiture of several lands, and other hereditaments, in the counties of Kildare and Westmeath, to the yearly value of £200, she was transplanted. Her decree dated 16 June 1656 by the Loughrea commissioners awarded her 364 acres in Tiaquin and the half barony of Killyan County Galway. These lands, included forty acres in the two quarters of Cregan and Ballinakill which she subsequently sold to John Bellew. While her former lands in County Westmeath have not been traced, the lands in Kildare were situated in the barony of Salt, parish of Straffan and consisted of 322 acres in Barbistown (Barberstown) together with a castle and stone house and estimated to have been worth £200 in 1641.[30] The letters patent, issued on foot of this petition were dated December 1677. They conveyed an estate of 600 acres to John Bellew 'in trust for and to the use of Thomas Dillon and his heirs', in the townlands of Kinclare, Carrowkeele, Liskelly, Glanloughra, Legan 'next to Glanloughra' all in the barony of Tiaquin, County Galway. They contained a savings of 45 acres in Liskelly to Robert Dillon 'an innocent' and his son Garrett. John Bellew's wife was the daughter of Robert Dillon of Clonbrock who, by his will dated 14 December 1628, left her as a marriage portion 'the interest out of the lands of Ballynadallon'. He also had two sons, the eldest, Richard, who died in 1676 leaving a son, Robert, and Luke who died in 1649 (?) leaving a son, Thomas. On the face of it the Thomas mentioned in the letters patent might have been the latter while the Robert for whom the 45 acres in Liskelly were saved was the son of Richard of Clonbrock whose estates were not forfeited in the Commonwealth period. Thomas Dillon's estate ultimately passed into the possession of the Bellews of Mountbellew in the eighteenth century following the marriage of

Michael Bellew, Christopher Bellew's great-grandson, and Jane, the daughter of Henry Dillon of Kinclare and descendant of Thomas Dillon.[31]

Apart from the lands granted in Connacht to John Bellew in the Commonwealth period and confirmed by the commission of 1676, the rest of the estate had been acquired privately, by purchase or otherwise, by either John himself, or by his son Patrick. Such acquisitions, not being held directly from the crown, carried some risk of challenge either by former proprietors, their heirs or assignees or by discoverers seeking a defective title. As there had been many such commercial transactions in land throughout the Restoration period, pressure grew for some means to enable such transactions to be regularised. In 1678 Ormond proposed the introduction of legislation to enable a commission to be established to secure defective land titles on payment of a fine. This proposal was resisted by such interests as the '49 officer security, the Duke of York and the nominees. In consequence, the suggestion was set aside until 1684, when the king issued a commission to enable 'those possessed under a doubtful title to purchase a confirmation at a moderate fine'.[32] Patrick Bellew took advantage of this arrangement and in September 1684 lodged an affidavit with the commission setting out the acreages and other details of the lands held by him in Louth and Galway amounting to 1,722 acres and 1,904 acres respectively. On payment of a fine of £20, he was enabled to pass letters patent including the creation of the manor of Clonoraneightragh alias Castlebellew in County Galway and the manor of Barmeath alias Bellewmount in County Louth.[33]

Patrick Bellew's letter patent from the commission had at last secured the Bellews in their estates. Though his father never recovered the ancestral lands of Lisrenny and Willistown, this loss was more than adequately compensated for by the additional lands he had acquired in Louth as well as Galway. They were to provide his children with a secure platform on which to build their future prosperity, and ensured that the fear that had dogged John Bellew for more than twenty years that his family would perish from the ranks of the gentry class was finally put to rest.

CHAPTER TEN

Epilogue

John Bellew died at Barmeath sometime before August in the year 1679 at the age of seventy-three years and was buried in a mortuary chapel constructed for the purpose of his burial by his wife Mary, who followed him in death two years later and was buried beside him. The chapel, which still stands in the grounds of Barmeath Castle, has over its entrance doorway a memorial shield quartering the arms of the Bellew and Dillon families with the inscription, 'This chapel was built by Mary Bellew relict of John Bellew, anno domini 1679. May their souls through the mercy of God rest in peace'. Already advanced in years, John made his last will and testament on 17 February 1673. It opened with a reference to the settlement made upon the marriage, in January 1664, of his son Patrick to Elisabeth, daughter of his comrade of the war years and the Commonwealth period, Sir Richard Barnewall baronet, of Crickstown, County Meath.[1] The latter had evidently defaulted on the payment of the marriage portion of £600, which remained unpaid at the time of the making of the will, and through 'which debt', John Bellew recorded that he was 'the more disabled from providing for his wife and children'. The marriage settlement, dated 7 January 1664, envisaged that, upon payment of the £600 by Barnewall, John Bellew would pay an annuity to the 'young couple' of £80, which was to continue to be paid to Elisabeth as her jointure should she outlive her husband.[2] The amount of the marriage portion had already been provided for in Barnewall's own marriage settlement, upon his marriage to his second wife Lady Julian Aylmer. The settlement between Bellew and Barnewall also provided, that John Bellew would create a trust to uses in respect of his estate, under feoffees of trust, 'to be indifferently chosen' by the parties. This provided for John's estate being held to his use for his lifetime, then to pass to his son Patrick and through him to Patrick's heirs and thereafter, as 'in course of descent ought to be'. An important provision limited to £300 the amount John Bellew might provide in his will for the preferment of his younger children 'in case he shall not otherwise provide for them in his lifetime'.

Sir Richard Barnewall had been transplanted to the barony of Clare, which lies contiguous to Tiaquin in County Galway where John Bellew had been transplanted. It seems likely therefore that the bond of friendship already established between them during the war had extended also to their respective families and that a social intercourse had developed between them. Like the Bellews, the Barnewalls were a prominent gentry family of the English Pale descended from the Barnewalls of Drumenagh and Terenure in County Dublin and settled in Crickstown, County Meath since the fourteenth century.[3] Two other prominent Barnewall families were descendants of the latter, the Viscounts Kingsland and the Barons Trimleston. Sir Richard, the second baronet, was born in 1602 and by his second marriage to Julia, daughter of Sir Gerald Aylmer of Donadea, had four sons and six daughters. Reflecting the social status of the Barnewalls at this period, his son and heir, Sir Patrick, was married to Frances, daughter of Richard Butler of Kilcash, County Tipperary, the Roman Catholic brother of the Lord Lieutenant James Butler, Duke of Ormond. Unlike Bellew whose landed estate was small, Sir Richard had in October 1641 an estate of over 8,900 acres, spread over the baronies of Deece, Rathoath, Moyfenrath, Duleek, Fore, Navan and Screen in County Meath, with the family seat at Crickstown in Rathoath. It consisted of a 'castle and stone house' described in the Civil Survey as ruinous.[4] The extent of his forfeited estate explains his Commonwealth land grant in Galway of between 2,500 and 2,852 acres profitable.[5] In the restoration land settlement Sir Richard, as a nominee, became entitled to recover Crickstown together with 2,000 acres adjoining thereto. No evidence has survived that he succeeded in making this recovery. Sir Patrick, his son and heir, is given in the *Abstract of Grants* as the recipient of letters patent in October 1677 for 1,261 acres plantation measure in County Galway, with a saving for Patrick Bellew and his wife Elisabeth.[6]

The evident intent of the marriage settlement between the Bellews and the Barnewalls was to give precedence to John's son Patrick over the rest of his brothers, notably Christopher. Since, by the rules of primogeniture, Patrick would have been automatically accorded such precedence, it is not clear why it should have been written into the marriage settlement, unless it was to prevent alienation of any part of the estate to the other sons. This arrangement was sought by Barnewall and enforced by him on John Bellew by reason of the fact that the latter was heavily in debt to him. This is revealed in a copy of a bond entered into by Bellew on 7 January 1664, the same date upon which the marriage settlement was concluded.[7] Each of these documents was witnessed by the Franciscan friar, Anthony Gernon and the lawyer, Augustine Darcy. The bond opens with an acknowledgement by John Bellew of a debt owed by him to Sir Richard Barnewall in the sum of £4,000 sterling. It required repayment to be made, at Sir Richard's 'will and pleasure', and to the repayment of which John bound himself, his administrators and trustees. It also referred to the provision in the marriage settlement whereby John would leave his entire estate to his son Patrick subject to the incumbrances of £300 for John's younger children and his wife's jointure 'as was agreed for her upon her intermarriage and no more'. 'All of this', was 'pursuant unto the agreement made on the intermarriage of the said Patrick and Elisabeth'. The bond concluded with a provision that if John Bellew, 'clearly and freely', should leave his estate including mortgages, leases and other properties and moneys, other than the incumbrances already provided for John's family, then Sir Richard agreed that the debt be made void. Otherwise it would be 'in full force by virtue of same'. Indebtedness was not an uncommon experience of the landed gentry of the seventeenth and eighteenth centuries and in many cases, whether Old Irish, Old English or British planter, often ended in bankruptcy and the enforced sale of the encumbered estate. Considering John Bellew's circumstances at this period, including his period of service as Carlingford's agent, it was to be expected that he would carry some level of debt secured upon his estate, but the amount of the debt was unusual, as also was Sir Richard's willingness to write it off in favour of his son-in-law. It is tempting to speculate that some portion of the debt may have been used to enable Patrick to acquire, by purchase, the 773 acres of lands in Connacht declared by him under the commission which dealt with the Connacht land titles in 1675. Barnewall's generosity may also have stemmed from his affection for his daughter Elisabeth, and her husband to be Patrick Bellew. In view of what subsequently transpired, an acquittance given by Patrick Bellew to his father on 7 January 1670 suggests that the debt due to Barnewall had been substantially repaid by that date.[8] The acquittance referred to a 'certain account stated between my father John Bellew and me', 'wherein all debts and demands' were acknowledged to be satisfied to £250 'due to Patrick'. The latter agreed in turn to acquit, discharge and indemnify his father, his heirs and assigns from 'the said sum or any part or parcel thereof'. The connection between this acquittance and the Barnewall debt is suggested by the fact that Sir Richard Barnewall's sons, Christopher and John, witnessed the acquittance.

Barnewall's failure to comply with the terms of his daughter's marriage settlement is reflected in John Bellew's will. There is no mention of a trust to uses having been established on foot of the marriage, while the provision for his younger children exceeded that provided for in the marriage settlement. The will also made provision, as a jointure for his wife Mary, the interest in the lands of Barmeath, Disart, Hitchestown, Graftonstown and Dromin. In return she was required to contribute an annuity of £40, together with the rents of Reynoldstown and Garvagh, towards the portions for his younger children, the 'first payment to be made twelve months after his death and not before'. He also left her his household stuff, corn, cattle and goods.

With regard to his heir Patrick, he left the marriage portion of £600 due by Barnewall, 'the more' to enable him to discharge 'such portions and moneys as shall fall due to be satisfied'. It was also intended as compensation for any loss he might sustain by the portion of £200 to be paid to his third son, Christopher, and of the lease to him of the town, lands and mills of both the Corgarrows in County Galway. He also left Patrick his great silver sault, his small silver sault, silver sugar box with two small silver spoons, great silver tankard, a dozen silver spoons, silver wine cup, small silver acquavitae cup, all of which Patrick was to have following the death of his mother 'and not before'. He also enjoined him 'to be assisting to his mother and his brothers and sisters upon all occasions and also to be themselves assisting and loving to each other'. As might have been expected, he left all his estates of inheritance in Leinster and Connacht to Patrick for life and then to Patrick's eldest son John with remainders in tail male to Patrick's younger sons, Richard and Christopher, with succession to any further sons. In default of Patrick's line, the estate would then pass to John's second eldest son, Robert, provided that 'he demean and match himself' to the satisfaction of his mother and the overseers of his will. Should he not do so, the estate would pass to his third and fourth sons respectively, Christopher and Nicholas, in tail male, provided that the latter 'demean and match himself' to the satisfaction of his mother and the overseers of the will. In default then the estate was to pass to his youngest son, James, with final remainders in tail male to Sir John Bellew of Castletown-Dundalk, the then head of the extended Bellew family with remainders to Sir John's second and third brothers, Matthew and Thomas.

While the will left to Patrick what he was strictly entitled to under the rules of primogeniture, it does seem clear that John held his third son Christopher in great affection and for whom he made the following special provision:

> Whereas upon my going into England a while since I left an authority with my said wife to prefer my said son Christopher Bellew who was much in my thoughts for his attendance and care of my concerns upon all occasions and what one should engage or do in that behalf. I would make good the same and therefore in pursuance thereof I bequeath to Christopher £200 and grants to him the town and lands of both the Corgarowes with the mills for the term of thirty-one years from the present date, paying after my death to my son and heir Patrick one grain of wheat yearly until the said £200 be paid to Christopher in one payment and for the rest of the thirty-one years £20 yearly. If Patrick does not pay the £200 within thirty-one years, Christopher shall hold the said lands and mills until it be paid, for a grain of wheat yearly. He shall hold them at £20 yearly for two years only after the £200 be paid, that he may provide himself with a convenient farm.[9]

If Christopher was his most favoured son, Robert, the second eldest, was much less favoured. In his case he was provided with, 'as a child's portion', the sum of £200 to be paid out of the annuity to be levied on his wife's jointure in the lands of 'Disart, Dromin, Reynoldstown and Garvagh'. This was made on the condition that Robert should 'betake himself to the profession which I did and have endeavoured to breed him unto, or unto some other honest vocation such as his said mother and my overseers shall approve of'. A similar provision was made in respect of the fourth son, Nicholas. He was to have 'as a child's portion', the sum of £100 to be paid by his mother out of the goods and stock of the estate. This was also conditional that he 'betake himself to some honest vocation approved of by his mother and the overseers of the will and match himself to their satisfaction'. His youngest son, James, was left 'as a child's portion' the sum of £100, to be paid by his mother out of the goods and stock of the estate. It was also provided that if John the testator 'happens not to die indebted', then James was also to have the money owing to John by his son-in-law Gerald Aylmer. While James had attained his majority by the date of the will, 'the charge of him' was left to his mother', 'to breed him according unto her best ability either religious or to the world'. In the event James seems to have followed a career as an attorney until his death in 1690 when he left his estate to his nephew, Patrick's second son Richard.[10] For John's daughter, provision was made in the will of a rent charge of £40 per annum out of Reynoldstown and Garvagh for two years after his death 'whereby she may have time to provide herself with another farm'. In accordance with the custom of the period, provision had already been made for her upon her marriage to Gerald Aylmer in January 1665 when John paid the sum of £600 to the groom's father, Christopher Aylmer of the prominent County Meath lawyer family of the period.[11] Robert must have taken his father's strictures to heart, as he is reported as being an apothecary in Dublin city in 1676 and to be married to a widow, Bridget Dillon née Seagrave.[12] The fourth son, Nicholas, seems to have settled as an attorney in the Dunleer area.

Leaving nothing to chance John Bellew established a series of trusts to uses, which substantially gave effect to its terms. One of these is in respect of his wife, Mary, and their second son, Robert, and is dated 22 May 1673. The other, in respect of their son Christopher, had its provisions 'saved' in the letters patent passed in March 1678 by Patrick Bellew on foot of the petitions, lodged by his father and himself to the commission for determining the claims of the transplanted persons in 1676.[13] Under the trust to uses established in respect of Mary and Robert, 'the castle, town and lands of Barmeath, Gallagh and Hainstown, the towns and lands of Disart, Hitchestown, Graftonstown, Dromin, Reynoldstown, Garvagh alias Garowlagh', were 'given, granted, bargained, sold, enfeoffed and confirmed' to named trustees consisting of, Sir Nicholas Plunkett of the city of Dublin Knight, Sir Gerald Aylmer of Thirstingstown County Meath and Richard Dillon of the city of Dublin esquire. The stated intent and purpose of the trust was, to secure that the lands and premises would stand to the use of John Bellew during his lifetime and thereafter to the use of his wife for her lifetime in satisfaction of all dowers she might otherwise claim from the estate. While the agreement records that she had brought a marriage portion of £500 with her upon her marriage to John, there is no mention of the marriage settlement which would have been concluded at the time by their respective parents. In turn, Mary and the feoffees of trust were required to pay the sum of £40 per annum to her son Robert out of the issues and profits of the estate, the first payment to be made within one year after John's death and to continue in equal amounts until the full sum of £200 be paid. The condition for such payment, also enshrined in the will was that Robert 'betake himself to the profession', his father 'did endeavour to breed him unto or some other honest vocation', that might be approved, either by his mother Mary or by the overseers of the will. Upon the determination of these bequests, the feoffees of trust were required to hold the estate to the uses of John's last will and testament. John's son James was empowered as his attorney to take possession of the estate comprising the trust and to convey freehold possession of same to the trustees. The witnesses to the latter were Christopher Bellew, James Bellew, Jane Barnewall and Brigitt Dillon. The same individuals also witnessed that James Bellew took possession of Barmeath, Gallagh and Hainstown, Disart, Hitchestown, Graftonstown and Dromin and delivered livery of possession of same to Richard Dillon who acted on behalf of the feoffees of trust.[14] As the townlands of Reynoldstown and Garvagh had been reserved for the payment of the sum of £200 to Robert Bellew, separate witnesses to the delivery of possession by James Bellew to Richard Dillon were involved. These were Christopher Bellew, James Bellew, Susan Bellew and Richard Kay. The same procedure must also have been resorted to on behalf of Christopher although the only surviving evidence is contained in John Bellew's petition of 1676, in which he excepted from his claim the 'quarter of Corgarrow' which he had demised to Sir Nicholas Plunkett of Dublin and his fourth son, Nicholas Bellew, in trust for his son Christopher and in respect of which he stated that the latter had submitted a separate petition. While the latter claim has not been discovered evidence that it was submitted is contained in the Savings to Patrick Bellew's letters patent which reserved Christopher's rights to a lease for 1,000 years passed by John Bellew to Sir Nicholas Plunkett and others of the lands of Corgarragh in trust for Christopher, 'nor any uses mentioned in a certificate of the said lands formerly granted to Sir Nicholas in trust for Christopher'. In an age when landowners readily resorted to law in pursuance of their landed rights, it is not surprising that, following their father's death, the brothers disputed their respective rights under the will resulting in a series of lawsuits which were conducted between them and Patrick during the years 1683 and 1684 and, again between Patrick and Christopher in 1709.[15] This was in direct contravention of the wishes of their father, who provided in his will that if any difference should arise concerning the same 'or any other matter which God forbid', they were required to leave the issue to be decided by the overseers of the will and 'such friends as they shall choose and not by any manner of suit in law'. Failure to do so, or, if 'any should deprive others', from the benefit of the will, he was to be excluded from his interests therein. As the storm clouds of family dissension gathered about the disputed will of their father, the death of Charles II in February 1685 saw the entire family once more engulfed in a period of political instability and strife and from which they were to emerge, if somewhat chastened by their experiences, with their estates intact, demonstrating that their capacity for survival was not the least important aspect of their family inheritance.

In March 1684 James, Duke of York and brother to the late king Charles II, ascended the thrones of the three kingdoms as James II, setting in motion a train of events which was to lead to a brief period of Roman Catholic ascendancy in Ireland followed by Protestant revolt, the Williamite wars, further land confiscations and the commencement in Ireland of the Protestant Ascendancy of the eighteenth century. As might be expected, the Bellews were to become deeply involved in all of these events. The initial reaction of the Protestant interest to the accession of James II was one of cautious optimism, occasioned as much by the fact that, being a Roman Catholic, James might persuade the Catholic interest to give their full allegiance to the new regime, as by the fact that James gave fulsome assurances following the death of his brother that he would maintain 'the religion and laws established in Church and State'. The preservation of their ascendancy as the ruling class within the state establishment and in particular the maintenance of the restoration land settlement were the prime Protestant concerns. In the town of Drogheda, the Protestant-dominated municipal corporation delivered an address, expressing sympathy with James upon the death of his brother and assured him of 'their unfailing resolution to serve his majesty in defence of his royal authority with their lives and fortune'.[16] In April 1685 his coronation was celebrated with a hogshead of wine 'hung up near the tholsel door to be drank on that occasion' and the provision of a barrel of beer with tobacco and pipes to every foot company in the army garrison 'to drink ye king's health'.[17] The corporation had every reason to be concerned with its position and sought, by demonstrating its loyalty to the new king, to pre-empt his support for the maintenance of that ascendancy.

The Catholic Old English merchant class of Drogheda had survived intact both the Commonwealth confiscations and the restoration land settlement. However, its long-established customary rights to participate in the affairs of the corporation had been denied them by virtue of the New Rules for Corporations introduced under the powers contained in the Act of Explanation of 1665, and which required Roman Catholics to take the Oath of Supremacy before admission to the Common Council, which was the ruling body of the Corporation.[18] In the closing years of the reign of Charles II that merchant class had acquired a sufficient political clout in the town to embark on a campaign for a restitution of its rights in the corporation. This was to culminate in a petition by Christopher Peppard and other leading Roman Catholic merchants to the Lord Lieutenant and council seeking an enquiry into the manner in which the affairs of the corporation had been administered since 'the beginning of ye wars'.[19] The matter had not been disposed of by the time of the king's death and had become a live issue again shortly after the coronation, when in July 1685, a number of Roman Catholic town merchants petitioned the corporation to be admitted as free merchants. Their petition was rejected on the grounds that the New Rules prohibited such admissions to any persons unwilling to take the Oath of Supremacy. In the following month this stance was completely abandoned when over forty overwhelmingly Catholic Old English of the town and its contiguous areas in the counties of Louth and Meath were elected freemen.[20] The onward march of a brief period of Roman Catholic ascendancy had begun. The appointment of Richard Talbot, Earl of Tyrconnell as Lord Deputy in February 1687 further quickened the pace of events. When Drogheda Corporation refused his nomination of Ignatius Peppard as mayor, *quo warranto* proceedings were begun against the Corporation culminating in the issue of a new town charter in November 1687 and the appointment of Peppard as mayor, Thomas Fitz-George Peppard as town clerk and Henry Dowdall as recorder.[21] Amongst the aldermen mentioned in the new charter was a Thomas Bellew of Gafney who was subsequently sworn freeman of the corporation.

The appointment of Roman Catholics to the Irish privy council, to the senior judiciary and as commissioned officers in the army was accompanied by similar developments in the local government arena where, as in Drogheda, *quo warranto* proceedings, followed by new charters, were instituted in most corporate towns, resulting in a substantial displacement of Protestants by Roman Catholics. This development was reflected in County Louth in all of the corporate towns where the new chief officers appointed were Catholics and, with the exception of Carlingford where the native Irishman Murtogh Magennis of Newcastle in County Down was appointed sovereign, all were Old English.[22] In the county Matthew Plunkett, Lord Baron Louth, was appointed to the lieutenancy with John Bellew's cousin, Roger Bellew of Thomastown, and John Babe appointed as his deputies. Patrick Bellew of Barmeath was appointed sheriff of the county in 1686, followed by Roger Bellew in 1687 and 1688 and John Taaffe in 1689. Patrick Bellew was also appointed to assist the commissioners of the revenue in the county.

The fact that James II was the 'Lord's anointed' far outweighed his Roman Catholicism with many sections of the Protestant interest, a fact testified to by the numbers of them who remained loyal even after the outbreak of revolution in England. Their interest in maintaining the political status quo, would also have been shared by those sections of the Catholic gentry class who had weathered the storms of the Commonwealth and Restoration periods, and had recovered their former estates or, as in the case of the Bellews, had acquired new ones. Dubbed the 'new interest' by Tyrconnell, their support for a full repeal of the restoration land settlement legislation would at best have been lukewarm, being satisfied instead for a more modest approach in which many deserving cases would be provided for while retaining the basic structure of the settlement intact. Bearing in mind that the legitimacy of their landed titles depended upon the latter, it was an understandable point of view. In County Louth the principal 'new interest' families were Nicholas Taaffe, Earl of Carlingford and Patrick Bellew of Barmeath, created baronet in December 1688. Their other Old English confrères, Matthew Plunkett, Baron Louth, and Sir John Bellew of Castletown-Dundalk, both of whom were to provide regiments of foot in the service of the king, would also have been like-minded, happy with the increased increment of engagement in political affairs, which the accession of James II brought about, but conservative where the land settlement was concerned. It may be significant, however, that while the Bellews of Barmeath made as full a contribution of loyalty and service to the king in the military field, they were not to the forefront in the political arena, Sir Patrick serving only one tour of duty as sheriff and, unlike their cousins, the Bellews of Thomastown and of Dundalk, their names are absent from the Jacobite hierarchy at the local and national levels. This may reflect the 'new interest' perception of them that existed in that hierarchy. However, as was the case in the late 1630s, the progressive destabilisation of the political situation in England was to have a corresponding development in Ireland. As was the case in Ulster in the period before the insurrection of 1641, there was in Ireland in 1688 a large body of displaced landed gentry, conscious of the losses suffered in the Commonwealth and Restoration periods, who saw the unfolding political scene, as an opportunity to secure the recovery of their long lost estates. This movement was to gather pace in the aftermath of James's deposition in England, and provided the Jacobite movement in Ireland with its own set of revolutionary objectives. These were not necessarily shared by James himself or by many of the Catholic landed gentry, who, like their Protestant counterparts, had rallied to the king out of their innate sense of loyalty to their lawfully appointed sovereign.

When King James's Irish Parliament was convened in May 1689, it became clear that the membership of the Commons was dominated by the faction seeking the total repeal of the Acts of Settlement and Explanation and their replacement by a Repeal Act which would restore landownership to the position obtaining prior to the commonwealth confiscations.[23] By this time large numbers of Protestant British settlers, dismayed by the turn of events since the deposition of James in England, had abandoned their properties in Ireland and fled either into England and Wales or Scotland. This development, together with the outbreak of the revolution in Britain, provided the pretext for the adoption by the Irish Parliament, in addition to the Act of Repeal, of an Act of Attainder in which over 2,500 persons were named; 1,340 of whom were described as having 'notoriously' joined in the revolt against the king and were outlawed, while others who had left Ireland were ordered to return, either by 1 September or 1 October 1689 or face outlawry. Those whose absence could be ascribed to age or infirmity were excluded from outlawry, subject to their estates being vested in the crown until they had returned. Outlawry proceedings, the age-old accompaniment of, and technical justification for, land confiscations in Ireland, would now be resorted to by the Jacobite Parliament, thus demonstrating that the behaviour of a Catholic ascendancy towards the Protestant underclass would differ little from the behaviour of the latter when they had the ascendancy.[24] The objective of these outlawries was not to inflict capital punishment on the delinquents, but, by the confiscation of their lands and properties, to provide a stock of reprisals to compensate those who, as in the case of the Bellews, had purchased or otherwise acquired lands during the Restoration period, which they would have to relinquish to their former owners under the provisions of the Act of Repeal. A prime example of these was Nicholas, Earl of Carlingford, for whom a special proviso was inserted in clause 34 of the Act of Repeal, requiring the commissioners appointed for the administration of the Act to compensate him for such relinquishments, by way of a grants of reprisals of other lands and properties forfeited to the crown either by the Act or upon account of any attainder for treason.

The spread of the revolt from Britain into Ulster, following the outbreak of hostilities in County Down in March 1689, and the commencement of the siege of Derry city in the following month, was the backdrop of King James's Irish Parliament and as Ireland prepared for war, local administrations broke down, giving way to the spread of disorders including the plundering of the properties of the absentee proprietors.[25] With the enactment of the Acts of Repeal and Attainder in the months of June and July, their implementation was put in train through provincial surveyors and collectors who were made responsible for securing, on behalf of the exchequer, the lands of the absentees, including those outlawed. These worked in turn with local commissions of enquiry who would have conducted, in a manner similar to the proceedings of the revenue commissioners in the Commonwealth period, the requisite inquisitions of the delinquents' properties and returning same to the exchequer. In County Louth the surviving evidence indicates that inquisitions were held, land and properties taken in charge and subsequently set out in custodium leases by the commissioners of the revenue.[26] All this occurred between June 1689 when the Repeal Act was enacted and the early months of 1690 before William marched on the Boyne. By this time most of the Protestants had fled the county some of whom, such as Henry Baker of Dunmahon, were to join with the defenders behind the walls of Derry and, in the case of Baker, to provide them with one of their most able commanders.[27] The plundering and pre-emptive occupation of lands and properties was not confined to the estates of the Protestant absentees. Sir Patrick Bellew, while serving as a captain in Simon Luttrell's regiment of Dragoons in Ulster, had his lands and other properties in Galway and Louth occupied by 'the old proprietors' and suffered, in consequence, the loss of a whole year's rent, £1,500 in stock, corn and hay. Suggesting that his houses in Clonoran and Barmeath had been plundered, he claimed the loss of £1,000 in household goods.[28] The fact that a man of such influence and standing should have suffered the arbitrary seizure of his lands and properties while he was engaged in the king's service, probably before the walls of Derry, suggests that a similar fate befell all of those named in the Act of Attainder. However, as the son of a man who had suffered confiscation of his estate in the Commonwealth period, he became entitled to a recovery of that estate under the Act of Repeal and the surviving evidence supports the possibility that he did in fact obtain such a recovery, probably on the basis of a custodium lease of the former Bellew estates at Willistown and Lisrenny, the restoration grantees of which had all fled or had been attainted.

Sir Patrick petitioned the commissioners of the revenue sometime before 1 July 1689 concerning the loss by him under the Act of Repeal of 'above five thousand acres' of land in the counties of Louth and Galway of the yearly value of £1,200.[29] He reminded them that he had already petitioned for a lease and reprise of the estates of Sir John Davis and Steven Stanley of Grangegorman and which had been first referred to the lords of the treasury and by them to the commissioners, 'long since' to which the petitioner had received no answer. Nothing seems to have been done on foot of this petition, leading Sir Patrick to petition the king himself complaining that he had not received any redress from the commissioners of the revenue. He pointed out that he had petitioned for a place called Edenderry, 'whereon there was a house fit for your petitioner's dwelling', he having lost by the Act of Repeal 'two good houses', and that that was the only place he could find undisposed of at his return (from the north of Ireland). He pointed out that he had offered to take £300 of his reprisal in the county of Down 'in the rebels possession' and some in the county of Louth, 'both of no value to your petitioner', he getting the estate of Sir Francis Blundell in and about Edenderry all of which he claimed was of far less value than his former estate and offered to leave the setting of the estate 'to themselves' giving him a moiety of the profit until 'your majesty were at better leisure to settle him or pay his wife and five daughters four hundred pound a year' until they were otherwise better provided for. He sought a speedy decision 'so that he may be dispatched to your majesty's service'. He also pointed out that his three sons and his other brothers, one of whom was killed at Cavan, were all in the king's service as well as nephews, friends and relations, all of whom he had induced, 'at the very beginning' to join that service.

On 1 July 1689, John Drummond, Earl of Melfort, one of those who had come into Ireland in King James's retinue sent a letter to the commissioners of the revenue on behalf of the king seeking information as to the reprisal of Sir Patrick and the 'best manner of doing it'. Details of Blundell's estate at Edenderry were compiled by Bellew later that month and in February 1690 he made an attested statement giving details of the lands that he had lost under the Act of Repeal, including the individuals from whom they had been purchased and which he reckoned had been worth £1,200 in 1686.[30] On 19 March 1690 P. Trant conveyed to Sir Patrick, on behalf of the commissioners of the revenue, a custodium lease of Blundell's estate in the barony of Coolystown, King's County and empowered him to enter upon the lands and to receive the profits thereof. It also conveyed a lease of the lands of Dundrum in the barony of Lecale, County Down, but which were at that time 'in rebel hands'. Even the Edenderry lands were of little profit to Bellew being encumbered by way of a jointure of £500 to 'the old Lady Blundell', a rent charge of £200 payable during his lifetime to Sir Edward Tyrell as well as the payment of quit rents on the estate and which were not payable in respect of the County Louth estate. In a statement conveying the details of the estate as well as the estates lost under the Act of Repeal it is remarked 'that Sir Patrick during the aforesaid encumbrances gets not a farthing profit out of the premises'.

The treatment of Sir Patrick was but a measure of the confusion and incompetence that attended James II's administration in Ireland, characteristics which extended into the military field as well. Considering the lateness of the decision of the commissioners of the revenue and the events at 'Boyne Waters' on 1 July it is not likely that Sir Patrick enjoyed for very long the profits, if any, of the Edenderry estates. This may also explain why he and many others of his class who had suffered in a similar manner, supported an early end to the hostilities and a negotiated settlement, which would at least restore them to the position obtaining before the hostilities had commenced. Nonetheless, Sir Patrick continued loyal to the king and in the course of the military campaign was promoted lieutenant-colonel of Luttrell's dragoons. His eldest son, John, hedged his bets by agreeing to being sent into Connacht in May 1691 by the Williamite Lord Justice Sir Charles Porter with instructions to 'do some considerable service' and with a promise that if he should be outlawed in his absence, it would be reversed and he would have the king's pardon.[31] While the outlawry was subsequently proceeded with, in order to avoid any suspicion being aroused that Bellew was engaged in the service of the Williamites, the ruse was not a successful one and John was imprisoned at Athlone by the Jacobites until after the battle of Aughrim. His brother Richard may have been a captain in Lord Bellew's regiment and Sir Patrick's brother Robert a captain in Lord Louth's regiment. It was either James, his youngest brother, or Nicholas who was killed in the action at Cavan in February 1690. As neither of these is mentioned in the post-Williamite period, it is likely that they did not survive the war.

In the wake of William's success at the Boyne, the Protestant proprietors began to return to their plundered estates in County Louth. For most of the period from May 1689 to July 1690 the county of Louth had been greatly disturbed by a variety of marauders, including the Jacobite forces sent into the county to oppose Schomberg in the autumn of 1689 and subsequently by Schomberg's and other Williamite forces in the period 1689–1690, before William's march on the Boyne finally put the county outside the reach of the Jacobites. To add to the general misery of war, the breakdown in law and order accompanying the war resulted in an extensive pillaging of lands and properties including those of the Protestant absentees, thus sowing seeds of bitterness and revenge which were to come to full flower in the Penal Laws against Roman Catholics, enacted in the early decades of the eighteenth century. One such absentee was Captain Thomas Aston, Sir William Aston's son and heir of the Aston estates in the barony of Ardee, including the former Bellew lands of Willistown and Plunkettsland.[32] The latter had been leased to Sir William's brother Alexander in July 1662 for a term of 99 years. After Alexander's death his wife Lettice (née Brownlow) sold her interest in the lease to a John Edmonds in January 1671–72 who in turn sold his interest in the lease to James Bellew, John's son, in August 1675 for £120, James to continue the payment of the original leasehold rent of £27 per annum. The lease terms contained a proviso that if the rent continued unpaid after a specified time, the lessor could levy a distress and recover the lands and properties comprehended in the lease.

Captain Aston had returned to County Louth in Duke of Schomberg's forces and was part of the Dundalk garrison in 1689. He participated in the battle of the Boyne in July 1690 and was subsequently given leave to attend to his estates in County Louth. He found Willistown laid waste and deserted and having entered into occupation of it on the basis of the proviso contained in the lease, he reset the lands to tenants 'at a very small rent', he being unable to settle there because he was on active service in Colonel Brudnell's regiment. He subsequently was transferred to England, thence to Catalonia and Flanders until the regiment was disbanded after which he returned to Ireland. He succeeded in recovering some rental arrears from the tenants he had previously set on the lands of Willistown and Plunkettsland and thereupon let the premises for a period of twenty-one years at an annual rent of £50. In a claim, which he laid before the trustees for the sale of the forfeited estates early in 1700, he sought a discovery of Willistown and Plunkettsland and on that basis sought the benefit of the lease as a forfeited interest. The latter was based upon a claim that James Bellew was in possession of the premises on 13 February 1689 and afterwards went into rebellion and was outlawed. Bellew had refused to pay any rent since the Earl of Tyrconnell had become Lord Deputy and was four years in arrears of his rent by the time of the Battle of the Boyne. James Bellew was dead by

March 1690, when his will was probated probably in favour of his nephew, Richard, and Aston's objective in taking the action was to break the lease so that the leasehold interest would come to him in reversion. While the outcome of these proceedings has not come to light, it seems reasonably certain that Aston quest for the lease was a successful one.

In April 1691 the Williamites published a comprehensive list of outlawries in respect of alleged supporters of James II in County Louth and which included all sorts of persons including landowners, tenants, merchants and Roman Catholic clergy.[33] Listed amongst them were Sir Patrick Bellew of Barmeath, his brother Christopher and son Richard, both described as of Tallonstown. Two other Bellews, Richard and John of Thomastown, were also included but whether they were of the Barmeath family or the collateral Thomastown family has not been determined. The Tallonstown address indicates that the former Bellew estates in the Lisrenny-Tallonstown district in the barony of Ardee had been recovered by the Bellews under the Act of Repeal. A similar pattern can be observed elsewhere in the county where many of those named as outlaws had addresses associated with the areas where their respective families had their estates at the time of the Commonwealth confiscations. These included such names as George Barnewall of Rathesker, Patrick Dowdall of Termonfeckin, Richard Hadsor of Cappock, James Moore of Barmeath, John Verdon of Clonmore and James Warren of Warrenstown. With the exception of Dowdall and Verdon, all these were from families who had been transplanted to Connacht during the Commonwealth period and who had succeeded in recovering, if only for a very short period, their former ancestral estates under the provisions of the Act of Repeal. These Williamite outlawries would have had the effect of clearing them from their newly recovered estates in County Louth and thus facilitated the returning planters, such as Thomas Aston, to recover title to their estates.

The ending of the Williamite War by the Treaty of Limerick in October 1691 was accompanied by the mass exodus of former Jacobite soldiery to the Continent either under Sarsfield, to enter into the French service or, under Brian Magennis, Viscount Iveagh, to enter into the service of the Emperor Leopold of the Holy Roman Empire. However, the beneficial provisions of that treaty toward landowners were such that most of the latter returned to their estates to pursue their claims for restoration. These included the Bellews of Barmeath and Connacht. The remarkable capacity of the Taaffes to survive in all political climates was exemplified by Francis Taaffe, who had succeeded to the estates and titles of his brother Nicholas, Earl of Carlingford after his death at the Battle of the Boyne. The latter had been a prominent supporter of James II, serving for a time on the English Privy Council and as ambassador to the Emperor Leopold before returning as a regimental commander to Ireland. His brother Francis was at this time marshal of the Emperor Leopold's Imperial army, then a principal ally of William of Orange in the struggle against France. It was necessary, therefore, in the interests of international diplomacy, to ensure that the Emperor's favourite soldier would succeed to his Irish estates. This necessitated the removal of any outlawries standing against the estate by virtue of his brother Nicholas's involvement with James. To this end, special provisions were made in an English Act of 1690 and an Irish Act of 1697 removing all such attainders thus enabling Francis to make a recovery of the estate.

In May 1692 Sir Patrick Bellew was adjudged by the Lords Justices and council to have been in Limerick on 3 October 1691 and that he had since submitted and taken the Oath of Fidelity provided for in an English Act of December 1690. Accordingly he was held to have been comprehended within the articles of the treaty and entitled to all the benefits thereof.[34] In the following February he was given a pass, dated at Dublin Castle, enabling him and his servant with their travelling horses to travel to the county of Louth and thence into Connacht 'upon his own affairs and to return again without let or hindrance, he behaving himself as becometh a loyal and dutiful subject of their majesties King William and Queen Mary'. His brothers Christopher of Connacht and Robert of Dublin received similar adjudications in October 1698 and July 1694 respectively as also did his son and heir John.[34] It was the beginning of their journey back from 'rebellion' and to the recovery of their estates. Christopher, who had married a Susanna Hill and had one son Michael, successfully claimed a reduction in his poll tax contribution in County Galway from the original levy of £10 to that of forty shillings.[35] His will is dated 1705.

Notwithstanding the fate of the Roman Catholic landed gentry under the eighteenth-century Penal Laws, the Bellews survived unscathed throughout that whole period and, in the case of Christopher's descendants, became one of the leading gentry families in County Galway, with an estate measured in 1871 at 10,516 acres statute measure and valued at £5,355 per annum.[36] In addition to their competence in estate management, they also engaged successfully in business and, not least in importance married well, each marriage adding its own increment to the expanding estate.[37] The ultimate display of their wealth and importance was to be expressed in the imposing mansion house and demesne constructed by them at Mountbellew, County Galway in the 1760s. When eventually the Penal Laws against landowners were repealed in the late 1770s, they purchased the Barmeath family lands at Castlebellew, estimated at 2,400 acres and valued at £2,000 per annum, for the then princely sum of £23,000.[38] Both families were prominent in the Catholic Relief Committee which agitated for the repeal of the Penal Laws and other reforms in the late eighteenth century, so much so that Sir Patrick Bellew of Barmeath was denounced as having carried 'his ideas of mischief as far as any in Ireland'.[39] Later on as the movement for reform was penetrated by the radicals of the United Irish Society, the parting of the ways was reached for the more conservative Barmeath Bellews who, dissociating themselves from the 'turbulent principles' of the republican radicals, seceded from the movement in 1791 arguing their reliance on Parliament for further relief.[40] This did not prevent one of their number Matthew Bellew, younger brother of Dominic, later Catholic Bishop of Killala, great-grandson of Robert Bellew of Tullydonnell County Louth, the fourth son of the original Sir Patrick, from involvement in the affairs of the 1798 insurrection.[41] Much to the disgust of his estranged brother Dominic, he was commissioned into the French General Humbert's army of Connacht and after a rather inglorious service with the French, he was captured at the Battle of Killala and after being, tried by Court-martial, was hanged in the nearby Protestant bishop's demesne.

The Barmeath Bellews exhibited all the characteristics of tenacity and endurance of their Galway cousins and like them also had good marriages. If the sale of their Galway estates in the late eighteenth century resulted in a reduced estate which in 1871 measured 5,109 acres statute measure, the valuation of £4,943 in County Louth was not significantly below that that of the Bellews of Mountbellew. They too engaged in conspicuous expenditure in respect of their mansion house and demesne at Barmeath, which in 1783 was a plain rectangular block, which incorporated the earlier Moore family tower house, two rooms deep and three storeys high with seven windows across the front and a main door. No doubt helped by the proceeds of the sale of Castlebellew, they were to engage in the early nineteenth century in an elaborate plan of reconstruction, the results of which survive to this day as Barmeath Castle. The architect was an Englishman named Thomas Smith of Hertfordshire who replaced the eaves cornice with battlements and after removing the end gables, added at each end of the original front round towers which rise a storey higher, with bold machicolations and huge arrow loops, the whole effect being described recently as a 'wild baronial fantasy'.[42] By comparison, the interior of the house is described as 'finished in a fine taste mostly with mid-eighteenth century rococo classical details'. Following their break with the Catholic radicals in the late eighteenth century, the Barmeath family pursued a conservative constitutional course which included support both for O'Connell's movement for Catholic Emancipation and the political establishment in Dublin, which resulted in the creation of Sir Patrick Bellew, the seventh baronet, as Baron Bellew of Barmeath in 1848. Some time before that he and his cousin Montesque, sometime commissioner for the National Board of Education, served as MPs for County Louth constituencies in the United Parliament in London. Unlike their cousins who have left County Galway, the Bellews occupy their ancestral seat at Barmeath to this day.

Epilogue

6. Aerial view of Barmeath Castle.

Appendices

APPENDIX I
TO THE HONOURABLE THE KNIGHTS, CITIZENS AND BURGESSES OF THE HOUSE OF COMMONS IN THIS PRESENT PARLIAMENT ASSEMBLED IN HIS MAJESTY'S KINGDOM OF ENGLAND.

THE HUMBLE PETITION OF [SEVERAL] OF THE KNIGHTS, CITIZENS AND BURGESSES OF THE COMMONS OF THE PARLIAMENT OF IRELAND WHOSE NAMES ARE UNDERWRITTEN [1]

Showing that whereas his most Sacred Majesty was graciously pleased to call a Parliament in this kingdom in the 10th year of his reign to consult of matters proper for that great assembly wherein the Commons of this kingdom as an entrance in that great service with unanimous consent granted unto his majesty six entire subsidies with this hope and assurance given unto them that by his majesty's favour fitting remedies should be applied for the redress of their grievances in the parliament but such was their misfortune that their humble request made in a petition of remonstrance presented to his majesty's Deputy of this kingdom did not meet with that success which the house well hoped for and whereas his majesty hath been likewise graciously pleased to assemble a parliament now held in this kingdom wherein having [?] taking into consideration his majesty's great and important occasions in full demonstration of their duty and affection to his majesty's service have presented his majesty with a free and cheerful gift of four entire subsidies with a real and true expression of their intentions for his majesty's further supply to the best of their abilities whereof his sacred majesty hath published that gracious answer that gave his people comfort and encouragement to hope in this parliament to have their grievances heard, represented and addressed but as yet they are so far from their expectations that by the continual interruptions given unto them in the House of Commons by frequent and unusual adjournments of the House by command of the right honourable the Lord Deputy without the consent of the House and by other delays and complaints of grievances and propositions for means or ways of redress are prevented or hopeless here.[?] Your petitioners therefore standing thus in a most perplexed state thought it high time to fly unto his most sacred majesty's Royal person with a humble remonstrance of the grievances of your kingdom but find themselves unable to make their personal addresses thither being restrained by proclamation to depart the kingdom without licence. The petitioners therefore calling to mind the near links and great ties of blood and affinity betwixt the people of this kingdom and the famous people of England, from whose loins they are descended, and being therefore, thus flesh of their flesh and bone of their bone, subjects to one gracious sovereign, and governed by the same laws, are emboldened humbly to beseech you, that you will be pleased to present the annexed petition of remonstrance of the grievances of this kingdom to his most sacred Majesty; and that you join with it your own desires and assistance in the behalf of the Commons of this kingdom, that by his majesty's grace and favour this kingdom may be relieved from such grievances as it now groans under that likewise you will be pleased to represent to his sacred Majesty the true affections of his people of this kingdom, and their desires to be eased of their grievances, and yet to preserve his Majesty's revenues without detriment, and to enable his subjects to give free and large supplies in Parliament to his Majesty, as his occasions hereafter shall require; and lastly that you would be pleased to join with us in our humble suit to his Majesty for his gracious and speedy directions and command that a committee, nominated by the House of Commons may be required and authorised to repair thither, in the name of the whole, to the effect and purpose as in our said petition of remonstrance is desired and your [petitioners shall pray etc.]

APPENDIX II
TO THE KING'S MOST EXCELLENT MAJESTY THE HUMBLE PETITION OF THE KNIGHTS CITIZENS AND BURGESSES, OF THE COMMONS HOUSE OF PARLIAMENT OF IRELAND WHOSE NAMES ARE UNDER WRITTEN

Showing that in all ages past, since the happy subjection of this kingdom to the imperial Crown of England, it was, and is a principal study and princely care of his Majesty, and his most noble Progenitors, Kings and Queens of England and Ireland, to the vast expence of treasure and blood, that their loyal and dutiful people of this land of Ireland, (being now for the most part derived from British ancestors), should be governed according to the municipal and fundamental laws of England: That the statute of Magna Charta or the great Charter for the liberties of England, and other laudable laws and statutes, were in several Parliaments here enacted, and declared, that by means thereof, and of the most prudent and benign government of his Majesty's and his Royal Progenitors, this Kingdom was, until of late, in its growth to a flourishing estate; whereby the said people where heretofore enabled to answer their humble and natural desires, to comply with his Majesty's Royal and Princely occasions, by their free gift of one hundred and fifty thousand pounds, sterling, and likewise by another gift of one hundred and twenty thousand pounds more, during the Government of the Lord Viscount Falkland; and after by the gift of forty thousand pounds, and their free and cheerful gift of six entire subsidies in the tenth year of his Majesty's reign; which to comply with his majesty's then occasions, signify to the then House of Commons, they did allow should amount in the collections unto two hundred and fifty thousand pounds, although as they confidently believe, if the said subsidies had been levied in a moderate Parliamentary way, they would not have amounted to much more than half the sum; besides the four entire subsidies granted in this present parliament. So it is, may it please your Lordship that by occasion of ensuing and other grievances and innovations, though to his Majesty no considerable profit, this kingdom is reduced to that extreme and universal poverty, that the same is now less able to pay two subsidies, than it was heretofore to satisfy all the before recited great payments; and his Majesty's most faithful people of the same do conceive great fears, that the said grievances and consequences thereof may hereafter be drawn into precedents, and to be perpetuated upon their posterity; which in their great hopes and strong belief, they are persuaded is contrary to his Majesty's Royal and Princely intention towards his said people: some of which said grievances are as followeth:

FIRST   The general and apparent decay of trades, occasioned by the new and illegal raising of the book of rates and impositions; as twelve pence a piece custom for hides bought for four or five shillings, and other heavy impositions upon native and other commodities, exported and imported; by reason whereof, and of extreme usage and censures, merchants are beggared, and both disenabled and discouraged to trade; and some of the honourable persons who gain thereby are often judges and parties; and that in the conclusion his Majesty's profit thereby is not considerably advanced.

SECONDLY   The arbitrary decision of all civil causes and controversies by paper petitions before the Lord Lieutenant and Lord Deputy, and infinite other judicatories upon references from them derived, in the nature of all actions determinable at then common law, not limited unto certain time, season, cause or thing whatsoever; and the consequences of such proceedings by receiving immoderate and unlawful fees by Secretaries, Clerks, Pursuivants, Sergeants at Arms and otherwise, by which kind of proceedings his Majesty loseth a considerable part of his revenue upon original writs and otherwise, and the subject loseth the benefit of his writ of error, bill of reversal, vouchers and other legal and just advantages and the ordinary course and courts of justice declined.

THIRDLY   The proceedings in civil causes at the Council Board, contrary to the law and great Charter, and not limited to any certain time or season.

FOURTHLY   That the subject is, in all material parts thereof, denied the benefit of princely graces, and more especially of the Statute of Limitations of 21 Jacobi, granted by his Majesty in the fourth year of his reign, upon great advice of the Councel of England and Ireland, and for great consideration, and then published in all the Courts at Dublin, and in all the Counties of this Kingdom, in open assizes; whereby all persons do take notice, that, contrary to his Majesty's pious intention, his subjects of this kingdom have not enjoyed the benefit of his Majesty's princely promise thereby made.

FIFTHLY   The extrajudicial avoiding of letters patent of estates of a very great part of his Majesty's subjects under the great seal, the public faith of the Kingdom, by private opinions delivered at the

Councel-Board, without legal evictions of their estates, contrary to law, and without precedents or example of any former age.

SIXTHLY   The proclamation of the sole emption and uttering of Tobacco, which is bought at very low rates, and uttered at high and excessive rates; by means whereof thousands of families within this Kingdom, and of his Majesty's subjects in several islands and other parts of the West Indies, as your petitioners are informed, are destroyed, and the most part of the coin of this Kingdom is ingrossed into particular hands; insomuch as the Petitioners do conceive, that the profit, arising and ingrossed thereby, doth surmount his Majesty's revenue, certain or casual, within this kingdom, and yet his Majesty receiveth, but very little profit by the same.

SEVENTHLY   The unusual and unlawful increasing of monopolies, to the advantage of a few, to the disprofit of his Majesty, and the impoverishment of his people.

EIGHTHLY   The extreme and cruel usage of certain late Commissioners and others [of] the inhabitants of the County and City of Londonderry, by means whereof the worthy plantation of that County is almost destroyed, and the said inhabitants are reduced to great poverty, and many of them forced to forsake the country; the same being the first and most useful plantation in the large Province of Ulster, to the great weakening of the Kingdom in this time of danger, the said plantation being the principal strength of those parts.

NINETHLY   The late erection of the Court of High Commission for causes ecclesiastical in those necessitous times; the proceedings of the said Court in many causes [cases] without legal warrant,; and yet so supported, as prohibitions have not been obtained, though legally sought for; and the excessive fees exacted by the Ministers thereof; and encroaching of the same upon the jurisdiction of other ecclesiastical Courts of this Kingdom.

TENTHLY   The exorbitant and barbarous fees and pretended customs exacted by the Clergy against the law: some of which are specified in a schedule annexed.

ELEVENTHLY   The petitioners do most heartily bemoan, that his Majesty's service and profit are much more impaired than advanced by the grievances aforesaid; and the subsidies granted in the last Parliament having much increased his Majesty's revenue, by the buying in of grants and otherwise, and that all his Majesty's debts, then due in this Kingdom, were satisfied out of the said subsidies; and yet his Majesty is of late, as the Petitioners have been informed in the House of Commons, become indebted in this Kingdom in great sums; and they do therefore humbly beseech, that an exact account be sent to his Majesty, how, and in what manner, your highness's treasure issued.

TWELFTHLY   The Petitioners do humbly conceive great and just fears at a proclamation, published in this kingdom in anno Domini 1635, prohibiting men of quality or estates for to depart this Kingdom into England, without the Lord Deputy's licence; whereby the subjects of this Kingdom are hindered and interrupted from free access and address to his Sacred Majesty and Privy Councel of England, to declare their just grievances, or to obtain remedies for them, in sort as their ancestors have done, in all ages, since the reign of King Henry 11, and great fees exacted for every of the said licences.

THIRTEENTHLY   That of late your Majesty's late Attorney General hath exhibited informations against many ancient Boroughs of this Kingdom, into your Majesty's Court of Exchequer, to show cause, by what warrant the said Boroughs, who heretofore sent Burgesses to the Parliament; and thereupon, for want of an answer, the said privilege of sending Burgesses were seized by the said Court; which proceedings are altogether coram non judice, and contrary to the laws and privileges of the House of Parliament; and if way should be given thereto, might tend to the subversion of Parliaments, and by consequence, to the ruin and destruction of the Commonwealth; and that the House of Commons hath hitherto, in this present Parliament, been deprived of the advice and councel of many profitable and good members by means thereof.

FOURTEENTHLY   That by the powerfulness of some Ministers of State in this Kingdom, the Parliament, in its members and action, hath not its natural freedom.

FIFTEENTHLY   That the fees taken in all the Courts of Justice in this Kingdom, both ecclesiastical and civil, and by other inferior officers and ministers, are so immoderately high, that it is an unspeakable burthen to all your Majesty's subjects of this Kingdom, who are not able to subsist, except the same be speedily remedied, and reduced to such a moderation, as may stand with the condition of this Kingdom.

AND LASTLY That the Gentry, Merchants, and other your Majesty's subjects of this Kingdom, are of late, by the grievances and pressures aforesaid, and other the like, very near to ruin and destruction; and Farmers of Customs, Customers, Waiters, Searchers, Clerks of unwarrantable proceedings, Pursuivants, and Gaolers, and sundry others, very much enriched; whereby, and by the slow redress of the Petitioners grievances, your Majesty's most faithful and dutiful people of this Kingdom do conceive great fears, that their readiness approved upon all occasions hath not been of late rightly represented to your Sacred Majesty. Your Majesty's Petitioners [therefore] wanting in respect of the Proclamation aforesaid a safe and free access to your Sacred Throne to implore remedies in the grievances aforesaid and not obtaining relief therein otherwise are necessitated to do that by this their petition of remonstrance under their hands which they cannot in person, most humbly beseeching, your most excellent Majesty, in your high wisdom to give order for your subjects relief against the said grievance and to signify your Majesty's good pleasure for the licensing a Select Committee from the House of Commons in the Parliament now assembled in this Kingdom and in case the Parliament be dissolved certain agents to be chose by the country from the several parts of this Kingdom to attend in person for expressing and demonstrating how your Majesty's revenue in this land may be preserved without detriment, the other many grievances of your Majesty's people of this land redressed, and they receive quiet repose and satisfaction and from that poverty that apparently is fallen upon them be raised and be enabled upon all right and honourable occasions most humbly and readily in Parliament to extend their utmost endeavours to serve your Sacred Majesty and comply with your royal and Princely designs and the petitioners as in duty bound will ever pray:

APPENDIX III
THE ACCOUNT TOUCHING THE TRAIN OF ARTILLERY c.1645–46[2]

1. There are in Athlone four serviceable pieces of cannon, the which must be fitted in all respects, before they can go to service. And to carry all necessaries belonging to the said four pieces, there will be four waggons requisite the which four pieces and four waggons will require eighty-eight oxen and twenty drivers.

There is a gun, a gun rope and a halew[?], with their tackling wanting.

There will be at present at least 300 shovels and spades, 50 pickaxes, 10 hatchets, 6 crowes and 3 polepikes [?].

2. As for bullets for the aforesaid artillery, I presume some may be had at Limbrick or Galwaie, if not, a course must be taken to get them made at Mr Dinnis in Munster from whence we had some heretofore and to that purpose I shall give the calibre of each piece as to the bullets height and weight.

3. There are in Limbricke two demi-cannons, one of a 22lb., bullet and another of a 34lb., bullet and how they shall be disposed of I humbly submit. As for Galwaie I know not what artillery is there, neither where any field pieces are, which were very useful, and fit to be looked after.

4. A list of the members requisite for the said train:
   A clerke of the store and one assistant.
   A carriage-master and two assistants.
   A quartermaster.
   Four gunners and fourteen assistants.
   A master carpenter and two under-carpenters.
   A master smith and two under smiths.
   20 drivers.
   100 pioneers with their officers viz., a captain, a lieutenant and two sergeants.

5. And as for a guard for the artillery, on the putting of that part of the army into any befitting posture, I must (with a deep sense of my own sufferings) confess that though the same be the groundwork and life of any army, yet hath it been always since these wars so sleighted that I may say it hath been a great meanes of the kingdom being brought to the condition its now in; for when armies have been readie to advance into the field, and gain the opportunity of service, both as to the enemy,

and time of year, then hath all been at a stand waiting for the fitting out of these things whereby the kingdom has been eaten out and the service lost, for hitherto there was never provision made for those things (let a man solicit as much as if his life lay on it) until the very time of service came, and things were put a work in a huddling manner, hand over head, and when the summer service were over no provision was made for laying up these things from the rain or weather, nor get from the members of the train, but all turned from winter quarters and so every year, they were forced to begin anew, as if the war were never thought of before. Whereas always a special care should have been had to choose amongst the whole army fit members for this employment and to continue them still. And such as should be fixed on for this employment should have a regiment given him, whereby he should not be to seek for men when there should be occasion of service of this kind, and those men by their constant attendance on the said charge when artillery were in service would become expert apt and fit to undergo and execute any thing belonging thereto, and when there were no occasion for artillery, a regiment of this practice and daring way would be found more useful and serviceable in all respects then can be imagined.

6. A convenient place, with a portion of land adjoining to it, is to be fixed on, where all the artificers and members belonging to the train, the cattle and necessaries unto them appertaining, shall be in probable security and that upon call all things may be forthcoming for service and without this, its in vain to be at expense for no sooner a man turns his back to these things, but all is in confusion, mislaid and quite lost, if they have not a place to themselves.

7. As for arms, armour, ammunition and what else shall belong to the store, I humbly offer that a convenient storehouse be appointed for such and an able clerk for the store, whereby such as shall command the artillery may receive and be able to give an orderly account of the comings in and issuings forth thereof.

Lastly inasmuch as the time of year is far spent and that the completing of these things will require much time and constant attendance, I humbly move that forthwith provision be made for the same, whereby they be suddenly got in hand with and that a punctual way of payment be prescribed for members of the train, or otherwise it is not to be expected that this part of the army can be out into any manner of equippage.

Endorsed 'a note touching the train'.

APPENDIX IV
A COLLECTION OF DOCUMENTS RELATING TO JOHN BELLEW'S TRANSPLANTATION TO CONNACHT[3]

DOCUMENT 1
The humble petition of the undernamed Submittees to the Kilkenny Articles

To the honourable Colonel Hewson, Colonel Sankey, Colonel Lawrence, Quarter-Master General Vernon and Doctor Jones, treators on behalf of the Parliament in the said Articles

Sheweth that your Petitioners acknowledge with thankfulness your Honourables' Justice in enlarging the rents and profits of their estates to be continued unto them until the Parliaments pleasure be made know touching the real estates, do most humbly pray your Honourables to take into your deep and serious consideration your petitioners' removal from their habitations being a people concerned and reduced to that extremitie and want, as if driven they may say, from the coast of Israel (Samuel 2 Chapter 21 Verse 5) must of necessity perish.

Your Petitioners therefore humbly beseech your Honourables (being their mediators and those with whom they made their covenant) that tender consideration may be had of their Articles and of your Honourables engagements, according unto the genuine and natural sense of honour [?] as they are laid down (a transplantation at that time being no more thought of by your Petitioners than their removal into America).

And accordingly that your Honourables may be pleased to mediate and interpose betwixt them and that heavy sentence of transplantation being as they most humbly offer in the annexed reasons repugnant to the express words of their said Articles and contrary to law, and they doubt not far from your Honourables intentions to expose them to such an inevitable ruin, though it were to your own hurt (Psalms 15 and 14).

And\your Petitioners poor concernments being not to be balanced with the consideration of Public Faith (ever held sacred and inviolably observed by all Nations) most humbly offer to your Honourables' Justice and probity [?] that whatever settlement shall be held forth unto them may be of their own estates and homes according to their Articles and the trust and confidence reposed by them in your Honourables upon their Submissions.

And they will Pray.

R. Barnewall, Pa. Netterville, John Bellew, L. Dowdall.

DOCUMENT 2
Reasons humbly offered by the petitioners, Submittees on Kilkenny Articles against their transplantation

FIRSTLY The words of the addition to the 5th., article speak of a moderate part of their estates and in another part of the Articles there is mention of passes to return to their homes for such as were not inclined to go beyond the seas, which estates and homes were explained by the Articles and the orders by which the Submittees were put in possession, to be the estates and homes formerly belonging to them, therefore a transplantation into other estates or homes may not be without violation of the Articles.

SECONDLY By the words in the additional article viz., 'we do promise faithfully and really etc.,' that the Submittees may enjoy such moderate part of their estates etc.,' the Treater's do interpose themselves between the Submittees and any Act that may hinder the enjoyment of their estates according [to the] Articles, Therefore a transplantation of the Submittees may not be without breach of trust.

THIRDLY The Treaters in behalf of the parliament knowing at the time of the treaty the engagement given to the undertakers and consequently the intended transplantation did by their subsequent engagement and public faith passed in the Articles provide against the same as to the Submittees, therefore the Act of Settlement (coming in time subsequent) cannot be intended to a violation of that faith.

FOURTHLY These words viz., the Treaters 'do promise faithfully and really to provide etc.,' that the Submittees may enjoy such moderate part of their estates etc., declare an intention of not transplanting the Submittees at the time of the Treaty and consequently a transplantation of them is contrary to that intention and contrary to the said expression which ought to over-rule the intention of all parties.

FIFTHLY The Act of Settlement holds forth a certain proportion of land to such as are thereby transplantable, that the said Act holds forth no certain proportion of land to such of the Submittees as are implied in the first qualification or expressed by name in the third therefore such are not transplantable by the said Act.

SIXTHLY The Articles hold forth to the Submittees a moderate part etc., but the Act of Settlement declares not what a moderate part is therefore the Act of Settlement extends not to the Submittees.

SEVENTHLY   The pleasure of the parliament being a trust and power settled in the parliament by special agreement and therefore until it be declared by Ordinance or otherwise by His Highness the Lord Protector, the Submittees ought to possess their estates and rents without transplantation. As it hath been adjudicated by the Court of Articles in England and confirmed by His Highness's letter and thereby the parliament being made the judge of the Moderate part which is to be held out unto the Submittees by the Articles, cannot transfer over that trust or power of adjudication unto any other.

EIGHTHLY   It hath been ingeniously confessed by the Treaters on behalf of the parliament that the mediation required by the Articles hath not been made, and consequently no pleasure of the parliament could be declared in pursuance thereof and therefore the Submittees ought to enjoy their estates until such mediation and judicature thereupon be declared.

NINTHLY   The proviso in the Act of Settlement saves to the Submittees the benefit of their Articles, and thereby to enjoy such moderate part of their estates etc., And the subsequent clause in that proviso deprives them of that enjoyment and exposes them to transplantation and consequently void for the ensuing reasons.

TENTHLY   If the subsequent clause in this Act of Settlement should over-rule the proviso it would render a void and fruitless and deprive the Submittees of the benefit intended them, by the said proviso in the Act and therefore repugnant, and subsequent clauses in Acts of Parliament repugnant to the body of the Act are void.

ELEVENTHLY   Justice requires that private or public faith and agreements grounded upon good considerations be performed, therefore what is repugnant thereunto is void.

R. Barnewall, Pa. Netterville, John Bellew, Lau. Dowdall.

DOCUMENT 3

The officers within named having considered of the within Petition of Sir Richard Barnewall and others the Submittees on Kilkenny Articles with the annexed reasons do return as their answer, that it is proper only for the lord deputy and council to be applied unto in the business of the said Petition mentioned, and therefore do not think fit to take any further notice thereof.

Dated 26 March 1655.

Signed by their order, Samuel Goodwin.

By the Lord Deputy and Council.

DOCUMENT 4

Whereas by an order of the lord deputy and council dated the 8th., of January last Sir Richard Barnewall Baronet and others of the Irish Party who submitted upon the Articles made at Kilkenny the 12 May 1652 and are comprehended therein and are persons excepted by name from pardon for life or estate (as appears by the third qualification in the Act for settlement of Ireland) should enjoy such proportion of their real estates respectively as shall not exceed one full third part thereof as by the said order doth more fully appear. Notwithstanding which order the said Submittees have hitherto refused to transplant in pursuance of the Declaration published in that behalf, pretending that by the letter of their Articles they are not comprehended within the acts for transplantation.

And whereas a petition has since been presented unto this board by the said Sir Richard Barnewall, John Bellew and Laurence Dowdall upon consideration had as well of the said petition as of the several reports made by the officers of the army at the head quarters (sundry of them being the commanders that were party and commanders to the said Articles and Treaty made at Kilkenny as abovesaid). The said lord deputy and council upon advice had and taken with the said officers of the army as aforesaid, do declare that the transplantation of the said petitioners into the Province of Connacht or county of Clare in pursuance of the said Act made in that behalf is not any breach or violation of their said Articles. <u>And therefore have thought fit and do hereby order that the said Sir Richard Barnewall and the rest of the Submittees above mentioned</u>, do transplant into Connacht or Clare as aforesaid at or before the fifteenth day of the present April, or otherwise incur the penalties mentioned in the several Declarations published in that behalf, and in the meantime the said Submittees are to make their applications to the Commissioners at Athlone appointed and authorised for the Adjudication of titles and qualifications relating to the Irish, to have their respective claims to their estates accordingly determined as also to the Commissioners sitting at Loughrea who are to set out unto the said Submittees and others comprised in the said Articles, their due proportions of lands pursuant thereunto and to the order of the 8 January above mentioned and their instructions in the like cases. And as to the other demands of the said Submittees touching the enjoyment of the profits of their real estates in pursuance of their said Articles since the 27 July 1653, it is further ordered that such of the petitioners as are comprehended within the third qualification in the said Act of Settlement and excepted by name as aforesaid shall enjoy the full profit issuing out of their real estates (over and above Contribution and paid into the Public Treasury from the 27 July aforesaid, deduction being first made for what hath already been received by the said persons from the Treasury or otherwise. Nevertheless for as much as it doth not at present appear unto the board what profit has arisen out of the respective estates of the said Submittees since the time aforementioned and which hath been paid into the public treasury, it is therefore further ordered that the Commissioners General of the Revenue do forthwith write unto the respective Receivers of the Revenue in the several Precincts where any of the estates of the said Submittees lie to certify unto them with what convenient speed they may, how much money hath been paid into the Treasury out of the estates of the respective petitioners since the time aforesaid over and above Contribution and what they or others in their behalf have respectively received [?] upon account and by what order and upon return made of what shall appear to be remaining and not yet paid unto them in pursuance of their Articles, orders shall be sent unto the Receiver of the Revenue at Athlone to make payment thereof unto such of the said persons as it shall appear of right to belong, and to that end the said petitioners are to repair to the said Receiver at Athlone who is hereby authorised upon notice given to him from the said Commissioners General to pay all such sums of money as shall appear to be due unto the said petitioners that are comprehended in the said third qualification as abovesaid.

Dublin the 3 April 1655
Thomas Herbert, Clerk of the Council.

The word fifteenth underlined by special order.
Thomas Herbert, Clerk of the Council.
A true copy Thomas Herbert, Clerk of the Council
By the Lord deputy and Council.

DOCUMENT 5

Upon reading the petition of Sir Richard Barnewall, Laurence Dowdall, Patrick Netterville and John Bellew and upon consideration had thereof and of their proposals annexed, it is thought fit and ordered in answer thereunto as follows:-

TO THE FIRST: Concerning their accommodation in Connacht (or Clare) order is given that the Commissioners at Loughrea do take special care that lands and other conveniences [?] be set out unto the petitioners pursuant to the late order of the lord deputy and council of the 3rd of this instant.

TO THE SECOND: Concerning the proving of their respective estates or having their proportions set out unto them upon the surveys thereof already made and returned, the council does not think it safe either for the State or the petitioners to rely upon those surveys. But the commissioners appointed for qualifications sitting at Athlone (to whom the petitioners have a liberty of application) and (upon such proofs and evidences as shall be produced before them for clearing the certain value of their respective estates) [are] empowered to determine and ascertain a full third part thereof to be set out by the commissioners at Loughrea accordingly in pursuance of the order of this board dated the 8th January last.

TO THE THIRD: Praying a competent time to stay at their now respective dwellings to order their concernments and prepare for their removal and that their wives and children may stay 'till their corn has been disposed of; it is thought fit and ordered that the petitioners be and are hereby permitted to stay from transplantation until the first day of May next ensuing and that their wives and families continue their present residence until the 20th day of the said month to follow their occasions without interruption and no longer. But the said petitioners are hereby ordered forthwith to depart this city of Dublin.

TO THE FOURTH: For satisfying them their arrears of rent due unto them since the 27th July 1653, order is given for paying unto them their due proportions of such of their said rents as shall appear to have been paid unto the public treasury which they are to receive from the treasurer at Athlone, the 1st June next over and above contribution.

TO THE FIFTH: Concerning arrears of rents due before the 27th., July 1653 and paid unto the treasury the council having made former orders in the case do not think fit to give any further order for payment thereof but (?) as for those rents which shall appear due by articles and not paid into the treasury nor assigned but remaining in the hands of the tenants who possesses any part of the petitioners estates, they are to have the same paid unto them by such tenants, all arrears of contribution and other public taxes being deducted.

TO THE SIXTH: For compelling tenants or servants who have been in arms with or aided or assisted the Irish to transplant with the petitioners into Connnaught, there being rules already given by the Declarations for transplantation in such cases, the council do not think fit to make any other orders therein.

TO THE SEVENTH: That the said petitioners may not be liable for any arrears of contribution or other taxes due or anyway payable out of such lands as shall be assigned them in Connacht before their removing into such lands, nor charged with contribution or any other tax for the insolvencies of others, the lord deputy and council do grant the same, that the said petitioners shall neither be troubled for any such arrears nor be charged for the insolvencies of others whereof all whom it may concern are to take notice.

TO THE EIGHTH: That after settling or improving their respective proportions in Connacht they may not be removed from the same. The lord deputy and council do agree thereto so far as the Commonwealths interest to such proportions may be concerned, but where the interest or title of any private person therein shall appear in such case the law is to decide the difference.

TO THE NINTH: Praying to be freed from payment of any sheaf out of their corn in ground in Leinster, they must conform to the orders already given in that case.

TO THE TENTH: Leave is granted by the answer to the third head for their wives and families to follow their occasions in the county without interruption 'till the 20th May next ensuing, whereof all whom it may concern are to take notice.

TO THE ELEVENTH: . . . suits out of Connacht in the Courts for administration of Justice at Dublin for debts or trespass, but left to the judication in the province of Connacht, the petitioners are referred to such orders as have already been given in the case.

TO THE TWELFTH: Setting forth that the petitioners, not transplanting as yet, hath not proceeded of disobedience but of their not having received a judgement on their Articles and therefore praying the same immunities held forth to such as did transplant before May 1654. It is ordered that the aforesaid petitioners shall have the benefit held forth to transplanting persons enjoining transplantation or by any subsequent Declaration pursuant thereof printed and published in that behalf.

Dublin 12th April 1655. Thomas Herbert Clerk of the Council.

A true copy examined, Thomas Herbert Clerk of the council.

DOCUMENT 6
Last page of a reply (other pages missing) to a petition and dated 20 April 1655

... Desired but in case any such persons as are transplantable according to the Declarations published in that behalf be discovered in any of the Provinces and brought before the commander-in-chief of the respective places where such persons live after the time of their stay is expired, within which they ought to have removed, such transplantable persons apprehended as aforesaid are ordered to transplant into Connacht, whereof all persons concerned are to take notice.

TO THE FIFTH: Desiring that the petitioners might have authorised copies of the orders mentioned in the ninth and eleventh proposals, the council do not think fit to grant their desires.

TO THE SIXTH: Desiring that leases and custodiums of land in Connacht might not hinder the petitioners from the present possession of such lands as shall be assigned them by the council at Loughrea, it is ordered that in case the petitioners shall receive any just grievance in reference to their settlement in Connacht, upon notice thereof the council will give such order therein as shall be agreeable to justice and their Articles.

Dat Dublin the 20th April 1655, Thomas Herbert Clerk of the Council.

A true copy examined Thomas Herbert Clerk of the Council.

DOCUMENT 7
By the Lord Deputy and Council
Upon reading the petition of Mr John Bellew praying that in regards he has transplanted himself according to orders, he may enjoy his crop of corn growing on the lands from where he removed in the province of Leinster, upon consideration had thereof and of the report from Sir Charles Coote knight and baronet Lord President of Connacht, Major General Hardress Waller and Colonel Sankey who certify it as their opinion that the petitioner having transplanted according to instructions may received the full benefit of the crop of his corn according to his contract and bargain. We do agree to the said report and hereby order the Commissioner General of the Revenue to take care that such servants as the petitioner shall employ for winning [?] of the said corn be not disturbed or molested therein. Provided no person be employed as aforesaid who is comprehended

in the Declaration of Transplantation. Athlone this 16 June 1655. Thomas Herbert Clerk of the Council.

24 September 1655, this is entered in the Commissioner General's office; P.W. Hopkins.

DOCUMENT 8

By the Commissioner General of the Public Revenue and Stores in Ireland

In pursuance of the within order from the right honourable the lord deputy and council we do hereby desire the sheriff of the county of Louth and all others whom these may concern to take care that the tenor of the said order be observed so as that the said Mr Bellew's servant be not in any wise molested in reaping and winning and disposing of the crop of corn belonging to the said Mr Bellew.

Dated the Custom House Dublin the 23 August 1655.

Signed by appointment of the said Commissioner, Stephen Allen Entered the 24 September 1655 P.W. Hopkin.

DOCUMENT 9

By the Commissioners for Adjudication of Claims and Qualifications of the Irish

The claim of John Bellew of Willistown in the County of Louth Esq., as well to his title as to his qualifications being this day in the presence of the Councel for the Commonwealth and Councel for the said Claimant, it appeared fully upon the evidence produced that the claimant hath made a good and legal title unto the several villages, hamlets, lands and fields of Lisrenny, Little Arthurstown, Nicholstown and Kenvickrath with their appurtenances lying in the barony of Ardee and County aforesaid, to the villages, fields and lands of Graftonstown and Hitchestown situated and being in the barony of Ferrard and County aforesaid. And hath also made an legal title by purchase unto the town and lands and fishings of Willistown and the appurtenances being in the barony of Ardee and County aforesaid. To the town and fishing of Adamstown in the barony and County aforesaid. To a parcel of land called Plunkettsland in Finvoy in the barony aforesaid. To the castle, townlands and fishing called Dawesland in Braganstown together with a Common in the whole town and fields of Braganstown which said fishings were of the clear yearly value of fifty pounds sterling. And hath also made a legal title unto the sum of £1200 sterling due to the said Claimant by several bonds of the staple from Oliver Lord Baron Louth, John Taaffe of Braganstown aforesaid Esq., and George Russell of Rathmullen in the County of Down Esq. The said bonds bearing date the one the seventh day of December one thousand six hundred and thirty eight and the other the nineteenth of March one thousand six hundred and thirty eight.

That the lands contain according to proof one thousand four hundred and sixty acres of profitable land and that the Claimant is comprised within the Articles of Kilkenny. The Court doth thereupon think fit and adjudge the said Claimant, his heirs and assigns for ever to have and enjoy (in Connacht or Clare) one third part of the quantity of the said lands hereinbefore mentioned and lands to the value of one third part of the said sum of fifty pounds yearly allowed in lieu of the said fishing; and lands also to the value of one third part of the said sum of twelve hundred pounds according to and in pursuance of the said Articles.

Saving to his Highness the Lord Protector, Commonwealth of England and all other persons all right and title that hereinafter may appear belonging to them out of the premises or any part thereof.

Dated at Athlone the twenty-sixth day of March 1656.

John Cooke, John Santhey, W. Halsey.

A true copy examined,
Thomas Burton, Deputy Registrar.

APPENDIX V
JOHN BELLEW'S CRITICAL COMMENTARIES ON THE PROPOSALS FOR THE LAND SETTLEMENT 1660–61

DOCUMENT 1[4]
A BRIEF OF THE DIFFERENCE BETWIXT HIS MAJESTY'S SUBJECTS OF IRELAND CLAIMING TO BE RESTORED TO THEIR FORMER ESTATES AND THOSE WHO NOW POSSESS THE SAME

Those who claim to be restored to their former estates are either innocent persons or such as submitted and constantly adhered to the peace concluded in Ireland in the year 1648 who since that time served under his majesty's authority and fought to the effusion of their blood against the usurper until he became . . . whereby his majesty's authority was interrupted and thereupon the usurper outed them of their estates.

Those who now possess their estates are either Adventurers or their assigns or such officers and soldiers as served the usurper against his majesty and his royal father and to whom the said usurper did for arrears or by way of gift grant what they now possess of the said estates as the reward of their service against his majesty and his royal father which estates hath been possessed by them since the interruption of his majesty's authority.

Those from whom their said former estates are yet detained conceive it just that as they lost the same serving his majesty so they should be restored thereunto on his majesty's restoration it being without precedent and repugnant to all reason and justice that the estates of such as served his majesty should be now the reward of those that fought against him and his royal father.

That as to those who possess the said estates at present, there may be a difference between the genuine Adventurer who issued money before his late majesty was separated from the parliament and those who issued money after such separation the first deserving more reward than the latter.

That there may be also a difference between the officers and soldiers who betrayed the houlls and towns they were intrusted in to the usurper and those who committed no such breach of trust, as also between the officers and soldiers who were instrumental in his majesty's restoration and those who were not.

As to the genuine Adventurer it may be thought reasonable that some course be prescribed for his satisfaction in forfeited lands, or in paying his disbursements wherein regard to be had to what he received hitherto out of the lands assigned for his disbursements.

As to the officers and soldiers who shall on examination appear to have been instrumental in his majesty's restoration it is fit that care be taken to satisfy their arrears pursuant to his majesty's letter from Breda wherein there is no engagement for assuring lands unto them and therefore after examination of the profits received hitherto enjoyed on that possession what shall appear to remain unpaid of those arrears to be satisfied in some equal way out of the Kingdom in general for discharge of his majesty's said engagement for those officers and soldiers who were instrumental in his majesty's restoration, have a great obligation in his majesty's subjects in general and merit well, full satisfaction of their arrears, yet it ought not to light only on the estates of those who are justly restorable as innocent persons or as adherers to the said Peace.

If this way of settlement for the several landed interests in Ireland be taken, then all genuine Adventurers and all officers and soldiers who can justly pretend any arrears will be put in a way of satisfaction and all innocent persons and all adherers to his majesty's peace will have their own without . . . any of those who were enforced upon pain of death by the usurper to transplant into Connacht and Clare and to take lands there.

DOCUMENT 2
REASONS ENFORCING THE PERFORMANCE OF HIS MAJESTY'S PEACE, MADE IN IRELAND IN THE YEAR 1648

That the peace granted to the Irish in the said year was not injurious or unjust for his majesty to grant for several reasons.

First he granted nothing to them but their own or what was formerly theirs, he gave them not the estates of any others of his subjects, that which some may complain of is the granting of Churches etc., by the said peace there is no tie on his majesty for those things but 'till a settlement and his majesty's pleasure be known in Parliament.

Is any man blinded with his own interest so much as to think it unreasonable for his majesty to give such a party his own subjects upon far harder terms than to give them an Act of Indemnity for all their former transgressions to endeavour to rescue his royal father out of the hands of his wicked murderers nay had heralded in the very Turks and given them the estates of such villains, how could they justly blame him.

Is it worthy consideration if that peace had been in itself unreasonable as it is not, whether the blame should not altogether be imputed to those who would now (right or wrong) hold the estates of the Irish were not those the men who put this necessity in part on his majesty, were not they the men who adhered to all interests and resolutions to serve their own turns those eighteen years past and not his majesty's; were not those the men who with hearts and hands enjoyed with the regicides and approved and justified the murder of the king, were not those the people who moved and voted the perpetual extirpation and banishment of the royal family and cried down Church and Nobility.

It is to be considered for what services they will keep his majesty's subjects' estates; is it not for their rebellion and service under Cromwell since the murder of our king; O God what an impudence it is for the greatest of rebels (if the Act of Indemnity had not interposed) to dare open their mouths to keep ones subjects' estates in recompense of such treachery and rebellion, if they be not blinded with too much self interests, would not they have thought themselves to have met the most gracious and indulgent crime that ever was, to confer honours and offices of profit and trust both in military and civil employments upon them and to give a general pardon for all their offences and such of them as had estates formerly to let them enjoy them, such as had not it were pity to reward their rebellion with granting them other mens estates.

Is there any colour to reward those people in Ireland better than the army in England who were the immediate actors in his majesty's restoration and had it been well examined many of those in Ireland did not know that the design was laid for restoring the king, if they had they would not join so freely; nay did not many of them oppose by surprising towns and forts and striving for the government there when they had a hint of bringing in his majesty.

It is likewise offered to consideration whether there hath not been a general . . . in the three nations and whether the Irish claiming the benefit of his majesty's said peace and who disowned the non adherers thereunto or any who had his immediate hand in murder ought not to have their own estates, rather than those who did worse to light only on the estates of those who are justly restorable as innocent persons or as adherers to the said peace.

The Irish had no hand in abetting the horrid murder of his sacred majesty and must they only be excluded from his mercy and an Act of Indemnity. It may well be asked why any officer or soldier who betrayed any of his majesty's garrisons during the war, especially to the regicides should have any arrears given them or who had not a hand in his majesty's restoration and certainly they who contrived his restoration in Ireland were not many and did not begin it until their army was broken in pieces amongst themselves. I pass by whether there was not a necessity on some of the greatest men in Ireland to prevent the malice of some of their own party had against them to bring in the king and were it not a sufficient reward for such as had a hand in his majesty's restoration, considering what they have done against his royal father and himself to give them an indemnity to confer titles of honour and places of profit in the civil and martial list on them and to enjoy their own estates without diminution as aforesaid.

It is worthy his majesty's consideration whether religion ought to admit so much inconvenience to fall on the one side and advantage to the other or whether on pretence of preserving an English Interest the Catholics of Ireland who are a considerable number of English extraction and who preserved the interest of the crown of England there for five hundred years must now be destroyed for a new sort of people who made it their work ever since they had a power in Ireland to destroy monarchy, Church, Nobility and Gentry, as appears by their former actions.

It is to be duly weighted how inconsistent it would be with his majesty's public faith, honour, interest and safety to give away his subjects estates that suffered so much and served so faithfully unto such persons and how inconsistent it would be to turn the Declaration and Instructions into a law in which there are so many ambiguities and contradictory expressions inserted that it cannot be put in execution before it be well explained; and how unreasonable the Bill is for making of it into a law may appear plainly by the aspersions cast in the Preamble on all the nation but such as were of Cromwell's party; and that it makes the dispossessions, sequestrations, transplantations and seizures of Cromwell the ground work of the forfeiture of estates in Ireland.

That those who were dispossessed by the usurper were such as holds their estates by the gift of his majesty's royal predecessors for service to them performed, and the now possessors of those estates deriving their interests from the usurper and their settlement as the reward of their activities against his majesty and his father's glorious memory. And the giving way to such possessions may tend to confirm the said now interests, established by a usurper, by which the obligation of enjoying those estates will pass to posterity as being the recompense of their service against the crown and become an encouragement to the like evil activities in the future.

APPENDIX VI
PATRICK BELLEW'S AFFIDAVIT TO THE COMMISSION OF GRACE 1684[5]

Patrick Bellew Esq., came this day before me and made oath that he is seized of the lands hereafter mentioned and is thereof by himself, his under-tenants and those deriving under him, in the present and actual possession and receiving the rents, issues and profits thereof these many years, that is to say:

The castle town and lands of Clonoraneighter containing 362 acres profitable and 294 unprofitable, the town and lands of Cloncalgy containing 172 acres profitable and 105 acres unprofitable, the town and lands of Tomree alias Moilagh containing 338 acres profitable and 128 unprofitable with two loughs thereon, the town and lands of Carrownaboe alias Carrownaborr containing 96 acres profitable and 36 unprofitable with the lough thereon, all lying and being in the barony of Tiaquin and county of Galway. The town and lands of Corgarragh alias Corgarroweighter and Corgarrowoughter with the mills and fishing weir containing 133 acres profitable and 33 unprofitable, lying and being in the half barony of Killyhan and county of Galway aforesaid. The town and lands of Clonoranoughter containing 142 acres profitable and 59 unprofitable, in possession of part by exchange and mortgage, the town and lands of Carrowneirigii alias Carrowneireggii containing 182 acres profitable and 111 are unprofitable, in possession of part by way of trust, in the four quarters of Mullaghmore 19 acres profitable and 14 acres unprofitable, in and about Keilneseire in the said 4 quarters with a wood thereunto belonging, in the town and lands of Loghmerisk alias Laghimorirty 117a.2r.27p., profitable and about 56 unprofitable in possession of part, lying and being in the said barony of Tiaquin and county of Galway. In the town and lands of Eskerow 11 acres profitable and about 44 unprofitable commonly called Killadow also lying and being in the said barony of Tiaquin and county of Galway. In the town and lands of Knockmackehill alias Knockmaskhall 3 acres profitable and about 7 acres unprofitable lying and being in the half barony of Bellamoe and county aforesaid. In the town and lands of Ballingarry, Cloghmoyle and Gortera 2 quarters 165 acres profitable and 1 acres unprofitable lying and being in the barony of Dunkellin and county aforesaid. In the town and lands of Ballinekill and Cregan 40 acres profitable and 21 unprofitable. In the town and lands of Ballinlassy 3 acres profitable. In the town and lands of Carrownegapul 20 acres profitable and a proportionable thereof unprofitable lying and being in the half barony of Killyan aforesaid and said county of Galway.

The castle town and lands of Barmeath with Gallagh and Hinostown parcels thereof containing 398a.1r.00p., profit' land. The town and lands of Dromin containing 76a.2.r.00p., profitable. The town and lands of Hitchestown containing 91a.1r.00p. The town and lands of Graftonstown containing 88a.1r.00 profitable. In the town and lands of Desart alias Disart 210 acres profitable land, the castle town and lands of Walshestown containing 110 acres profitable. The town and lands of Baggotstown containing 241a.1r.00p., profitable. The town and lands of Killcallaght alias Killtallaght containing 207a.3r.00p., profitable lands. In the town and lands of Rathdrumore 7 acres profitable, and a house and backside part of Drumgoother. The town and lands of Drumgoother containing 74 acres profitable. The town and lands of Reynoldstown containing 187a.1r.00p., profitable land. The town and lands of Garolaugh alias Garulagh alias Garrvagh containing 39 acres profitable land, lying and being in the barony of Ferrard and county of Louth.

DETAILS OF THE LANDS CONVEYED BY LETTERS PATENT TO PATRICK BELLEW [IN THE COUNTY OF LOUTH][6]

X:	The manor, castle town and lands of Barmeath, now to be called Bellewmount, with Heinstown, Gallagh and Mooregrange, sub-divisions of Barmeath.	398a.1r.00p.
X.	Dromin.	76a.2r.00p.
X.	Hitchestown and its sub-denomination of Bellewgrane.	91a.1r.00p.
X.	Gratistown alias Graftonstown.	88a.1r.00p.
X.	Dishard alias Desard and its sub-denominations of Levinsgrane and Dowdallsgrane with a lough.	210a.0r.00p.
0:	The castle, town and lands of Welshestown to be called Bellewscourt	110a.0r.00p.
O.	Baggotstown.	241a.0r.00p.
O.	Kiltalaght with two mills. 207a.3r.00p.	
O.	Dromgooter. 74a.0r.00p.	
O.	More of Dromgooter with a house and garden intermixed in lands of Rathdruminure.	7a.0r.00p.
X.	Reynoldstown with several Warrens thereunto belonging.	179a.1r.00p.
X.	Garralaugh alias Garvagh.	39a.0r.00p.
	[TOTALS]	[1722a.1r.00p.]

To hold the lands thus O marked to his heirs and assigns for ever; to hold the lands thus X marked to the use of himself for life; subject to the jointures, debts, legacies etc., of the last will of his father John Bellew Esquire dated 17 February 1672; remainder to his son and heir apparent Patrick Bellew and the heirs male of his body, remainder to his second son Richard and the issue male, remainder to his third son Christopher and his heirs male, remainder to the heirs male of his own body, remainder to the uses limited and appointed by his father's will, remainder to his own right heirs for ever.

[IN THE COUNTY OF GALWAY]

DENOMINATION	ACREAGE PROFITABLE	ACREAGE UNPROFITABLE
BARONY OF TIAQUIN		
The castle manor towns and lands of Clonoraneightragh now to be called Castle-Bellew, 2 quarters	362. 0.00	294.0.00
Tomree alias Moylagh 2 quarters	338.0.00	118.0.00 & lough
Cloncalgy 1 quarter	172.0.00	105.0.00
Carrowneboe alias Caronobber 1 quarter	96.0.00	36.0.00 & lough
Clonoranoughter 1 quarter	142.0.00	59.0.00
Carrownecreggy 1 quarter	182.0.00	111.0.00
In Mullaghmore	19.0.00	14.0.00
In and about Killneshiere with a wood thereunto belonging. In Loughmericke alias Laghtmurierty being one cartron called ye Creggans of Laghtmuriety	57.3.00	
More in John Bodkin's proportion of said quarter in Common	5.1.00	56.0.00 to both
The quarter of Eskeroe called Killedowan	117.0.00	49.0.00
BARONY OF KILLYAN		
Corgarrow alias Corgarroweighter and Corgarrowoughter 1 quarter with the mills and fishing weares thereunto belonging	133.0.00	33.0.00
Ballynekill & Cregane	40.0.00	21.0.00
In Ballinlassy	3.0.00	
In Carrownegapill 1 quarter in Common	20.0.00	proportion
BARONY OF BELLAMOE		
In Knockmaskehill alias Knockmaskall	3.0.00	7.0.00
BARONY OF DUNKELLIN		
In Ballingarry Cloghmoyle and Gortroe	165.0.00	1.0.00

The lands in Galway created the manor of Clonoraneightragh alias Castlebellew, with power to hold courts leet and baron, a law day or court of records, to build and keep a prison, to appoint bailiffs, seneschals, gaolers and other officers, to enjoy all waifs, strays, fishings etc., and to make a park with free warren and chase, to erect dove and pigeonhouses.

The lands in County Louth to be created the manor of Barmeath alias Bellewmount with the like privileges.

APPENDIX VII
THE MARRIAGE SETTLEMENT OF PATRICK BELLEW AND ELISABETH BARNEWALL[7]

The ensuing are the agreements concluded upon betwixt Sir Richard Barnewall of Crickstown in the county of Meath Baronet and John Bellew of Willistown in the county of Louth Esq., this 7 January 1663 which agreement is by them desired to be drawn up in form of law:

FIRST: It is agreed betwixt the aforenamed parties that Patt. Bellew son and heir apparent of the said John, and Elisabeth Barnewall one of the daughters of the said Richard shall according unto the laws of holy Church be married unto each other, at any time upon the reasonable request of the said Sir Richard or the said John, at or before the last day of this present Jan.

ITEM: In consideration of the said marriage the said Sir Richard is to give unto the said John as a portion and preferment in marriage with his said daughter, the full sum of six hundred pound str., pursuant unto a feoffement made by the said Sir Richard upon intermarriage with the Lady Julian Barnewall alias Alymer mother of the said Elisabeth.

ITEM: In consideration of the said portion the said John is to maintain the young couple until the said portion shall be paid, and upon payment of the said portion, the said John is to give unto them the said young couple, four-score pounds str., yearly during the said John's life, and in case the said Elisabeth shall overlive the said Patrick then she is to have the said eighty pounds str., yearly during her natural life as a dower or jointure.

ITEM: The said John at the reasonable request of the said Sir Richard to settle and conveigh (sic) all such real estate and leases which he shall have (or shall any wayes acquire) unto such feoffees in trust, as shall be indifferently chosen by the said Sir Richard and the said John ; to the use of the said John for life, the remainder to the said Patt. For life, the remainder to the first begotten son of the said Patt., and so to the rest of the sons begotten by the said Patrick on the body of the said Elisabeth, and so with remainders over, as in course of descent ought to be, to the heirs of the body of the said John, the remainder in fee to the right heirs of Sir John Bellew of Bellewstown in the county of Meath knight forever, with a proviso that the said John may charge his said estate with the sum of three hundred pounds str., and no more, towards the preferment of his youngest children, in case he shall not otherwise provide for them in his lifetime and that the said John's wife, shall have such jointure or dower as the said John did agree to make upon his intermarriage, and that such children as the said Patt., shall have by the said Elisabeth shall have such portions respectively as the said Patt., and the said feoffees shall think fit to appoint for them, after the death of the said John.

In witness of all and singular the premises the said Sir Richard and the said John have to these presents interchangeably put their hands and seals the day first within written.

R. Barnewall John Bellew.

Being present at the signing sealing and delivering hereof:
Anthony Gearnon: Augustine Darcy.

Patrick Bellew Esquire Plaintiff -v- James Bellew Gentleman

These Articles were produced unto Augustine Darcy at the time of his examination on the plaintiff's behalf dated the 29 January 1684. William Scott.

APPENDIX VIII
COPY OF BOND DATED 7 JANUARY 1664 BETWEEN JOHN BELLEW AND SIR RICHARD BARNEWALL

Know all men by these presents that I John Bellew of Clonoran in the county of Galway Esquire do hereby acknowledge [myself] to be injustly owing and indebted unto Sir Richard Barnewall Baronet in the just and full sum of four thousand pounds sterling current and lawful money of . . . in England to be paid unto the said Sir Richard Barnewall his heirs, executors administrators or assignees at his or their will and pleasure for which payment well and truly to be made and done I the said John Bellew do by these presents bind myself my executors and administrators and trustees firmly by these presents in witness whereof I have hereunto put my hand this 7 day of January 1663.

Whereas the abovesaid Sir Richard Barnewall has married Elisabeth Barnewall one of his daughters to Patt.Bellew son and heir of the abovesaid John Bellew upon condition and in consideration that the said John Bellew should leave to his said son and heir all the estate, mortgages and leases that he then had [or] should have or that any other in trust or otherwise acquire with any of the said John's money be it in whose name soever and that . . . with any manner of incumbrance whatsoever be it by lease or otherwise except the incumbrance of three hundred pounds which three hundred pounds the said John hath power to leave on the said estate it he should leave of his younger children otherwise unprovided for as also leave unto his wife all such jointure as was agreed for her on her intermarriage and no more, all which is pursuant unto the agreement made on the intermarriage of the said Patt. and Elisabeth.

The condition therefore of the above obligation is such that if the said John Bellew shall clearly and freely leave unto the said Patt Bellew the estate he now hath in his possession as also all the estate, mortgages and leases he has or shall acquire be it in his own name or any other name or that he or any other shall acquire with the said John's money during the said John's life without any incumbrance whatsoever except the above said incumbrance and the said John shall in every point upon the request of the said Sir Richard do settle upon the said Patt.Bellew and his heirs forever the said [estate] then the obligation to be void otherwise to be in full force in virtue of same.

John Bellew.

Being present we whose names . . . Anthony Gearnon: Augustine Darcy.

Patrick Bellew Esquire Plaintiff -v- James Bellew Gentleman

This Bond was produced unto Augustine Darcy at the time of his examination on the plaintiff's behalf dated the 29 January 1684. William Scott.

Notes

CHAPTER ONE

1 See Harold O'Sullivan, 'The march of south-east Ulster in the fifteenth and sixteenth centuries: a period of change' in Raymond Gillespie & Harold O'Sullivan (eds.), *The Borderlands: Essays on the History of the Ulster Leinster Border* (Belfast, 1989), chapter 5.
2 For the O'Hanlons of Orier in the early seventeenth century, see George Hill, *An Historical Account of the Plantation in Ulster at the Commencement of the Seventeenth Century 1609–1620* (IUP Reprint, Shannon, 1970), p. 64.
3 For Sir Patrick Gernon of Killencoole, see Brendan Bradshaw, *The Irish Constitutional Revolution of the Sixteenth Century* (Cambridge, 1979) p. 212; for Chamberlain of Nistlerath, see Harold O'Sullivan, 'Letitia Brownlow' in 'Women in County Louth in the seventeenth century' *JLAHS*, xxiii, no. 3 (1995), p. 351; for Richard Hadsor, see Evelyn P. Shirley, *The History of the County of Monaghan* (London, 1879), pp. 107–8.
4 J.C.W. Wylie, *Irish Land Law*, 2nd edn (London, 1986), pp. 4–6.
5 See Brendan Smith, 'The medieval border Anglo-Irish and Gaelic Irish in the late thirteenth and early fourteenth century Uriel', in Gillespie & O'Sullivan, *Borderlands*, chapter 4 and Brendan Smith 'The English in Uriel 1170–1330', Unpublished Ph.D. thesis University of Dublin 1990.
6 O'Sullivan, 'The march of south East Ulster' in Gillespie and O'Sullivan *Borderlands*.
7 Harold O'Sullivan, 'The landed gentry of the county of Louth in the age of the Tudors' in *JLAHS*, xxii, (1994), no. 1, pp. 71–73.
8 NA, Bellew Papers, no. 5228 Chancery Bill O'Neill v Bellew, 1614 and Tomás O'Fiaich, 'The O'Neills of the Fews' in *Seanchas Ardmacha*, vii, no. 1, (1973), pp. 50–51.
9 NA, Bellew Papers 1121/2/5; Grant dated 1 November 1399 from John Kennefer to John Bedelew Knight and John Boscome the younger of 'all his lands in Kenferarath, Lestrany, Little Arthurstown, Nicholestown, Mochlistraney, Louth, Ardee and all his other lands in County Louth'; 6 June 1408, Quit claim William Kenefer to John Kennefer.
10 O'Sullivan, 'The landed gentry of the county of Louth', pp. 68–69.
11 Charles McNeill and A.J. Otway-Ruthven, *Dowdall Deeds* (Dublin 1960), p. x; A.J. Otway-Ruthven, 'The partition of the De Verdon lands in Ireland in 1332' in *Proceedings of the Royal Irish Academy*, vol. 66, section C, no. 5, p. 417 (1968).
12 Otway-Ruthven, 'The partition of the De Verdon lands', pp. 417 and 425.
13 *Ibid*, p. 425.
14 See 'Manuscript History' of the Bellew family by The Hon. Mrs Richard Bellew, NA, Bellew Papers 1121/2/1.
15 *Ibid.*, Bellew Papers 1121/2/2 and 3 (Sir John Bellew, 1622–1600).
16 For the early history of the Bellews of Lisrenny and Willistown, see NA Manuscript History John Bellew and Patrick Bellew of Lisraney & Graftontown 1121/2/5.
17 *IORCHAL*, Car.I, no. 42, 9 August 1638, NA, 'Manuscript History' 1121/2/5.
18 NA, 1121 1/5 no. 37; BP, 'my father's will'.

19 John Foster, (ed.), *Register of Admissions to Grey's Inns 1521–1889* (London, 1889), no. 182, described as John Bellew, son and heir of Patrick Bellew of Graftonstown.
20 BP, Entitled 'Hadsor's acknowledgement unto me', 30 November 1630.
21 BP, entitled 'Articles William Moore for the 95 acres in Hitcheston'.
22 BP, no. 52 entitled 'copie of the Statute Staple dated the 7 December 1638 for £400 acknowledged by John Taaffe, George Russell and George Taaffe to John Bellew Willistown'; NA,'Bellew Papers', 1121/1/2.
23 BP, no. 25, entitled Patrick McEntire the younger, Patrick Conlan, Patrick Hoey, Patrick Kenedy, George Fulchagh, Nicholas McEntire, Jo.Crooly, Patrick Crooly, Thomas Frydy, and Patrick Dawe all of Clogher, fishermen their bond to pay £31.10 stg., at will and pleasure.
24 NLI, *Report on Private Collections, no. 3*, Dillon Papers, calendar of will of Robert Dillon dated 14 December 1628; The Honourable Mrs. Richard Bellew, 'John Bellew of Willistown 1606–1679' in *JLAHS*, vi, no. 4 (1928) pp. 229–237; BP, several documents dealing with the sale of Willistown to John Bellew by George Gernon of Dunmahon through trustees, Gerard Colley Ardee and Peter Barnewall of Terenure County Dublin.
25 Bellew, 'John Bellew of Willistown', p. 230.
26 *Ibid.*, p. 230.

CHAPTER TWO

1 For the Old English at this period, see Aidan Clarke, *The Old English in Ireland 1625–42*, (London 1966), and 'Colonial Constitutional Attitudes in Ireland 1640–1660' in *Proceedings of the Royal Irish Academy*, 90, C, no. 11 (1990).
2 For the Graces, see Aidan Clarke, *The Graces 1625–41* (Dundalk, 1968).
3 For the 1640 Parliament, see Hugh Kearney, *Strafford in Ireland 1633–41 A Study in Absolutism*, (Cambridge, 1989), chapter 13 and for the members of this Parliament, see Appendix 11, and M. Perceval-Maxwell, *The Outbreak of the Irish Rebellion of 1641* (Dublin 1994), pp. 67–91 and 92–117.
4 For the Remonstrance, see *JHCI*, v. 1, p. 279–282 and Edmund Curtis and R.B. McDowell (eds.), *Irish Historical Documents 1172–1922* (London, 1943) pp. 142–146.
5 *JHCE.*, p. 32, 20 November 1640, 'Remonstrance given in and noted'; p. 39, 30 November 1640 'The two gents John Bellew and Oliver Cashell who brought over these petitions were called in and the Speaker told them the House has taken into account your petitions'.
6 Copies of these petitions are in NLI Mountbellew papers, Ms.31884 (a); a copy of the petition to the king is also to be found in BL, Add.Chart. 9324; a copy of the petition to the English Parliament is in BL Egerton 1048 p. 13 (1); see also J.T. Gilbert *Facsimiles of the National; Manuscripts of Ireland*, (Dublin, 1884), v. l, pp. 316–7 which gives the signatories to the petitions.
7 For the Select Committee and their instructions, see Curtis and McDowell, *Irish Historical Documents*, pp. 146–7.
8 *JHCI*, 1, pp. 295–6.
9 *JHCI*, 1, pp 305–481.
10 Karen J. Harvey, 'The Family Experience: The Bellews of Mount Bellew' in T.P. Power and Kevin Whelan, *Endurance and Emergence: Catholics in Ireland in the Eighteenth Century* (Irish Academic Press, 1990), pp. 190–191.
11 J.T. Gilbert, *A Contemporary History of Affairs in Ireland from 1641–1652* (Dublin, 1880), 1, ii, 'Deposition by George Creichtonn' [sic] 15 April 1643, p. 543.

12 *JHCI*, pp. 378–381.
13 *Ibid.*, pp. 380–381.
14 M. Perceval-Maxwell, *The Outbreak of the Irish Rebellion*, pp. 179–191.
15 *JHCI*, i, pp. 507 and 516.
16 M. Perceval-Maxwell, *The Outbreak of the Irish Rebellion*, p. 186.
17 William J.Smith and Kevin Whelan (eds.), *Common Ground Essays on the Historical Geography of Ireland, presented to T. Jones Hughes*, (Cork University Press), 1988, pp. 60 and 65 and J. Edwards, 'A Rural Geography of County Louth' (Unpublished Masters Thesis, UCD, 1965); Sir William Brereton *Travels in Holland, the United Provinces, England, Scotland and Ireland 1635*, edited by Edward Hawkins (Chetham Society, 1884).
18 Nicholas Bernard, *The Whole Proceedings of the Siege of Drogheda in Ireland* (Dublin, 1736), p. 1.
19 NLI, Peppard Papers, D.!6,186 13 July 1653, testimonial by Doctor N. Bernard in favour of Mr George Peppard.
20 For the evil effects of the 'drinking shops' of Dundalk on a party of Owen Roe O'Neill's army who tarried too long in them before marching off with a consignment of gun-powder and were subsequently slaughtered by a force under Inchiquin on the 15 July 1648, see Gilbert, *Affairs in Ireland*, ii, pp. 37–38; for County Louth and the export of linen yarn, see Kearney *Strafford in Ireland*, pp. 154–159.
21 William J. Smith and Kevin Whelan (eds.), *Common Ground*, pp. 60 and 65.
22 Brereton, *Travels*.
23 For McKiernan, see Harold O'Sullivan, 'The Franciscans in Dundalk', *Seanchas Ardmhacha*, iv, no. 1, (1960–61), pp. 58–59.
24 M. Hickson (ed.), *Ireland in the Seventeenth Century: The Irish Massacres of 1641-2, their Causes and Results*, (London, 1884), i, Appendix R, pp. 341-3.
25 Robert C. Simington, *The Civil Survey* AD *1654–1656*, 'County of Kildare', viii, (Dublin, 1952), pp. 175–177; Public Library Armagh, 'Claims appointed to be heard and determined by his majesty's commissioners appointed to execute the Act for the settlement of Ireland 1662–1668': no. 198; claim by Sir Paul Davis in respect of the lands of Thomastown near Ballina County Kildare, setting forth that Roger Moore late of Dundalk, in the county of Louth, esquire, being seized in fee of and in the premises, did in consideration of £300 paid to him by Margaret Gibbons . . . did demise [by deed 1635] all and singular the premises . . . for the term of 1,000 years . . . provision for redemption; NA 'Book of Survey and Distribution', Quit Rent Office Copy shows lands in the parishes of Kilsleve and Loughilly in the barony of Orier as held by Roger Moore these lands were subsequently recovered in the Restoration Land settlement by the earl of Castlehaven; see Harold O'Sullivan 'The Restoration Land Settlement in the Diocese of Armagh', in *Seanchas Ardmhacha 1660 to 1684*, xvi, no. 1. (1994) p. 22; For the Castlehaven interests in these lands, see Hill, *Plantation*, p. 535.
26 NA, Bellew Papers 1121/1/1, appointed by Parsons and Borlace 29 October 1641.
27 *JHCI*, i, p. 495.
28 For recent studies of the insurrection of 1641, see Brian Mac Cuarta (ed.), *Ulster 1641: Aspects of the Rising* (Belfast, 1993), Chapters 5–7; Perceval- Maxwell, *The Outbreak of the Irish Rebellion* (Dublin, 1994), chapters 9 to 12; Jane H. Ohlmeyer, *Civil War and the Restoration in the Three Stuart Kingdoms: The Career of Randal MacDonnell, Marquis of Antrim 1609–1683* (1993), chapter 4 and Jane H. Ohlmeyer (ed.), *Ireland, 'From Independence to Occupation 1641 –1660'*, (Cambridge, 1995), chapters 1 and 2.
29 Bernard, *Siege of Drogheda*, pp. 4–5.

CHAPTER THREE

1. The Depositions of the county of Louth have been transcribed from TCD Ms., F.3.5, fol. 1–57, by Thomas Fitzpatrick and edited for publication by T. Gogarty in *JLAHS.*, iii, nos. 1 and 2, (1912–1913).
2. Perceval-Maxwell, *The Outbreak of the Irish Rebellion of 1641* (Dublin 1994) pp. 242–46.
3. Bernard, *Whole Proceedings*, p. 10.
4. For the commission of martial law issed to John Bellew, see NLI, Mountbellew Papers, Ms.31883, 30 October 1641 signed by Borlace and Parsons; Bernard, *Whole Proceedings*, p. 14, 'before this regiment [Tichborne's] came to us, at the earnest request of the said sheriff of Louth [John Bellew], the State was so far moved as to send down three hundred arms, for the defence of that county (who had not then declared themselves) with about forty more for the guard of Dundalk, but the suspicion of their treachery scenting stronger here than possibly it might twenty miles further, were by my Lord Moore stopped in their passage'.
5. Gilbert, *Affairs in Ireland*, 1i, p. 370–1.
6. Gilbert, *Affairs in Ireland*, 1i, Appendix 38, Proclamation by the Lords Justices at Dublin 8 February 1641-2, P.383–393; *Bellings*, ii, Appendix 34 22 June 1642 'List of members expelled from the House of Commons in Ireland on charge of High Treason.
7. NLI, Mountbellew Papers, Ms.31, 882.
8. For Read's deposition taken on the rack, see *Bellings*, i, pp. 298–299.
9. Robert Dunlop, *Ireland under the Commonwealth*, 2 vols, (Manchester, 1919), i, pp. cxx–cxxi.
10. Richard Bellings, *History of the Irish Confederation and the War in Ireland*, edited by J.T. Gilbert (Dublin, 1891), i, pp. 259–61; Karl S. Bottigheimer *English Money and Irish Land*, (Oxford, 1971) pp. 40–44; M. Perceval-Maxwell, *The Outbreak of the Rebellion*, pp. 260–84, See also BL, Egerton Ms, 1048 p. 14 (1) 7 (2), 'Articles of the Treaty concerning the reducing the kingdom of Ireland to the obedience of the King's Majesty and Crown of England agreed between the Commissioners for Scotland authorised by His Majesty and the parliament of that Kingdom and the Commissioners for England authorised by His Majesty and the Parliament of that Kingdom at Westminster.'
11. *JLAHS.*, 'Depositions', ii, no. 1 (1912), p. 78 and no. 2 (1913), pp. 168–9.
12. NLI, Mountbellew Papers, Ms.31,946.
13. Robert C. Simington, *The Civil Survey 1654–6, Miscellanea*, (Dublin, 1961) x, p. 66.
14. Fynes Moryson, *An History of Ireland, from the year 1599 to 1603: with a short narration of the state of the kingdom from the year 1169, to which is added a description of Ireland*, 2 vols. (Dublin, 1735), i, p. 185–188.
15. *JLAHS*, iii, no. 1, (1912), p. 79.
16. Bernard, *Whole Proceedings*, pp. 13–16.
17. *Ibid.*
18. BP.
19. See Bellings, *History*, i, pp. 236–253 for various submissions by the Pale gentry as conveyed by Lieutenant-Colonel Read.
20. HMC, *Ormond Manuscripts*, N.S., ii, pp. 24–7.
21. BP, the pass is signed by Tichborne and Lord Moore.
22. *Bellings*, i, *History*, appendix XIX pp. 268–285, 'Contemporary Account of Proceedings of Confederates in Leinster 1641-2', including depositions.
23. Bernard, *Whole Proceedings*, pp. 38–40.
24. *Affairs in Ireland* i, pp. 374–379.
25. Bernard, *Whole Proceedings*, pp. 39–40

26 From the arrival of Ormond to the taking of Dundalk see Bernard, *Whole Proceedings*, pp. 85–93
27 Sir John Temple, *The Irish Rebellion* (7th. edn Cork, 1766), Tichborne's letter to his wife; for the hanging of the bailiff of Dundalk and others, see King's Inn Library, 'Prendergast Papers; Ormond's letter on behalf of Lord Dungannon', viii, pp. 810–817.
28 The Hon. Mrs Bellew, 'John Bellew of Willistown 1606–1679' in *JLAHS*., vi, no. 4 (1928), pp. 229–237.
29 Ibid., p. 235, BP, letter dated 19 June 1654, evidently obtained by Bellew as part of his case against transplantation.
30 NA, Bellew Papers, Manuscript History 1121/2/5.
31 *Gilbert, Affairs in Ireland*, i, p. 536 and 543.

CHAPTER FOUR

1 Bellings, *History*, ii, p. 213
2 Mrs Bellew, 'John Bellew of Willistown', p. 231.
3 For an appraisal of the Leinster army of the Confederation including artillery, see Rolf Loeber and Geoffrey Parker, 'The Military Revolution in Seventeenth Century Ireland', in Jane Ohlmeyer (ed.), *Ireland*, pp. 70–88
4 NA, Bellew Papers, 1121/1/7 no. 24, pp. 25–7; Bellings, *History*, v, p. 30.
5 Ibid., p. 74.
6 Jerrold I. Casway, *Owen Roe O'Neill and the Struggle for Catholic Ireland* (Philadelphia, 1984), pp. 84–88.
7 Ibid., p. 88.
8 NLI, Mountbellew Papers Ms.31,998, testimony by Owen Roe O'Neill on behalf of Lieutenant-General John Bellew, 19 September 1643; O'Neill marked the victory at Portlester by giving a financial reward to the party which was involved in the defence of the mill.
9 Ibid., pp. 88–9.
10 See David Stevenson, *Scottish Covenanters and Irish Confederates: Scottish-Irish Relations in the mid-seventeenth century* (Belfast, 1981) pp. 103–139.
11 IORCHAL, 39 Car.1 inquisitions postmortem taken at Beaulieu 18 March 1644, nos. 50 and 51, on the estates of John Babe of Darver and William Plunkett of Beaulieu both of whom had been captains in Barnewall's regiment.
12 JHCI, li, p. 329 Petition May 1644 by Nicholas Gernon.
13 Dawe's freehold in Braganstown is referred to in *IORCHAL*, 16–23 Car.1, no. 23, 23 April 1633; inquisition postmortem, Christopher Taaffe of Braganstown; BP, Deed 1 November 1644 by Thomas Dawe of Dunany, heir apparent to Patrick and Richard Dawe late of Braganstown who 'by these presents demise, sett and to farm let unto John Bellew of Willistown . . . for divers good and valuable considerations as also for that the said John doth relieve myself my wife and family in these miserable times as likewise for and in consideration of the sum of £10stg'; BP, 11 January 1645 bond by Thomas Dawe to give seizen of the town lands and fields of Braganstown, Mansfieldstown, Drumcashell, Milltown and Dundalk to John Bellew.
14 BP, entitled the Deed of Malanescreagh, Finvoy and Simonston dated 20 May 1645 certified by Nicholas . . . Patrick Plunkett and Richard Carwell that they were present when William Moore delivered a clod of earth to John Bellew, in the field over against the tavern of Verdonstown and likewise at St Patrick's Well.
15 BP, endorsed 'my brother Darcy's acknowledgement for the £26 due unto me on Taaffe of Braganstown.'

16 This Richard Dillon may be identical with the Richard Dillon of Cloonbroke County Galway who recovered forfeited estates in Dublin, Westmeath, Galway and Roscommon in the restoration land settlement; he had two brothers Thomas and Lucas both of whom died in the year 1647; the estates at Clonbrock had not however been confiscated; as this was the family of John Bellew's wife Mary, these may have been her brothers, Public Library Armagh, 'Submissions and Evidence', 'Claims appointed', no. 241 and PROI, *Appendix to the Nineteenth Report of the Deputy-keeper*, 'Abstract of the Decrees of the Court of Claims', p. 53, no. 226.

17 Harold O'Sullivan, 'Military operations in County Louth in the run-up to Cromwell's storming of Drogheda', *JLAHS*, xxii, no. 2 (1990); see also Proclamation concerning the 'protection of Roman Catholic subjects . . . occasioned by the advance of some forces out of the north, 3 April 1647 in *HMC*, 'Ormonde Manuscripts', ii, part 1, pp. 56–7.

18 Bellings, *History*, vi, p. 145; see also Thomas L. Coonan, *The Irish Catholic Confederacy and the Puritan Revolution* (Dublin, 1954), chapter 16, 'The Clerical coup d'etat'.

19 Bellings, *History*, v, pp. 30–33.

20 Coonan, *The Irish Catholic Confederacy*, pp. 230–1.

21 *Ibid.*, pp. 235–37

22 *Ibid.*, p. 237.

23 *Ibid.*, pp. 239–40.

24 Bellings, *History*, vi, p. 80 and 84.

25 *CSPI 1633–1647*, p. 540, 2 November 1646, 'muster of the Leinster army'.

26 Barnabas O'Ferrall and Daniel O'Connell, (eds.), *Commentarius Rinuccinianus* (Dublin 1932–1949), iv, p. 291 and ii, pp. 431–2.

27 Mrs Bellew, 'John Bellew of Willistown', p. 233.

28 Thomas L. Coonan, *Catholic Conferences*, pp. 244–248.

29 Bellings, *History*, vii; Bellings comments on Bagnall's speech was that it moved the General Assembly 'to compassion, and some of the prelates had a feeling sense of his discourse. But their resolution had cast roots too deep to be shaken'.

30 Mrs Bellew, 'John Bellew', pp. 233–4; Bellings, *History*, vii, p. 348; payments to army of Leinster, Portlester Camp, 5 August 1647, mention of the pay for the train of artillery; see also p. 346 for the pay of the 'officers and others of the train of artillery' which provided eight shillings per diem for the commander of the artillery.

31 Padraig Lenihan, 'The Leinster Army and the battle of Dungan's Hill 1647' in *The Irish Sword*, xviii, no. 71 (1991), p. 145.

32 NA, 'Carte Transcripts', xxi, p. 101, Ormond to the Commissioners for the county of Louth, 28 May 1647, 'granted unto Lieutenant-Colonel John Bellay a custodium of the town and lands of Willistown and Cashellstown in the county of Louth, lately belonging to John Bellew now in rebellion'.

33 Bellings, *History*, pp. 236; 244–245; Mrs Bellew, 'John Bellew' p. 234 and NLI, 'Mountbellew Papers, Ms.31,966, commission signed by Ormond to John Bellew as captain to command 'the company now under his command' 'for the train of artillery'.

34 His commission as 'lieutenant of the ordnance throughout the kingdom' is dated 11 August 1650 and is in NLI Mountbellew Papers, Ms.31,966.

35 NA, Carte Transcripts, vol. 25, p. 1 and Bellings, *History*, vii, p. 123.

36 G.A. Hayes-McCoy, *Irish Battles* (Dublin, 1969). 'Rathmines 1649', pp. 206–211.

37 BP, Mrs Bellew 'John Bellew', p. 234.

38 Ormond's letters to Cromwell are in Gilbert, *Affairs in Ireland*, ii, p. 483 (August) and p. 453 (September).

39 BP.
40 BP.
41 Gilbert, *Affairs in Ireland,* ii, pp. 66 and 68–9; Coonan, *Catholic Confederacy,* p. 304–305.
42 Gilbert, *Affairs in Ireland*, vol. 2, p. 91–96; Richard Bagwell, *Ireland under the Stuarts* 3 vols. (London, 1963), ii, pp. 233–4.
43 These articles are in Gilbert, *Affairs in Ireland*, ii, pp. 489–50.
44 *HMC*, Ormond Manuscripts, N.S. i, p. 155–6
45 BP.
46 Liam Cox, 'Athlone in the Civil War 1641–1652', *Irish Sword*, xxxix, part 2 (1972), pp. 161–166.
47 Gilbert, *Affairs in Ireland*, ii, pp. 149–50.
48 *Ibid.*, iii, pp. 215–6.
49 Gilbert, *Affairs in Ireland*, ii, p. 270.
50 NA, Carte Transcripts xxvii, p. 244.
51 For a list of those executed see Gilbert, *Affairs in Ireland*, iii, p. 264.
52 For a critical commentary on the negotiations leading to the Kilkenny Articles including John Bellew's participation, see Gilbert, *Affairs in Ireland*, iii, pp. 88–94.
53 For the Kilkenny Articles and the Explanations regarding same, see Gilbert, *Affairs in Ireland*, iii, pp. 94–99; see also NLI, Mountbellew Papers, Ms.31,966, a manuscript copy of the Articles.
54 Thomas L. Coonan, *Catholic Confederacy*, p. 318–319.
55 NLI, Mountbellew Papers, Ms.31,966.
56 R. Dunlop, *Ireland under the Commonwealth* 2 vols. (1913), ii, p. 321.

CHAPTER FIVE

1 Harold O'Sullivan, 'Military operations in County Louth in the run-up to Cromwell's storming of Drogheda', *JLAHS*, xxii, no. 2 (1990), pp. 187–208.
2 *Ibid.*, pp. 190–1.
3 Harold O'Sullivan, 'The Plantation of the Cromwellian soldiers in the Barony Of Ardee', *JLAHS.*, xxi, no. 4 (1988), p. 438.
4 *Ibid.*, p. 451 (Ardee); Harold O'Sullivan, 'The Cromwellian and Restoration settlements in the civil parish of Dundalk', *JLAHS.*, xix, no. 1 (1977), p. 30.
5 T. Gogarty (ed.), *Council Book of the Corporation of Drogheda* (Drogheda, 1915), i, pp. 29–31, 'A true and Exact Particular of the Survey of Several Parcells of Lands . . . on the Meath Side of Drogheda', in many instances the lands are mentioned as 'lately held' or the tenancy is in doubt.
6 For this period see T.C. Barnard, *Cromwellian Ireland, 1649–1660* (Oxford, 1975), pp. 1–26.
7 Robert Dunlop, *Ireland under the Commonwealth*, 2 vols, (Manchester, 1913), i, p. 1.
8 For studies of the Commonwealth land confiscations and transplantations, see Dunlop, *Ireland*, John P. Prendergast *The Cromwellian Settlement of Ireland*, 3rd edn (Dublin, 1922), G.E. Howard, *A Treatise of the Exchequer and Revenue of Ireland* (Dublin) NLI Joly Ms.61; chapter 21, Karl S. Bottigheimer, *English Money and Irish Land* (Oxford, 1991), Peter Berresford Ellis, *Hell or Connacht* (London, 1975) and Robert C. Simington, *The Transplantation to Connacht 1654–58* (Dublin, 1970), Introduction and Explanatory Note.
9 C.H. Firt and R.S. Rait, *Acts and Ordinances of the Interregnum 1642–1660*, ii (London, 1891) pp. 598–652 and pp. 1100–1110.
10 For Drogheda, see Gogarty *Council Book*, pp. 24–33; O'Sullivan 'The Plantation in Ardee', pp. 415–27.

11 For Ponsonby and Fowke, see O'Sullivan 'Plantation in Ardee', p. 415 and O'Sullivan 'Military Operations in Louth' p. 187; for Lowe, see National Library of Wales, 'John Jones Letterbook' pp. 89–91.
12 O'Sullivan, 'Plantation in Ardee', part 3.
13 For the Commonwealth confiscations and plantations in County Louth, see, Harold O'Sullivan, 'Landownership changes in the County of Louth in the Seventeenth Century', i and ii (Unpublished Ph.D. thesis, University of Dublin 1992), chapter 3 and Appendix F.
14 For the particulars, see the 'Gross Survey' in O'Sullivan, 'The Plantation in Ardee' pp. 428–449.
15 *Ibid.*
16 *Ibid.*, p. 416
17 NA, The Bellew Papers, 1121/1/2, p. 24; for William Aston, see O'Sullivan, 'The Plantation in Ardee'; for Oliver Tallant, see O'Sullivan, 'Landownership Changes' pp. 296–7.
18 Batten's deposition is in Gogarty (ed.), 'County Louth Depositions 1641'.
19 James L.J. Hughes, *Patentee Officers in Ireland 1173–1826* (Dublin, 1960) p. 4.
20 That this alleged trespass was still awaiting judgement when Bellew transplanted is suggested by the decision of the Lord Deputy and council in paragraph 11 of Document 5 in Appendix IV.
21 For their joint petition and subsequent correspondence see Appendix IV, which also contains copies of documents pertaining to John Bellew's transplantation.
22 His address is given as Termonfeckin County Louth and holding 115 acres in Killineer; he was the third son of Viscount Netterville; he had an estate of inheritance from his uncle Richard Netterville of Corbollis, County Dublin of lands in Kilkenny and Tipperary; see Public Library Armagh, 'Lists of Claims of Innocents', 'Claims appointed' no. 130.
23 For a successful petition to the Committee or Court of Articles, see the case of the Ulster Protestant Planter Lord Claneboy's petition of August 1653 against transplantation (which was also a test case for the Ulster Protestants who had sided with Ormond) in C.W. Russell and J.P. Prendergast, *The Carte Manuscripts in the Bodleian Library Oxford* (London, 1871), pp. 134–138.
24 Dunlop, *Ireland*, ii, pp. 419–421; T. Birch (ed.), *A Collection of the State Papers of John Thurloe* (London, 1742) ii, p. 343.
25 See Appendix IV, Documents 1 & 2.
26 Dunlop *Ireland*, ii, pp. 419–421.
27 Appendix IV, Documents 3 and 4.
28 *Ibid.*, Document 4.
29 *Ibid.*, Document 5.
30 Gerard Lyne, 'Three Certified Gross Survey transcripts for County Galway', in *AH.*, no. 35 (1992), pp. 159–209; that the authorities were unsure of the accuracy of the Strafford Survey is referred to in p. 168.
31 Appendix IV, Document 6.
32 'De bene esse', i.e., 'For what it is worth'; to allow or accept for the present until the matter can be fully examined and to stand or fall on the outcome; this phrase was used at this time to refer to cases where a temporary occupation of land was authorised pending the determination of the actual amount to be granted.
33 For the Bellews transplanted to Connacht in the Autumn of 1655, see Appendix Documents 7 and 8; for the decision of the Athlone Commissioners dated 26 March 1656 see Appendix Document 9, and the decision of the Loughrea Commissioners dated 12 June 1656, BP.
34 Appendix IV, Document 9; NLI, Townley Papers: 'Surveyor's Book of the Down Survey, County Louth 1657, from which the acreages given have been abstracted.

Notes

35 BP, Taken from a petition by John Bellew of Barmeath to 'the commissioners for hearing and determining the claims of the transplanted persons . . .' circa 1676.
36 Appendix IV, Documents 7 and 8.
37 Robert C. Simington, *The Transplantations to Connacht 1654–1658*, p. 131.
38 *Ibid.*, p. 247.
39 *Ibid.*, p. xxiii.
40 *Ibid.*, p. x.
41 For the settlement of Coote's regiments, see Mary O'Dowd, *Power Politics and Land: Early Modern Sligo* (Belfast, 1991) Chapter 8.
42 *Ibid.*, xxiii.
43 *Ibid.*
44 John P. Prendergast, *The Cromwellian Settlement of Ireland* (London, 1996), p. 194.
45 Mrs Bellew, 'John Bellew'.
46 For the twilight years of the English Commonwealth in Ireland, see J.I. McGuire, 'The Dublin Convention, the Protestant Community and the Emergence of an Ecclesiastical Settlement in 1660', in Art Cosgrove and J.I. McGuire (eds)., *Parliament and Community*, (Dublin, 1983) pp. 121–146.
47 Harold O'Sullivan, 'The Trevors of Rosetrevor: a British Colonial Family in Seventeenth Century Ireland' (Unpublished M.Litt. thesis, University of Dublin, 1985) pp. 158–159.
48 Dunlop, *Ireland*, ii, pp 702–3
49 For the end of the Commonwealth period in Ireland see O'Sullivan, 'Trevors of Rosetrevor', pp. 159–163.

CHAPTER SIX

1 J.I. McGuire 'The Dublin Convention' pp. 122–129.
2 Richard Bagwell, *Ireland under the Stuarts, and during the Interregnum*, 3 vols. (London, 1963) ii, pp. 370–371.
3 NA, Carte Transcripts, xxx, p. 470.
4 *Ibid.*
5 Carte Transcripts, xxx, p. 474.
6 William Montgomery, *The Montgomery Manuscripts*, edited by G. Hill (Belfast, 1869), pp. 238–39.
7 O'Sullivan, 'Trevors of Rose Trevor' pp. 155–63.
8 The full list of members is in *CSPI 1660–62*, pp. 141–142.
9 For Ormond's instructions to the crown forces in Ireland to transfer their allegiance to the parliamentary commissioners, see NA, Carte Transcripts, xxi, p. 130; for his dealings with the parliamentary commissioners, including the Articles of Dublin of the 18 June 1647, see BL, Thomason Tracts, E.394 (14) and Short Title Catalogue 'Severall Papers of the Treaty', no. 378 (4), the former provided under article 9 'upon performance of what he had undertaken', for the payment to Ormond of £3,000 'to answer his occasions until his transportation' together with bills of exchange in the sum of £10,877 to be paid one half at fifteen days after sight and the rest six months later; the latter consists of copies of correspondence which passed between Ormond and the commissioners between October 1646 and November 1646 in which there are several references to monies to be paid to Ormond.
10 English Statute, 12 Car. 11, c 11 s.25.
11 R. Steele (ed.), *Tudor and Stuart Proclamations* (Oxford, 1910) i, no. 3220.
12 NA, Carte Transcripts, xxx, p. 443, dated 6 May 1660; the signatories were Lords Fitzwilliam and Dillon, Edward Fitzharris, W. Fogarty, Dudley Bagnall,

John Seagrave, Patrick Porter, Thomas Plunkett, Christopher Alymer, Ulicke Burke, Lord Barnewall, Nicholas Plunkett, Oliver Cashell, Peter Bath, Lords Mayo and Netterville, William Burke, Garrett Moore, Piers Butler, B. Bryan and Christopher Dillon.
13 For the Articles of Peace 1649 see Bellings, *History*, vii, pp. 184–211.
14 For the Gracious Declaration as incorporated into the Act of Settlement, see *The Irish Statutes*, revised edn: *3rd Edward II to the Union, By Authority* (London 1885) pp. 90–165 and Curtis & McDowell *Irish Historical Documents*, pp. 158–169.
15 *The Irish Statutes*, clause 11, pp. 110–111.
16 *Ibid.*, clause 20–24, pp. 113–114.
17 L.J. Arnold, *The Restoration Land Settlement in County Dublin 1660–1668*, (Irish Academic Press, Dublin, 1993) p. 46.
18 *Ibid.*, Chapter 2, pp. 37–52.
19 NLI, Mountbellew Papers, D.31,885.
20 Charles II was not entirely out of sympathy with the cause of the Catholic Party; see Arnold, *Settlement*, p. 46.
21 NLI, Mountbellew Papers, D.31,948.
22 For a guide to developments in Ireland in the years 1660–1662 including petitions to the king and instructions given for the implementation of the Gracious Declaration, see R.P. Mahaffy's Preface to *CSPI, 1660–1662*; see also J.P. Prendergast, *Ireland from the Restoration to the Revolution, 1660–1690* (London, 1887) chapters 1 and 2.
23 NLI, Mountbellew Papers, D.31,948.
24 NLI, Mountbellew Papers, D.31,948.
25 Harold O'Sullivan, 'Landownership changes in the County of Louth in the seventeenth century' unpublished Ph.D. thesis, University of Dublin, 1991, i, p. 114–115.
26 For Ismay Bellew, see 'Bellew Inscriptions' and pedigree, *JLAHS*, i, pp. 104–7.
27 For the Taaffe connections with Sligo, see Mary O'Dowd, *Power Politics*.
28 For the Taaffe family, see *Dictionary of National Biography*, pp. 284–89; Lodge, *Peerage of Ireland*, pp. 287–99 and Viscount Charles Taaffe, *Memoirs of the Family of Taaffe* (Vienna, 1856), pp. 1–27.
29 *Affairs in Ireland* li,.p. 145.
30 Bellings, *History*, vii, p. 236.
31 Gilbert, *Affairs in Ireland*, iii, pp. 330–1.
32 Ronald Hutton, *Charles II, King of England, Scotland and Ireland* (Oxford, 1989) pp. 77 and 123–25.
33 Harold O'Sullivan, 'Landownership changes', ii, appendix G. 'John Bellew's Statement of Account', hereafter as 'Bellew's Account', p. G205.
34 NA, Bellew Papers, 1121/1/2, pp. 136–7
35 NLI, Mountbellew Papers, D.31,948
36 NLI, *ibid*.
37 NLI, *ibid*; NA, Bellew Papers, 1121/1/2, pp. 115–6
38 'Bellew Account', '10 April 1661 to 29 May 1662', p. G122 'entering the order for the custodium in the county of Louth'; p. G123 'spent in my journey to the county of Louth'.
39 The Widow Humpherey's or Widd Vmphry's House in Cook Street, St Audoen's Parish, was a big house with ten hearths, see *The Fifty-Seventh Report of the Deputy-Keeper of the Records in Ireland* (1936) pp. 528 and 561.
40 'Bellew Account', pp. G120–G207.
41 *CSPI, 1660–1662*, for Hardress Waller's estate, see p. 261; for the Collooney estate, see p. 177 and for the reprisal lands in Louth, see p. 453, October 1661

Notes

for the reversion of Braganstown and Cookstown estates, see p. 343; for his ancestral estates, see pp. 246 and 412 which also ordered the release of mortgages on his lands in Sligo.

42 *Ibid.*, p. 356.
43 For the Taaffes of Braganstown and Cookstown, see *ibid.*, p. 343.
44 'Bellew Account' '10 April 1661 to 29 May 1662', pp. G120–G131.
45 DNB.
46 BP, see also NA, Bellew Papers, 1121/1/2, pp. 24–27 for particulars of the estate as set out to him by order of Parliament, 22 March 1652.
47 BP, a bond dated 2 November 1661 between Patrick Bellew of Clonoran County Galway 'who was on the 7 October last was by virtue of his majesty's writ by the sheriffs of the city put in possession of the said lands of Drumroe to and for the use of the right honourable Theobald Taaffe earl of Carlingford is to receive the rent thereof since the first day of May last past to the use of the said Lord Taaffe' and David Elliot 'undertenant to Robert Wade'.
48 'Bellew Account', 10 April 1661 to 29 May 1662, pp. G128– G131.
49 BP, for the full text, see O'Sullivan 'Landownership Changes' i, pp. 125–6.
50 For particulars of these, see O'Sullivan 'Landownership changes', i, pp. 117– 123.
51 The limitation of the 1 August 1661 on the lands in Louth which could be reckoned as reprisals for the loss of the Collooney estate is in Taaffe's proviso in the Act of Settlement clause 225; the details of the rentals received from the custodium lands in County Louth in the period May 1661 to May 1663 are in 'Bellew Account', pp. G152–G154, these lands also included most if not all of the lands which had been allotted to Bellew as his custodium lands.
52 For Gernons recovery of their estates at Milltown under the Act of Settlement, see O'Sullivan, 'Landownership changes' i, pp. 181–186.
53 For Trevor and Montgomery, see O'Sullivan, 'The Trevors of Rose Trevor' pp. 167–74 and Arnold, *Restoration Land Settlement in Dublin*, pp. 77–8.
54 For details of the procedures involved, see the case of Major John Pepper, Ballygarth, County Meath in O'Sullivan 'Landownership changes' ii, Appendix F.
55 For details of the acquisitions made by the Trust in the town of Drogheda by March 1662, see *ibid.*, ii, Appendix B.
56 For the '49 Officers Trust, see Kevin McKenny, 'Charles II's Irish Cavaliers' in *Irish Historical Studies*, no. 28, (1993), pp. 409–25.
57 For the events leading up to the passing of the Act of Settlement in 1662, see Arnold, *Restoration.*, Chapters 11 and 111.
58 For the enactment of the Act of settlement see Bagwell, *op.cit.*, iii chapter XLI.
59 *The Irish Statutes*, revised edn, pp. 85–88.
60 BP.
61 These are set out in the Act of Settlement.

CHAPTER SEVEN

1 'Bellew Account'; for some of Bellew's dealings with the Irish Privy Council circa June 1663, see pp. G148–G150; for dealings with Ormond February–March 1664 see pp. G163–G165 including the payment of two shillings and six pence to the 'doorkeeper at the back-stairs to give me access to my Lord Lieutenant about that of my Lord's letter touching the custodium lands 22 February 1664'.
2 The correspondence between Jones and Legge for the period 1663–1667 concerning the acquisition of lands in County Louth is in the 'Dartmouth Papers' *H.M.C. Report 15 Appendix 1*, (1896), pp. 109–113.
3 'Bellew Account,' p. G162.

4 Mary Bellew's letter is in NLI, Mountbellew Papers, Ms.31,947; the reference to Keating's employment at this time is in 'Bellew Account', p. G1341–138; Christopher was employed in John Bellew's office in Dublin in April 1665, *ibid.*, p. G183.
5 Ingoldsby's proviso enabled him to recover the sum of £2,000 with interest since the year 1658 out of Waller's estate.
6 'Bellew Account', p. G134.
7 *Ibid.*, pp. G134–G135; pp. G140–G142.
8 *JHCI*, 1i, p. 226, 10 December 1662.
9 BP, no. 46, entitled earl of Carlingford's order for a lease of Sir Hardress Waller's estate and dated 20 September 1662 signed by the duke's commissioners Messrs. Maurice Eustace, Anglesey, Kingston, G. Lane, Orrery, J. Berkeley and Broderick, copied in NA, 1121/1/2, p. 48, no. 46. together with particulars of the estate.
10 BP; the text is in O'Sullivan 'Landownership changes' i, pp. 126–6.
11 P.M. Souars, *The Matchless Orinda* (Massachusetts 1931); that Carlingford participated in such affairs, see 'Bellew Account', 'to the play for a box my lord had at the playhouse 22 November 1662' cost £2, probably the Smock Alley Playhouse.
12 The house had six hearths, *Fifty-Seventh Report of the Deputy-Keeper of the Public records in Ireland* (Dublin, 1936), p. 563.
13 NA, Bellew Papers, 1121/1/5, pp. 58–62, letter no. 59.
14 For some details of Bellew's dealings in respect of the Taaffe household in Dublin, including the arrival of Carlingford, see, 'Bellew Account', pp. G134–G140.
15 'Bellew Account' p. G157; for the events at Kilkenny at this time, see HMC, 15th Report, App. 7 p. 171. 17 September 1663.
16 'Bellew Account', wine cellar, p. G146, Mrs Hales, p. G149.
17 For details of these, see Appendix, Deputy-Keeper's *Report of the Public Records in Ireland* (Dublin, 1887), 'Abstract of the decrees of the court of claims', and NA, Ferguson Manuscripts, 2/446/10 xxxvi, 1A/52/1.
18 Harold O'Sullivan, 'The Restoration Land Settlement in the Diocese of Armagh', in *Seanchas Ardmhacha*, xvi, no. 1 (1994), p. 19–36.
19 For the procedures in the Court of Claims, see O'Sullivan, 'Landownership changes', pp. 147–149.
20 NA, Rev. Exchequer 16, presented to the Public Record Office by E.J. French, 20 May 1926; see also O'Sullivan, 'Landownership changes', ii, Appendix H.
21 *CSPI*, 1660–62, p. 343.
22 O'Sullivan, 'Landownership changes', 1, pp, 131–132; see also 'Bellew Account', Bellew's dealings with the Council Board, p. G137, and pp. G148–G156.
23 The Record Office Kent County Council, Maidstone, Sir John Deering's notes on the proceedings of the Court of Claims, appendix IV, no. 387, Saturday 15 August 1663.
24 For details, see 'Bellew Account', pp. G155–G160; among the witnesses who gave evidence on behalf of Carlingford were 'Moore of Barmeath' who was a Connacht transplanter, George Taaffe, probably of Sligo, and Jenico Taaffe, formerly of Athclare, a Connacht transplanter.
25 In November 1663 the king issued instructions to Ormond reducing the quit-rents on the restored estates to what they were in 1641 and which was given effect 12 February 1664, NA, Bellew Papers, 1121/1/1 pp. 47–8; also BP, Carlingford to Bellew, letters dated 20 February and 8 March 1664 regarding Aston; a rentroll in NLI, Ms.13,836 'Lord Carlingford's Rent Roll' sets out the estates held by the Taaffes at that time; 'Bellew Account', pp. G173–174, Clintonsrath; pp. G174–G177, Sligo, p. G177 Aston and Stickillen rents circa December 1664.

26 John J. Prendergast, *Ireland from the Restoration to the revolution* AD *1660–1690* (London, 1887) p. 29.
27 O'Sullivan, 'Landownership changes', 1, pp. 209–10.
28 BSD, Louth and Sligo.
29 'Bellew Account', p. G147 circa 1662–63 'for entering the king's letter at the Rolls Office, the same requiring the earl of Carlingford being continued the possession and profits of the lands in the county of Louth until finally settled and for the clerk's expediting the same my Lord's custodium being then much opposed by my Lord Chief Baron', 12 shillings.
30 'Bellew Account', pp. G142–145, and G155–G156.
31 Details in O'Sullivan, 'Land Settlement Armagh', pp. 22–35.

CHAPTER EIGHT

1 O'Sullivan, 'Land Settlement Armagh', pp. 40–63, Arnold, *Land Settlement County Dublin*, chapters 5 and 6.
2 'Bellew Account', pp. G164 and 196–198 Dungannon; pp. G193–G194 Erasmus Smith; pp G194–G195 Massarene.
3 For Bayly, see O'Sullivan 'Land Settlement Armagh', p. 51.
4 O'Sullivan, 'Landownership changes' 1, pp. 122, and pp. 224–32.
5 *JHCI*,1i, pp 224–295.
6 Simington, *Transplantation to Connacht*, p. 247, 'Bellew Account' p. G135 mention a 'George Warren of Darver' who may have been a tenant to the Earl of Carlingford who held a custodium lease of lands at Darver at this time.
7 This may have been the origin of the list of certificates and passports issued to all 'sheriffs, Sargents and Bayliffs' in the years 1662–63, identifying the servants of members of the Lords and Commons who under 'the ancient laws and customs of this realm' were exempted from all arrests etc. during sessions of Parliament and forty days thereafter, published in T. Gogarty, *Council Book of the Corporation of Drogheda* (Drogheda, 1915), pp. 9–15 in which an Ambros Antill is mentioned as servant to the Earl of Carlingford.
8 Arnold, *Land Settlement Dublin*, pp. 100–104; C.W. Russell and J.P. Prendergast, *The Carte Manuscripts in the Bodliean Library Oxford* (London, 1871), p. 180.
9 'Bellew Account', p. G168.
10 *Irish Record Commission Report no. 15*, 'Abstract of Grants under the Acts of Settlement and Explanation AD 1666–1684', pp. 72, 187, 189, 190, 191.
11 'Bellew Account', p. G186.
12 Ronald Hutton in *Charles II* (Oxford 1989), p. 231 expresses the view that Carlingford was sent as ambassador 'in the hope that his hard drinking, swashbuckling ways would endear him to the Austrians as Rochester had done'; for correspondence connected with Carlingford's embassy to Vienna, see, Carlingford Papers, Osborn Collection, Yale University USA.
13 BP, letters of 11 May 1666, 8 July 1666 (a copy of this letter is in NA, Bellew Papers 1121/1/1 and 2) and 11 July 1666.
14 BP, Address given on a letter from Nicholas 'my lord Carlingford', dated 11 October 1666.
15 'Bellew Account', pp. G200–201, details of moneys paid by their son to his mother, and which she paid 'to such as I was engaged unto for his lordship's occasions when I went to England'.
16 BP, see also Hutton, *Charles II*, pp, 237–8.
17 BP, May 1655.
18 For Boyle, see Arnold, *Land Settlement Dublin*, pp. 104–107.

19　BP, letter 29 July 1666, 'for Captain John Bellew at London'.
20　BP, 14 September 1677.
21　*Ibid.*, 8 July 1666.
22　This may have been the letter calendared in *CSPI 1666–69*, pp. 312–3 giving the duke precedence before all others in the acquisition of custodium lands in Ireland.
23　BP, dated 'Dublin 23rd', referring to the ex-soldiers, he urged Bellew 'to be sure you have a letter to reprise the soldiers in the barony of Cossca [?] and above all things our lands in Louth'.
24　BP.
25　*CSPI 1669–70* pp. 586–88.
26　BP, and NA, Bellew Papers, 1121/1/2, full text in O'Sullivan, 'Landownership changes', i, pp. 222–223.
27　BP, *CSPI 1666–69*, p. 343, NA, Bellew Papers, 1121/1/1 and 2.
28　BP.
29　'Bellew Account', p. G176, reference to a plea in the Court of Common Pleas to remove Wetherall's arrest; G.188, meetings in Galway with Bayly concerning 'the lands in controversy betwixt my Lord and the said captain', 24 October 1665.
30　Record Office Kent County Council Maidstone Dering Papers, full text in O'Sullivan, 'Landownership changes' 1, pp. 226–228; BP, letter dated November 6, Nicholas Taaffe to Bellew in London referring to a letter from Sir Heneage Finch to Dering indicating 'that would do all our business he approving of it'; a second letter dated 11th, '67 from Warrenstown referring to Braganstown and Cookstown and a conversation he had had with Sir Winston Churchill who advised 'we might very well lose those lands if we did not take out our certificate, which I thought very strange, not being sure of reprisals for the soldiers, but he told me it was the common practice, it were a most lamentable thing that those estates that have caused so much labour and trouble, both to you and my father and the enemies he purchased upon that account now should be lost for want of three score pounds, presumably the cost of taking out the certificate from the Court of Claims; a further letter from Warrenstown dated 31 January 1667/8 after Bellew's return from England advising him to delay proceeding in the court of claims on the grounds that he was sick and could not attend and which may have been a pretence as he continued (should) 'they press you, tell them you have orders from my father not to proceed till he comes, they may do what they please but make you no defence, you know he will bring along with him both the king's private letter and public letter to the commissioners.'
31　BP, witnessed statement by George Rawdon, dated 28 November 1668.
32　*Ibid.*, witnessed statement by John Bellew, dated 30 November 1668; also a certified true copy of a letter dated 3 December 1668 from Rawdon to Dering of the Court of Claims; *ibid.*, memorandum dated 30 November 1668 of the commission for executing the Acts of Settlement and Explanation certifying Mr Samuel Bull's statement signed by Paul Brazier [Deputy Registar] decree and certificate issued by the commissioners dated Thursday 17 December 1668.
33　William Strickland is listed by Bottigheimer as an adventurer who drew Irish land in Waterford for an adventure of £600, Karl S. Bottigheimer, *English Money and Irish Land* (Oxford, 1971) Appendix B, p. 210.
34　A copy of Carlingford's letters patent, taken from NA, Pyke-Fortesque' Papers, 1004/1/6/1 is in O'Sullivan 'Landownership changes', 2, Appendix J.
35　BP, letter 7 December 1669.
36　*IRC Report* no. 15, 'Abstract of Grants', pp. 72, 187, 189, 190, 191.
37　The Rent Roll is in the NLI, Ms.13,836.
38　R.C. Simington, *The Civil Survey of County Meath*, v, Irish Manuscripts Commission, barony of Slane, pp. 341–376; the 1677 Rent Roll identifies the lands

Notes

in Slane as Gernonstown and Roosland part of Roostown, Littlefootstown, Crivagh, Biggstown and part of Biggsnowrath; the acquisition of custodium lands in Tipperary etc. is mentioned in 'Bellew Account', pp. G180, 3 March 1664; £3.10 paid, 'to him I sent to let my lords custodium lands in Wexford, Kilkenny and Tipperary' G186, writs of sciere facias taken out in respect of lands in Tipperary and Wexford; details of land in Meath in 'Abstract of Grants' *IRC*, Report no. 15, p. 210; see also *ibid.*, p. 277 for details of letters patent passed 3 July 1683 by Nicholas Earl of Carlingford in respect of 3,828 acres of lands acquired by him in the baronies of Corren and Tirrerell, County Sligo.

39   For details of the acquisition of the lease of Warrenstown, see 'Bellew Account', p. G183 hire of horses to go to Louth 'about getting a place for my lady to reside in', dealings with Dillon re Warrenstown, p. G184, bargain concluded with Dillon re Warrenstown.
40   BP, and NA, 'Bellew Papers', 1121/1/5, p. 61.
41   'Bellew Account', pp. G183–G186.
42   'Bellew Account', p. G203.
43   Benignus Millett, *Collectanea Hibernica*, nos. 6 and 7 (1963–64), p. 143.
44   John Hanly, (ed.), *The Letters of Saint Oliver Plunkett 1625–1681* (Dublin, 1979), pp. 70–75.
45   Hutton, *Charles II*.

CHAPTER NINE

1   See clause 16 of the Act of Settlement, 1662.
2   NLI, Mountbellew Papers, Ms.31,945.
3   *ibid.*
4   O'Sullivan, 'Landownership changes', 1, pp. 186–194.
5   *CSPI 1660–1662*, p. 55.
6   HMC, 'Hastings', ii, p. 376, 24 September 1677.
7   For a statement of Lord Iveagh's case, see NA, Carte Transcripts 35, p. 139; for details of letters patents and savings see *IRC Report no. 15*, 'Abstracts of Grants', p. 252 in the name of his daughter, Elisabeth Magennis.
8   See note 313, Chapter 8.
9   NLI, Mountbellew Papers, Ms.31,948 and BP, undated petition and claim by John Bellew, 'to the commissioners for putting into execution the Act of settlement and the Act of Explanation'; the schedule gives details of the lands assigned to him in Galway.
10 BP.
11 BP, addressed to Mr John Bellew at Reynoldstown.
12 T.C. Barnard, *Cromwellian Ireland English Government and Reform in Ireland 1649–1660*, (Oxford University Press, 1975), Chapter 9.
13 'Bellew Account' pp. G203–205.
14 NA, 'Bellew Papers' 1121/1/1, p. 120, indenture between John Bellew of Clonoran, County Galway and Theobald, Earl of Carlingford dated 17 February 1668/9.
15 NA, Bellew Papers, 1121/1/1, p. 122.
16 NA, Bellew Papers, 1121/1/1, p. 122.
17 NA, Bellew Papers, 1121/1/18, 1681 Earl v Bellew; *ibid.*, 1121/1/2, pp. 52–3 and 57.
18 As calculated from the BSD.
19 O'Sullivan, 'Landownership changes', 1, pp. 158–9; NLI, Mountbellew Papers, Ms.31,948; *JLAHS* O'Sullivan, 'An Arbitration Award regarding Intermixed Lands in the Parish of Dysart, dated 1671, xxiii, no. 4 (1995) pp. 405–412.

20 *IRC*, Report no. 15, 'Abstracts of Grants', Richard, Earl of Westmeath, p. 255, Luke Dowdall, pp. 235 and 254, Barnewall, pp. 244 and 312 (Sir William Petty Savings) and Geoghegan, p. 278, Byrne son/heir of Conley Geoghegan.
21 O'Sullivan 'Landownership changes' 1, Oliver Plunkett, Baron Louth and his son Matthew, pp. 186–193, Sir John Bellew, pp. 177–181, Nicholas Gernon, pp. 181–186, Thomas Clinton p. 167–169, Taaffe Earl of Carlingford, Chapter 5.
22 O'Sullivan, 'Landownership changes', 1, pp. 118–121.
23 L.J. Arnold, *Land Settlement Dublin*, Chapters 7 to 10.
24 BP, Petition: 'To the Honourables the Commissioners for hearing and determining the claims of the transplanted persons in the Province of Connacht and County of Clare and NA, Bellew Papers Ms.1121/1/2, pp. 101–103.
25 Christopher's rights were saved in Patrick Bellew's letters patent as follows: 'To.Christ. Bellew; This patent not to prejudice a lease for 1,000 years, passed by John Bellew to Sir Nicholas Plunkett of Dublin Knt., and others of the lands of Corgarragh, in trust for said Ch'.Bellew, one of the sons of the said John; nor any uses mentioned in a certificate of the said lands formerly granted to said Sir Nicholas, in trust for the said Christopher, *IRC* 'Abstract of Grants', p. 321.
26 *Ibid.*, p. 247. The lands marked with an asterisk were those in the original Commonwealth grant by the Loughrea Commissioners to John Bellew in 1656–see p. 68.
27 BP, A statement entitled 'Sir Patrick Bellew came before me this 22 February 1689 and made oath that the within lands were bought from the within named persons and were worth in the year 1686 the sum of £1220'.
28 Robert C. Simington, *Transplantation to Connacht*.
29 Robert C. Simington, *The Civil Survey AD 1654–1656*, viii, 'County of Kildare', Irish Manuscripts Commission (Dublin 1952), p. 16.
30 Karen J. Harvey, 'The family experience – The Bellews of Mountbellew' in Thomas P. Power and Kevin Whelan, (eds.), *Endurance and Emergence Catholics in Ireland in the Eighteenth Century* (Irish Academic Press, Dublin) 1990, p. 180–181.
31 For the background to this Commission see L.J. Arnold, *Land Settlement, Dublin*, Chapter 19.
32 For documentation concerning these transactions, see Appendix VI.

EPILOGUE

1 NA, Bellew Papers, 1121/1/5 p. 46; an Account of £95 incurred by the executors of the will, Mrs Mary Bellew and her son James submitted to the Prerogative Court for approval has survived in BP, dated August 1689 the expenses related to servants wages, £30, the cost of burial, £40 and bequests, £20; a sum of £5 seems to have been disallowed.
2 BP, printed in full in Appendix VII.
3 Burke's *Peerage and Baronetage*.
4 Robert C. Simington, *The Civil Survey AD 1654–1656 County of Meath* (Dublin, 1940), p. 95.
5 Robert C. Simington, *Transplantation to Connacht*, p. 85.
6 See Burke, *Peerage*, under Sir Patrick; *Abstract of Grants*, p. 244; The BSD for County Meath shows Sir Richard Barnewall, in the Restoration period, as the proprietor of 182 acres plantation measure in the parishes of Screen, Crickstown and Ballymaden; a Matthew Barnewall had 93 acres in Rathoath and a Jane Barnewall had 25 acres in Kilbrew.
7 BP, printed in full in Appendix VIII.

Notes

8   NLI, Mountbellew Papers, Ms.31,949.
9   NA, Bellew Papers, 1121/1/5 – see note 361.
10 BP, Prerogative Will, the sole executor was his nephew Richard, and the overseers were the Venerable Doctor Dromgoole and his cousin Roger Bellew of Thomastown.
11 BP, The acquittance is signed by Sir Gerald Alymer and witnessed by Laurence Taaffe, Robert Cadell, Christopher Bellew and Andrew Plunkett dated 24 January 1665.
12 NA, Bellew Papers, 1121/1/5 pp. 7, 25, 32–40 65–70 and 1121/1/11 p. 26–28.
13 IRC, 'Abstract of Grants', Patrick Bellew, p. 247 and 'Savings' p. 321.
14 NA, Bellew Papers, 1121/1/1, p. 12, details of a 'final concord' made between John Bellew and Richard Dillon of the city of Dublin dated 20 May 1575 in the King's Bench of lands and premises in Barmeath, Callagh, Hainstown, Dizart, Hitchestown, Graftonstown, Dromin, Reynoldstown and Carrolagh, evidently giving legal effect to the trust.
15 NA, Bellew Papers, 1121/1/2, p. 54–55 and 1121/1/11, p. 32.
16 T. Gogarty, *Council Book of the Corporation of Drogheda 1649–1734*, 1, (Drogheda, 1915) p. 209.
17 *Ibid.*, p. 209.
18 For Drogheda during the Commonwealth and Restoration periods see O'Sullivan, 'Landownership changes' 1 and 2.
19 T. Gogarty, *Council Book*, pp. 207 and 211.
20 *Ibid.*, pp. 210–211 and 221.
21 *Ibid.*, p. 220.
22 See J. Dalton, *History of Drogheda* (Dublin, 1844) [Vol ii] pp. 298–9 and W. Harris, *The History of the Life and Reign of William* (Dublin, 1749), pp. x–xii.
23 Those elected to the Parliament for the County of Louth were Thomas Bellew, Thomastown, and William Talbot, Haggardstown; Hugh Gernon, Killencoole and John Babe Darver for Ardee; Robert Dermott and John Dowdall for Dundalk; Christopher Peppard Fitz-Ignatius and Bryan Dermott for Carlingford; Henry Dowdall and Christopher Peppard Fitz-George for Drogheda; list from T. Davis, *The Patriot Parliament*, (London, 1893), pp. 161–165.
24 For the list of those outlawed etc. in County Louth, see Harold O'Sullivan 'The Jacobite Ascendancy and Williamite Revolution and Confiscations in County Louth 1684–1701, in *JLAHS.*, xii no. 4 (1992), pp. 433–4.
25 W. King, *The State of the Protestants in Ireland under the late King James's Government* (London, 1691), pp. 390–2 and 'Instructions' by the Marquis D'Albaville, James II's principal secretary of state to the Lord Chief Justice Nugent to enforce the law, *Ibid.*, pp. 392–5; O'Sullivan, 'Landownership changes', pp. 341–345.
26 W. King, *Protestants in Ireland*, pp. 390–2; O'Sullivan 'Landownership changes', pp. 392–5., and Dalton, *Drogheda*, [Vol ii] p. 304.
27 For Baker, see O'Sullivan, 'The Jacobite Ascendancy', pp. 441–4.
28 *Ibid.*, pp. 434–5 and B.P. see also O'Sullivan 'Landownership changes, pp. 345–6.
29 O'Sullivan, 'The Jacobite Ascendancy', p. 435.
30 *Ibid.*
31 J.G. Simms, *The Williamite Confiscation in Ireland 1690–1703* (Connecticut, 1976), p. 76; Simms was of the view that the 'considerable service' envisaged was to prepare the way for a negotiated settlement of the hostilities.
32 BP, undated copy of petition to the Trustees of the Forfeited Estates circa 1700 by Captain Thomas Aston.
33 O'Sullivan, 'The Jacobite Ascendancy', p. 436.
34 BP.

35 BP, and NA, Bellew Papers, 1121/1/11, pp. 76–9.
36 *Ibid.*, 1121/1/11, pp. 76–9.
37 B. Banks, (ed.), *Land Owners in Ireland* (Dublin, 1676), p. 293; Karen J. Harvey, 'The Bellews', pp. 171–197.
38 *Ibid.*, p. 183.
39 *Ibid.*, p. 189.
40 *Ibid.*, pp. 188–192.
41 NA, The Bellew Papers, 'The Bellews of Tullydonnell County Louth, 1121/2/7.
42 Christine Casey and Alistair Rowan, *The Buildings of Ireland: North Leinster* (Penguin Publications, 1993), p. 154.

APPENDICES

1 Copies of these petitions are in NLI, Mountbellew papers, Ms.31,884 (a); a copy of the petition to the king is also to be found in BL, Add.Chart. 9324; a copy of the petition to the English Parliament is in BL, Egerton 1048 p. 13 (1); see also J.T. Gilbert, *Facsimiles of the National: Manuscripts of Ireland* (Dublin, 1884) v.l pp. 316–7 which gives the signatories to the petitions.
2 NA, Bellew Papers, 1121/1/7, no. 24, pp. 25–7.
3 Documents 1 to 5 in NLI, Mountbellew Papers, Ms.31996; documents 6 to 9 in BP.
4 These documents are in NLI, Mountbellew Papers, Ms.31,885.
5 BP.
6 NA, 'Lodge Record of the Rolls', p. 317; the lands marked O were those acquired by Patrick Bellew from Tomlinson and those marked X were lands acquired by John Bellew in his lifetime.
7 These two documents are from the BP.

Glossary

ATTAINDER. The condition of a person convicted of treason or on whom a judgement for outlawry has been pronounced; as well as suffering forfeiture of property the individual was liable to the death penalty.

BENEFICIAL INTEREST. A right of substantial enjoyment or equitable interest, as opposed to merely nominal ownership or legal interest.

COMMON LAW. The ancient unwritten law of England [and Ireland] embodied in judicial decisions, as opposed to statute law, and administered in the common law courts.

COMMONWEALTH. The republican form of government which existed in Ireland and England from the execution of Charles I in 1649 and the restoration of Charles II in 1660.

CONCEALMENT. The practice of non-disclosure of a land title to avoid payment of a feudal incident or because of some defective title which could lead to a resumption of the land by the State.

CUSTODIUM. A lease from the crown under the seal of the exchequer whereby the custody of lands seized into the king's hands was demised to another as custodee or lessee.

DEBENTURE. A charge in writing of specified property with the repayment at a fixed time of the money loaned; the word was used in the Commonwealth period to describe the document that was issued to a soldier stating his arrears of pay and confirming his entitlement to compensation for such arrears by an allocation of land of equal worth and value out of the confiscated lands in Ireland.

DECREE. The sentence of the court of chancery delivered on the hearing of a cause; the word was also used to describe a decision of the court of claims under the Act of Settlement of 1662 enabling forfeited lands to be restored to the former proprietor his heirs or assigns; such decisions were based either on the 'innocence' of the claimant or on the basis of a 'proviso' in favour of the claimant contained in the Act.

DISCOVERER. A person employed or engaged for reward in the search of legal records for the purpose of discovering defective titles in lands; discovers were employed inter alia by the Courts of Claims established under the Acts of Settlement and Explanation.

INCUMBRANCE. A charge or mortgage on a real or personal estate, the incumbrancer being the person entitled to enforce the charge or mortgage.

INQUISITION. An inquest of office or enquiry conducted by an officer of the crown such as a sheriff or escheator, concerning any matter that entitled the crown to the possession of lands or tenements.

JOINTURE. The estate settled on a husband and wife before marriage in satisfaction and bar of the woman's dower.

LETTERS PATENT. Writings on a parchment given by the king and sealed with the great seal, authorising the recipient to do or enjoy anything which of himself he could not do; the word patent signified that the writings of the document were open, ready to be shown for confirmation of the authority given by them; this was the usual form of conveying a grant of land by the crown to an individual in Ireland in the seventeenth century.

OUTLAWRY. Putting a man outside the protection of the law so that he became incapable of bringing an action for the redress of injuries and forfeited all his goods and chattels to the king. Usually commenced by a writ of exigent issued by the Court of King's Bench to the sheriff who was required to put it into execution by calling out the name of the person charged at local 'hustings'; if the person came forward he would have been arrested and sent for trial; if after calling his name five times at hustings he failed to appear, he was named by judgement of the coroner as outlawed. The fifth call was termed the quinto exactus. (A failure to comply with the procedure laid down was often a good defence against a charge of outlawry.)

PROVISO. A condition entered into a deed. The word was also used to denote a special provision made in the Acts of Settlement and Explanation in favour of a named individual i.e., the proviso-man.

PLANTATION MEASURE. The land measure adapted by Sir Josias Bodley in the surveys done for the Ulster Plantation, based upon a twenty-one foot perch and which by the 1630s had became known as Irish Plantation Measure. To convert plantation measure to statute measure, multiply the former by 196 and divide the result by 121.

QUIET. A direction to the sheriff or to his official to put a person into possession of an estate and to secure him against disturbance.

REPRISAL. A taking in return; used in the Acts of Settlement and Explanation to describe the estate of 'equal worth and value' granted to a person ousted from an estate to make way for another in accordance with the provisions of the Acts.

REVERSION. The residue of an estate left in the grantor to commence in possession after the determination of some particular estate granted to him; a reversionary lease was one to take effect in the future usually after the previous one had ended its time.

SAVINGS. A clause in a letters patent providing for the saving of a reservation or exception usually in favour of another, to the provisions of the patent.

SEQUESTRATION. A writ directed to commissioners commanding them to enter the lands and take the rents and profits and seize the goods of the person against whom it is directed.

STATUTE STAPLE. Bond of record entered into under the supervision of the mayor and constable of the Staple, in Staple towns such as Dublin and Drogheda, enabling recognisances to be entered into for the lending of money and its subsequent repayment under penalty of estreat.

TRUSTEE. A person to whom an estate has been conveyed, devised or bequeathed in trust for another

USE. The equitable right to receive the profit or benefit of lands and tenements, divorced from the legal owning of them.

Bibliography

MANUSCRIPTS

British Library London

Additional Charter 9324
Egerton Manuscripts 1048
Short Title Catalogue 'Several Papers of the Treaty' no. 378(4)
Thomason Tracts E.394(14)

King's Inns Library, Dublin

Prendergast Papers

National Archives

Bellew Papers
Books of Survey and Distribution, Quit Rent Office Copies, Louth, Meath and Sligo
Carte Transcripts
Ferguson Manuscripts
Lodge John, Summaries of Entries on the Irish Chancery Rolls
Pyke-Fortesque Papers

National Library of Ireland

Dillon Papers
Mountbellew Papers
Peppard Papers
Reports on Private Collections
Taaffe Papers Ms.13836
Townley Papers: The Surveyors' Book of the Down Survey of County Louth 1657

National Library of Wales

John Jones Letterbook

Public Library Armagh

Claims appointed to be heard and determined by his majesty's commissioners appointed to execute the Act for the Settlement of Ireland 1662–1668

Papers in Private Keeping

Bellew Papers, Barmeath Castle County Meath
Pepper Papers, Ballygart Castle County Meath, (Mrs F.C. Delaney Pinecroft, Julianstown County Meath)

Kent Archives Office, Maidstone

Dering Papers

University of Dublin

The Transplantation proceedings of the Revenue Commissioners of the Precinct of Trim

Yale University USA

Osborn Collection, The Carlingford Papers

PRINTED PRIMARY AND CONTEMPORARY MATERIAL

Historical Manuscripts Commission

Dartmouth Papers Report 15 Appendix 1 (1896)
Fifteenth Report, App. 7
Hastings ii
Ormond Manuscripts N.S. ii

Irish Manuscripts Commission

Analecta Hibernica no. 35
Hughes, L.J. (ed.) and *Patentee Officers in Ireland 1173–1826* (1960)
O'Ferrall, Barnabas and O'Connell Robert, *Commentarius Rinuccinianus*, Six Volumes (Dublin, 1932–49)
Simington Robert C. (ed.) and *Books of Survey and Distribution and Distribution*, 4 vols. (Dublin, 1944–1967), Roscommon, Mayo, Galway and Clare
—— *The Civil Survey* AD *1654–1656*, Limerick, iv; Meath v; Kildare, viii, and Miscellaneous x (1938–1961)
——*The Transplantation to Connacht 1654–1658* (1970)

Irish Records Commission Publications

Inquisitionum Officia Rotulorum Canncellaria Hibernice Asservatorum Lagena (Dublin 1826–1829)

Abstract of Grants of Lands and other Hereditaments under the Acts of Settlement and Explanation AD 1666–1684, Report no. 15

Legal Texts

Kenelm Edward Digby, *An Introduction to the History of the Law of Real Property, with Original Authorities*, 5th edn (Oxford, 1897)

E.R. Hardy Ivamy, (ed.), *Mosley and Whiteley's Law Dictionary*, 10th edn (London, 1988)

Howard G.E., *A Treatise of the Exchequer and Revenue of Ireland*, NLI, Joly Manuscripts, 61, Chapter xxi

J.C. Wylie, *Irish Land Law* (London, 1975)

Records of Parliament

Dunlop R., *Ireland under the Commonwealth*, 2 vols. (Manchester, 1913)

Firth C.H. and Raith R.S., *Acts and Ordnances of the Interregnum, 1642–60*, 3 vols. (London, 1911)

The Journals of the House of Commons England

The Journals of the House of Commons of the Kingdom of Ireland (Dublin, 1753)

The Irish Statutes, Revised Edition, Third Edward III to the Union, by Authority (London, 1885)

Public Records Office England

Calendar of State Papers Ireland

Public Record Office Ireland, Reports of the Deputy-Keeper

'Abstract of Decrees of the Court of Claims for the trial of Innocents', 19th Report (Dublin, 1887)

'List of Houses in the City of Dublin and the number of hearths in each 1664' 57th Report (Dublin, 1936)

Other Contemporary Material

Banks, B. (ed.), *Land Owners in Ireland* (Dublin, 1876)

Bernard, Nicholas, *The Whole Proceedings of the Siege of Drogheda in Ireland* (London, 1642)

Bellings, Richard, *History of the Irish Confederation and wars in Ireland*, edition by J.T. Gilbert, 7 vols. (Dublin, 1891)
Birch, T. (ed.) *A Collection of the State Papers of John Thurloe* (London, 1742)
Bereton, Sir William, *Travels in Holland, the United Provinces, England, Scotland and Ireland, 1635*, edited by Edward Hawkins, (Chetham Society, 1884)
Curtis, Edmund and McDowell R.B., *Irish Historical Documents 1172–1922* (London, 1943)
Foster, John (ed.), *Register of Admissions to Gray's Inns 1521–1889* (London, 1889)
Gilbert, J.T., *A Contemporary History of Affairs in Ireland from 1641 to 1652*, 3 vols, 6 pts. (Dublin, 1880)
———, (ed.), *Facsimiles of the National Manuscripts of Ireland* (Dublin, 1884)
Gogarty, T. (ed.), *Council Book of the Corporation of Drogheda* (Drogheda, 1915)
———, (ed.), Fitzpatrick Thomas, 'Transcripts of the 1641 Depositions of the County of Louth', *Louth Archaeological and Historical Journal*, iii, nos 1 and 2 (1912–13)
Hanley, John (ed.), *The Letters of Saint Oliver Plunkett 1625–1681* (Dublin, 1979)
Hickson, M. (ed.), *Ireland in the Seventeenth Century: The Irish Massacres of 1641-2, their Causes and Results* (London, 1884)
King, W., *The State of the Protestants in Ireland under the late King James's Government* (London, 1691)
Loeber, Ralph and Parker, Geoffrey, 'The Military Revolution in seventeenth century Ireland', *Ireland from Independence to Occupation 1641–1660* (Cambridge, 1995)
Montgomery, William, *The Montgomery Manuscripts*, edited by G. Hill (Belfast, 1869)
Moryson, Fynes, *An History of Ireland from the Year 1599 to 1603; with a short narrative of the State of the Kingdom from the year 1169, to which is added a description of Ireland*, and 2 vols. (Dublin, 1735)
Millett, Benignus, *Collectania Hibernica*, nos 6 and 7 (1963–64)
Otway-Ruthven, A.J., 'The partition of the De Verdon lands in Ireland in 1332' in *Proceedings of the Royal Irish Academy*, vol. 66, Section C, no. 5, (April, 1968)
Russell, C.W. and Prendergast, J.P., *The Carte Manuscripts in the Bodleian Library Oxford* (London, 1871)

Steele, R., (ed.), *Tudor and Stuart Proclamations* (Oxford, 1910)
Temple, Sir John, *The Irish Rebellion*, 7th edn (Cork, 1766)

SECONDARY SOURCES

Arnold, L.J., *The Restoration Land Settlement in County Dublin 1660–1668* 3 vols. (Dublin, 1993)
Bagwell, Richard, *Ireland under the Stuarts and during the Interregnum* 3 vols. (London, 1963)
Barnard, T.C., *Cromwellian Ireland: English Government and Reform in Ireland 1649–1660* (Oxford, 1975)
Bellew, the Honourable Mrs Richard, 'John Bellew of Willistown 1606–1679', *JLAHS*, vi, no. 4, (1928)
Bellew, Ismay, 'Bellew Inscription and Pedigree', *JLAHS*, i, no. 1, (1904)
Bereford-Ellis, Peter, *Hell or Connacht* (London, 1975)
Bottigheimer, Karl S., *English Money and Irish Land* (Oxford, 1971)
Bradshaw, Brendan, *The Irish Constitutional Revolution of the Sixteenth Century* (Cambridge, 1979)
Casey, Christine and Rowan, Alistair, *The Buildings of Ireland: North Leinster* (Penguin, 1993)
Casway, Jerrold I., *Owen Roe O'Neill and the Struggle for Catholic Ireland* (Philadephia, 1984)
Clarke, Aidan, 'Colonial Constitutional Attitudes in Ireland 1640–1660' in *Proceedings of the Royal Irish Academy*, v. 90, C, no. 11 (1990)
——, *The Graces 1625–41* (Dundalk, 1968)
——, *The Old English in Ireland 1625–42* (London, 1966)
Coonan, Thomas L., *The Irish Catholic Confederacy and the Puritan Revolution* (Dublin, 1954)
Cox, Liam, 'Athlone in the Civil War', *Irish Sword*, xxxix, part 2 (1972)
Dalton, J., *History of Drogheda* (Dublin, 1884)
Davis, T., *The Patriot Parliament*, 2nd edn (London, 1893)
Dictionary of National Biography from the Earliest Times to 1900, 22 vols. (London, 1908–09)
Edwards, J., 'A Rural Geography of County Louth, Unpublished M.A. thesis, UCD (1965)
Gillespie, Raymond, *Colonial Ulster: The Settlement of East Ulster 1600–1641* (Cork, 1985)
Gillespie, Raymond and O'Sullivan, Harold (eds.), *The Borderlands: Essays on the History of the Ulster Leinster Border* (Belfast, 1989)

Harvey, Karen J., *The Bellews of Mount Bellew* (Dublin, 1998)
——, 'The Family Experience: The Bellews of Mount Bellew' in T.P. Power and Kevin Whelan, *Endurance and Emergence: Catholics in Ireland in the Eighteenth Century* (Dublin, 1990)
Hayes-McCoy, G.A., *Irish Battles* (Dublin, 1969)
Hickson, M., (ed.), *Ireland in the Seventeenth Century: The Irish Massacres of 1641–42, their Causes and Results* (London, 1884)
Hill, George, *An Historical Account of the Plantation in Ulster at the Commencement of the Seventeenth Century 1609–1620*, (IUP Reprint Shannon, 1970)
Hutton, Ronald, *Charles II, King of England, Scotland and Ireland* (Oxford, 1989)
Kearney, Hugh, *Strafford in Ireland 1633–41 'A Study in Absolutism* (Cambridge, 1989)
Lenihan, Padraig, 'The Leinster Army and the Battle of Dungan's Hill', *The Irish Sword*, xviii, no. 1, (1991)
Lodge, J., *The Peerage of Ireland*, edited by Mervyn Archdall (Dublin, 1879)
Mac Cuarta, Brian (ed.), *Ulster 1641, 'Aspects of the Rising'* (Belfast, 1993)
McGuire, J.I., 'The Dublin Convention, the Protestant Community and the Emergence of an Ecclesiastical Settlement in 1660', Cosgrove Art and McGuire J.I., *Parliament and Community*, (Dublin, 1983)
McKenny, Kevin Joseph, 'Charles II Irish Cavaliers', *Irish Historical Studies*, no. 28, (1993)
——, The Landed Interests, Political Ideology and Military Campaigns of the North West Ulster Settlers and their Lagan Army in Ireland 1641–1685', Unpublished Ph.D., thesis State University of New York at Stony Brook, (1994)
O'Dowd, Mary, *Power Politics and Land: Early Modern Sligo*, (Belfast, 1991)
O'Fiaich, Thomás, 'The O'Neills of the Fews', *Seanchas Ard Mhacha*, vii, no. 7, (1973)
Ohlmeyer, Jane H., *Civil War and the Restoration in the Three Stuart Kingdoms: The Career of Randal MacDonnell, Marquis of Antrim 1609–1683* (Cambridge, 1993)
——, (ed.), *Ireland, 'From Independence to Occupation 1641–1660* (Cambridge, 1995)

O'Sullivan, Harold, 'An arbitration award regarding Intermixed lands in the Parish of Dysart, dated 1671' *JLAHS*, xxiii, no. 4 (1996)

——, 'Landownership changes in the County of Louth in the seventeenth century', Unpublished Ph.D., thesis University of Dublin (1992)

——, 'Military Operations in the County of Louth in the run-up to Cromwell's storming of Drogheda', *JLAHS*, xxii, no. 2, (1990)

——, 'The Cromwellian and Restoration Land Settlements in the Civil Parish of Dundalk', *JLAHS*, xix, no. 1, (1977)

——, 'The Franciscans in Dundalk', *Seanchas Ard Mhacha*, iv, no. 1, 1960–61

——, 'The Jacobite Ascendancy and Williamite Revolution and Confiscations in County Louth 1684–1701'. *JLAHS*, xii, no. 4 (1992)

——, 'The landed gentry of the County of Louth in the age of the Tudors', *JLAHS*, xxii, no. 1 (1989)

——, 'The Plantation of the Cromwellian soldiers in the Barony of Ardee' *JLAHS*, xxi, no. 4, (1988)

——, 'The Restoration Land Settlement in the Diocese of Armagh', in *Seanchas Ard Mhacha 1660 to 1684*, xvi, no. 1, (1994)

——, 'The Trevors of Rosetrevor, a British colonial family in seventeenth-century Ireland', Unpublished M.Litt. thesis, University of Dublin (1985)

——, 'Women in County Louth in the seventeenth century' *JLAHS*, xxiii, no. 3 (1993)

Perceval-Maxwell, M., *The Outbreak of the Irish Rebellion of 1641* (Dublin, 1994)

Prendergast, John P., *Ireland from the Restoration to the Revolution 1660–1690* (London, 1887)

——, *The Cromwellian Settlement of Ireland* 3rd edn (Dublin, 1922)

Shirley, Evelyn P., *The History of the County of Monaghan* (London, 1879)

Simms, J.G., *The Williamite Confiscations in Ireland 1690–1703* (Conneticut, 1976)

Smith, Brendan, 'The English in Uriel 1170–1330', Unpublished Ph.D. thesis, University of Dublin (1990)

Smith, William J., and Whelan, Kevin, (eds.), *Common Ground: Essays on the Historical Geography of Ireland* (Cork, 1988)

Souars, P.M., *The Matchless Orinda* (Massachusetts 1931)
Stevenson, David, *Scottish Covenanters and Irish Confederates* (Belfast, 1981)
Taaffe, Viscount Charles, *Memoirs of the Family of Taaffe* (Vienna, 1856)

Index

Act for Adventurers (1642) 29, 55
Act for the Settlement of Ireland (1652) 55, 56–7, 60, 66, 67, 72, 73, 75, 173
Act of Attainder 150, 151
Act of Explanation (1655) 108, 147
  Bellew and 123, 125, 129
  Carlingford and 97, 106, 115, 116
  Connacht transplanters and 123–4
  and Court of Claims 102
  repeal 150
  successor to Act of Settlement (1662) 86, 91, 111
Act of Repeal viii, 150, 151, 152, 154
Act of Settlement (1662) 77, 86, 91, 92, 127
  Bellew and 96
    arguments against bill 77–8, 180–3
  Carlingford and 97, 98, 99, 100, 111, 118
  Connacht transplanters and 124
  Court of Claims 94, 95, 134, 136
    Bellew and 32, 127–30, 135
    Carlingford and 97, 98, 101–7, 111, 113, 115, 116
    Connacht transplanters and 123–5
    termination 108
  enactment 93–4
  provisos for named individuals 95, 99
  repeal 150
Annesley, Arthur 128–9
Arlington, Earl of 112–13
Aston, Sir William 59, 106, 119, 127, 154
Athlone, Co. Westmeath 50, 51
  transplantation commission 58, 63, 64, 65, 66, 82, 124, 175
Aylmer, Gerald 37
Aylmer, Mary (née Bellew) 37

Bagnall, Sir Henry 46
Bagnall, Colonel Walter 46, 52, 69
Baltinglass, Lord 80, 82
Barmeath, Co. Louth viii, 5, 32, 42, 116, 117, 133–4, 136, 139, 140, 143, 145, 146, 148, 151, 157, 158, 188

Barnewall, Christopher 29, 31, 32–3, 34, 142
Barnewall, Lieutenant-Colonel James 67, 70
Barnewall, Sir Richard 170, 172, 173, 174, 191
  and Act of Explanation 125
  and Act of Settlement 67
  arrest ordered by General Ludlow 70
  and Articles of Kilkenny 52, 60, 61, 62
  and Gracious Declaration 80
  marriage of daughter Elisabeth to Patrick Bellew 140–2, 189–90
  restoration land settlement 135
Bath, James 28, 34
Bayly, Major Nicholas 91, 108, 110, 116, 122
Bellew, Sir Christopher (MP) 8, 26, 84
Bellew, Christopher (son of John Bellew) 17, 68, 86, 100, 145, 146, 156, 186
  and Galway estates viii, 37, 136, 143, 144
  legal training 98
Bellew, Elisabeth (née Barnewall) 136, 140, 141, 142, 189–90, 191
Bellew, James (son of John Bellew) 37, 144, 154
Bellew, John 4, 5
  career and social position
    background vii
    conscious of social position 69
    financial affairs 142–6
    High Sheriff of Louth 23
    Justice of the Peace 8
    as lawyer 7
    legal training in London 6–7, 14
    member of declining Old English elite 9, 10
    money-lending activities 7–8
  under Commonwealth settlement
    arrest ordered 70
    outlawed by Act of Settlement 1652 57

Bellew, John *(cont.)*
    transplantation 59–61, 63, 64, 65, 66, 67, 68, 76, 170–9
    in Confederate Wars vii, 38, 68, 85
        'account touching train of artillery' 168–9
        assault on Tecroghan Castle 49–50
        capture at battle of Rathmines 48
        estate plundered 54
        under Ormond's command 47–8
        signs Articles of Kilkenny 52–3
    death 140
    and Earl of Carlingford *see* Taaffe, Theobald
    estates *see also* Barmeath, Co. Louth; Willistown, Co. Louth
        acquires lands 8
        acreages 64
        increases by purchase 68
        plundered 54
        sequestered by Ormond 47
    family
        children 36–7
        establishes trusts for 145–6
        marriage settlement for son Patrick 140–2, 189–90
        Patrick Bellew and Elisabeth Barnewall's family settlement 191–2
        wife *see* Bellew, Mary
        will 146, 186
    House of Commons
        in 1641 23–4, 25
        appointed to committee to treat with rebels 26, 27, 32
        election as member 8, 10
        expulsion from 26
        and 'Just Remonstrance' 12–16, 20
        member of select committee 18
        on Select Committee 16, 18
    insurrection of 1641 26–7, 32–6, 46
    abandons estate 37
    capture by Parliamentarian forces 48
    in Confederate Army 38, 43, 44, 45, 47, 125
    considered traitor 37
    negotiations with Ulster Irish 27–8, 84
    under Ormond's command 47–8
    praised by Owen Roe O'Neill 40, 41
    returns to estate 42
    at Tullyesker 32
    under Restoration vii–viii, 77, 80–3, 108, 123, 124, 127, 129, 130, 132, 134, 135, 138, 139, 141
        see also Taaffe, Theobald
        petitions commissioners 136–7
        petitions Lords Justices 86–7
        views on land settlement proposals 95–6, 180–3
Bellew, John, of Castletown-Dundalk 94–5, 143, 149
Bellew, John (of Lisrenny) 5
Bellew, Mary (daughter of John Bellew) 37
Bellew, Mary (née Dillon) vii, 37
    assists husband 86, 98–9, 112
    background 8
    death 140
    during husband's absences 43, 47, 68
    and provisions of husband's will 143–5
    transplantation 66
Bellew, Matthew 143, 157
Bellew, Montesque 158
Bellew, Nicholas (son of John Bellew) 136, 144, 145, 146
Bellew, Patrick (cousin of John Bellew) 109
Bellew, Patrick (d. 1610; father of John Bellew) 5–6, 7
Bellew, Sir Patrick (eldest son of John Bellew) 36
    assists father 86, 98, 100
    dispute with Nicholas Taaffe 134
    and estates 89, 119, 136, 137–8, 139, 184–6
    and James II viii, 148, 149, 151, 152, 153
    marriage to Elisabeth Barnewall 140–2, 189–90, 191
    and provisions of father's will 143–5
    upbringing 68
    and Williamites viii, 155, 156
Bellew, Patrick (grandfather of John Bellew) vii
Bellew, Sir Patrick (seventh baronet) 158
Bellew, Philip 4
Bellew, Richard 3–4
Bellew, Richard (son of John Bellew) 36, 186
Bellew, Robert (son of John Bellew) 36, 144, 145, 156

Bellew, Roger vii, 4, 148
Bellew, Thomas (brother of John Bellew) 143
Bellew, Thomas (son of John Bellew) 68
Bellew, Walter 4, 5
Bellew, Sir Walter 4
Bellew, William 4
Bernard, Dean Nicholas 21, 24, 26, 32, 34, 35, 36
Blundell, Sir Francis 152
Borlace, John 14, 15, 24
Boyle, Michael (Bishop of Cork) 89, 99, 113
Boyle, Roger (Baron Broghill, Earl of Orrery) 69, 70, 71, 72, 77, 79, 87, 88, 94, 101, 113
Brereton, Sir William 22
Broderick, Sir Allen 105, 113
Butler, James *see* Ormond, Duke of

Carlingford, Earl of *see* Taaffe, Theobald
Carlingford, Lady 85, 101, 119, 120, 121, 134
Cashell, Oliver 12–16, 20
Castlehaven, Lord 23, 49, 94
Catholic Confederacy vii, 39, 51, 80, 84
  see also under Bellew, John
  Articles of Kilkenny vii–viii, ix, 51–3, 59, 61, 62, 63, 70, 80, 170–2, 173
  cessation of war 41–2
  divisions within 43–4, 51
  'Nuncioists' 46, 47, 51, 76, 84, 85
  'Ormondists' 46, 47, 60, 69
  General Assembly 38, 46, 47
  Leinster army 38, 43, 45, 46, 47, 68, 85, 109, 125
  Munster army 47, 48
  Rinuccini 38, 43–4, 45, 47, 76
  Supreme Council 44, 45, 46, 47
Catholics and Catholic Church *see* Roman Catholics and Roman Catholic Church
Charles I 122
  Bellew and 32, 33
  English Civil War 43
  execution 73, 89
  Graces *see* Graces
  and Irish forces 40
  'Just Remonstrance' presented to 12, 14, 161–2
  raises 'New Irish Army' 18–19
  and Wentworth 11
Charles II 59, 81
  and Bellew's case 123, 125, 126, 127
  Carlingford earl of and 85, 91, 92, 95, 111–12, 114, 115, 122, 128
  Convention of 1660 71
  Gracious Declaration *see* Gracious Declaration
  and Irish land settlement 74, 75, 79, 86, 90, 108, 113, 139
  Irish royalists under Commonwealth 69–70
  Ormond and 49
  succeeded by brother James 146–7
Chichester, Arthur (Earl of Donegal) 80, 82
Churchill, Colonel Winston 105, 131
Clanricard, Lord 45, 49, 80
Clotworthy, Sir John 11
Commonwealth viii, ix, 21, 50, 51, 52, 53, 56, 57, 61, 71, 72, 73, 75, 76, 80, 119, 138, 139, 147, 151, 155
  army 56
  ex-soldiers 100, 104, 135
  and Convention of 1660 71–2, 75
  Irish resistance to 51
  land forfeitures 9
  land settlement 55, 57, 60, 66, 76, 80, 119, 138, 139, 147, 151, 155
  structures of government established in Ireland 53, 55
  transplantations viii, 58–70, 72, 76
  see also transplantation commissions
Confederate Catholics *see* Catholic Confederacy
Convention of 1660 70, 71–2
Conway, Viscount 129, 130
Coote, Richard (Baron Collooney) 85–6, 90
Coote, Sir Charles 44, 50, 67, 69, 70, 71, 72, 79, 85–6, 87, 94
Corren, Viscount *see* Taaffe, Theobald
Cromwell, Henry 69–70, 89
Cromwell, Oliver 48–9, 51, 55, 61, 69, 77, 89

Dawe, Thomas 42, 65, 68
Dering, Sir Edward 104, 105, 116, 117, 129
Dillon, Captain Arthur 59, 119, 120

Dillon, Robert vii, 8, 138
Dillon, Lord Robert 8
Dillon, Sir James 39, 40, 50
Dowdall, Laurence 60, 61, 67, 70, 125, 170, 172, 173, 174
Drogheda, Co. Louth 7, 21, 22, 24, 25, 26, 28, 54, 55, 56, 57, 69, 106, 147, 148
  Cromwell and 51
  insurrection 26, 29, 31, 32, 34
  siege of 1641-2 21-2, 24, 29, 36
  mercantile class 21
Dundalk, Co. Louth 4, 21-2, 24, 54, 55, 56, 69, 91, 92
  assault by Ormond 36
  fall to insurgents in 1641 23, 24, 25, 29

England
  Civil War 10, 40, 89
  Committee for Articles 60-1
  Commonwealth *see* Commonwealth
  Convention Parliament 73
  Parliament 12, 19, 20, 23, 29, 35, 40, 44-5, 46, 47, 57, 60, 61, 75
    House of Commons 11, 12, 13, 14, 89, 136 *see also* Act for the Settlement of Ireland (1652)
  Privy Council 14, 93, 128
  Puritans 11, 47
Eustace, Sir Maurice 72, 87, 113

Finch, Sir Heneage 112, 136
Fingal, Earl of 39, 80
Fitzgerald, George 70, 80
Fitzgerald, Sir Luke 50, 67, 70
Fleetwood, Lord Deputy 61, 67, 89
Fortesque, Sir Faithful 22, 24, 29
Fowke, Colonel John 56, 58

Gloucester, Duke of 72, 129
Gorge, Dr Robert 108, 110, 112, 113, 115, 133
Gormanston, Lord 26, 34, 38
Gormanston, Viscount 80
Graces, The 11, 12, 17, 18, 20
Gracious Declaration 75, 76, 77, 78, 79, 83, 84, 85, 86, 88, 92, 93
  commissioners 88, 92, 94
    Instructions of February 1661 to commissioners 76, 77, 78, 79, 83
  Trust for the '49 officers 93, 94, 139
Guire, Major Luke 49

Inchiquin *see* O'Brien, Murrough
Ingoldsby, Sir Richard 99, 100
insurrection of 1641 vii, viii, 9, 10, 17, 18, 20, 74
  background 12, 22
  and Bellew *see under* Bellew, John
  'New Irish Army' and 19-20
  Old English and 20
Ireton, Henry 55

James II
  ascent to throne 147
    defeat at William's hands 152-3, 155-6
    Irish Parliament of 1689 150-1
    Irish Protestant reactions to 149
  and Bellew's petition 86
  Convention of 1660 72
  and Irish lands 94, 95, 99, 100, 104, 110-11, 119, 122, 139
    dispute with Carlingford 108, 113-16, 118, 128, 133
  Jacobite-Williamite wars viii
  and Richard Talbot 77
Jones, Colonel John 69, 70
Jones, Colonel Michael 54
Jones, Michael vii, 47, 48-9
Jones, Sir Theophilus 70, 72, 79
Just Remonstrance *see* Petition of Remonstrance

Kilkenny 38, 43, 47, 57, 101
  Articles vii-viii, ix, 51-3, 59, 61, 62, 63, 70, 80, 170-2, 173
King, John (Baron Kingston) 80, 82, 90

Lane, George 94
Legge, Colonel William 91, 94, 97, 122
Leopold, Emperor 111, 155, 156
Lisrenny, Co. Louth vii, 4, 6, 7, 54, 64, 82, 139, 151, 155
Lorraine, Duke of 85
Loughrea, Co. Galway
  transplantation commission 58, 63, 64, 65, 66, 67, 82, 124, 136, 137, 173, 174, 175, 177
Louth, Lord 24, 31, 97
Ludlow, Lieutenant-General 70, 89

Magennis, Arthur (third Viscount Iveagh) 129, 130
Magennis, Brian (Viscount Iveagh) 155
Magennis, Hugh (Viscount Iveagh) 52

Index

Magennis, Sir Con 23
Maguire, Lord 22–3
Massareene, Viscount 91, 94, 108
Maxwell, Robert (Earl of Nithsdale) 17, 69
Monck, General George (Duke of Albemarle) 71, 72, 79, 108
Montgomery, Viscount 69, 72, 92
Moore, Lord 26, 27, 29, 32, 39–40, 56
Moore, Sir Garrett 56
Moore, William 7, 32–3, 36, 42, 109
Mountbellew, Co. Galway 138, 157
Mountgarrett, Viscount 80
Mountrath, Earl of *see* Coote, Sir Charles
Muskerry, Lord 52

Netterville, Patrick 60, 61, 66, 67, 170, 172, 174
Netterville, Viscount 80
New English vii, 9, 10, 46
'New Irish Army' 18–19
Newry, Co. Down 23, 31, 109
Nithsdale, Earl of (Robert Maxwell) 17, 69
northern Irish *see* Ulster Irish
Nugent, Richard (Earl of Westmeath) 52, 67, 70, 80, 124, 135

O'Brien, Murrough (Lord Inchiquin) 40, 47, 48, 56, 79, 89, 105
O'Connell, Daniel 158
Old English vii, 6, 33, 34, 35, 36, 122, 141, 142, 147, 148
    Anglo-Norman background 1–2
    coalition with New English against Wentworth 11–12, 17–18
    and Common Law 2
    Commonwealth land settlement 60
    in Confederate Wars 42
    in County Louth 21
    displaced by New English 9, 10–11
    and Graces 18, 20
    and Insurrection of 1641 20, 23, 24, 25, 27, 29, 31
    merged with Old Irish after defeat 51–2
    and restoration land settlement 135
    Roman Catholicism 10
    transportation of 'New Irish Army' to Spain 19
Old Irish 1, 2, 19, 43, 51, 142
Old Protestants 69, 70, 71, 72, 73, 80
O'Moore, Rory 22–3

O'Neill, Art McBaron 23
O'Neill, Hugh 2, 23, 31, 84
O'Neill, Owen Roe 23, 39–40, 41, 43, 44, 45, 51
O'Neill, Sir Phelim 23
Ormond, Duke of (James Butler) 43, 44, 91, 94, 115, 136, 141
    and Bellew's petition for restoration of lands 81, 97
    Carlingford and 84, 112
    and Catholic efforts to have lands restored 74–5, 76–7, 80, 125, 130, 135, 139
    and Charles I 73, 74–5, 79
    commissions Bellew as lieutenant-general of artillery vii
    in Confederate wars 36, 40, 43, 44, 46, 47, 48, 49, 50, 51, 54
    convenes privy council in Kilkenny 101
    insurrection of 1641 28
Ormond Peace vii, 47, 74, 75, 77, 78, 80, 84, 181–3

Pale Englishry *see* Old English
Parliament (English) *see under* England
Parliament (Irish) 42, 100, 109–10, 110
    in 1641 25
    in 1661 93–4
    Bellew's election to 10
    Jacobite Parliament 150–1
    'New Irish Army' 19–20
    Petition of Remonstrance 12–13, 16, 17, 20, 163–7
    Wentworth and 11–12, 13, 17–18, 60
Parsons, William 14, 15, 20, 24
Penal Laws viii, 17, 154, 156, 157
Petition of Remonstrance 12–13, 16, 17, 20, 163–7
plantations 11, 12, 23
Plunkett, Archbishop Oliver 120
Plunkett, Colonel Richard 39
Plunkett, Margaret 5
Plunkett, Matthew (Baron Louth) 119, 148, 149
Plunkett, Oliver (Baron Louth) 8, 44, 65, 129
Plunkett, Oliver (first baron Louth) 5
Plunkett, Sir Nicholas 50, 77, 93, 136, 145, 146
Plunkett, Thomas 91
Ponsonby, Colonel 56
Porter, Sir Charles 153

Poynings's Law 16, 18, 93
Preston, Thomas vii, 39, 43, 44, 45, 46, 69, 109, 125
Privy Council of Ireland 15, 67, 73, 101, 103, 148
Protestants 11, 51, 74, 76, 77, 79, 93, 94, 120, 124, 127, 147, 149, 150, 151, 153
  in County Louth 21
  'delinquents' 56
  Episcopalians 70, 73, 75
  New English settlers 9, 10
  in 'New Irish Army' 18
  Old Protestants 69, 70, 71, 72, 73, 80
  in Parliament 13
  Presbyterians 11, 71, 73
  restoration of Charles II 71
Puritans 11, 34–5, 44, 47
Pym, John 13, 19

Rathmines, battle of vii, 48, 51
Rawdon, George 71, 117, 129
Read, Sir John 28, 29
restoration land settlement viii, ix, 3, 85, 86, 122, 123, 127, 135, 147, 149
Reynolds, John (commissary-general) 49, 50, 53
Reynolds, Sir Robert 81, 109
Rinuccini, Giovanni Battista 38, 43–4, 45, 47, 76
Roman Catholics and Roman Catholic Church 43, 52, 68, 72, 73, 76, 77, 79, 93, 94, 120, 136, 147, 148, 149, 154, 156
  see also Catholic Confederacy; Penal Laws
  Catholic Committee 17, 157
  Counter Reformation 22
  disturbed by Protestant faction in parliament 12
  English Parliament and 23
  insurrection of 1641 34–5
  in 'New Irish Army' 18
  of Old English 9
  representatives in Parliament 11, 13
  under restored monarchy 74–5
  divisions 76
Rupert, Prince 136
Russell, George 65
Russell, Patrick 6, 7

St Laurence, Bartholomew 31
Sarsfield, Patrick 155

Schomberg, Duke of 153, 154
Scots
  army in Ireland 40, 43
  Catholics in Ireland fear army of 35
  Charles I's war with 11, 18–19, 84
Smarmore, Co. Louth 19
Smith, Erasmus 91, 94, 108
Smith, Thomas 158
Smith, W.J. 22
Spain 19, 20, 85
Stanley, Sir Thomas 82
Strafford *see* Wentworth, Thomas

Taaffe, Christopher 42, 87, 98
Taaffe, Francis (Earl of Carlingford) 155–6
Taaffe, James 120
Taaffe, Jenico 100, 109, 120
Taaffe, John 42, 54, 65, 103, 148
Taaffe, John, Viscount 104
Taaffe, Major-General 52
Taaffe, Nicholas 101, 112, 113, 114, 118, 120, 122, 130–4
Taaffe, Nicholas (Earl of Carlingford) 149, 150, 156
Taaffe, Robert 122
Taaffe, Sir John 84
Taaffe, Theobald (Viscount Corren, Earl of Carlingford) 19, 26, 120, 124, 125, 128, 142
  attempts to use influence on Bellew's behalf 123
  Bellew as agent for viii, 86, 88, 95, 96, 98, 100, 101, 107, 117–20, 134, 142
  Court of Claims petition 106, 114–19, 135
  dispute with son Nicholas 130–3
  in Dublin 87–9, 97, 99
  Bellew serves under command 81
  career and character 84–5, 122
  Collooney lands 90–2
  created Earl of Carlingford 88
  dispute with Duke of York 128
  dispute with George Warren 109–10
  at Emperor Leopold's Court in Vienna 111–13
  return from 115
  friendship with Bellew 84
  wife 85, 101, 119, 120, 121, 134
Taaffe, Viscount 80
Taaffe, William 114, 122, 134
Taaffe, Sir William 84
Talbot, Henry 113

Talbot, Richard (Earl of Tyrconnell) 77, 113, 136, 148, 149, 154
Talbot, Sir Robert 49, 50, 52, 67
Tallant, Patrick 59
Tecroghan, Co. Meath 45, 49–50, 51, 67, 81
Tichborne, Sir Henry 25, 26, 28, 29, 32, 34, 36, 37, 39, 91
Tichborne, William 39
Tisdell, William 109–10
transplantation commissions 53, 60
  Athlone, Co. Westmeath 58, 63, 64, 65, 66, 82, 124, 175
  Loughrea, Co. Galway 58, 63, 64, 65, 66, 67, 82, 124, 136, 137, 173, 174, 175, 177
Treaty of Limerick viii, 155
Trevor, Colonel Mark (Viscount Dungannon) 69, 72, 91, 92, 108, 122
Trimleston, Baron 80, 141
Tyrell, Thomas 52

Ulster Irish 2, 22, 24, 25, 26, 27, 28, 29, 32, 33, 34, 35, 36, 50
  see also O'Neill, Owen Roe

Vienna 111, 112, 113, 115, 128

Waller, Hardress 70, 87, 88–9, 91, 95, 99, 100, 113, 115, 177
Wandesford, Sir Christopher 11, 12, 13, 14, 16
Ware, Sir James 88
Warren, Colonel 69
Warren, George 100, 109, 110
Warren, William 7, 31
Wentworth, Thomas (Earl of Strafford) viii, 8, 10, 60, 69, 84
  impeachment 16
  parliamentary coalition against 11–12, 13, 17–18
Westmeath, Earl of (Richard Nugent) 52, 67, 70, 80, 124, 135
William of Orange 151, 153, 154, 156
Williamson, Sir Joseph 112, 113
Willistown, Co. Louth 8, 36, 42, 47, 57, 64, 82, 139, 151, 154

York, Duke of *see* James II